Marya Ho

lives in Minne

from the reviews:

'Eating disorders may seem to hold few mysteries in a confessional age, but this book will silence the critics. It is a memoir of a neurotic young woman's attempt to kill herself by refusing food, but it is so much more than that. *Wasted* sheds light on the psychology of all women who fear gaining weight. Hornbacher pulls this off because of her intelligence which is ferocious and her research, which is exhaustive. Her vividly written memoir interweaves findings from studies of eating disorders, comments from her parents and extracts from her case notes. The result is a morbidly compelling read – difficult to put down, hard to forget…She leads us through her short life – the five hospitalisations, the spell in a mental asylum, the botched education – with painful honesty, including all the grisly details – the sewers clogged by her vomiting sessions, the spell in a mental asylum, the elaborate lies and inexorably plunging weight – but the reader is carried along by the humour and wisdom with which they are recounted…A remarkable book, one of the best biographies you are likely to read this year. Women will recognise themselves in its pages; men will recognise their wives. Those with daughters should pay particular attention.'

MARIANNE MACDONALD, *Observer*

'The extraordinary diary of a 23-year-old bulimic who gives us in intimate, infinite detail the growth of self-loathing and alienation, how her parents used her as a football in their dreadful marriage and the process of starvation and sickness. Hornbacher provides the missing link, an insight, in prose as harshly illuminating as neon, of how easily it begins.'

ANGELA NEUSTATTER, *Independent*

'Compulsive reading, which ought to be compulsory.'

VICTORIA NEUMARK, *TES*

'A coruscating account of what it feels like to be anorexic and bulimic...an excoriating condemnation of our culture and the pressures it puts on women: to be clever and thin; and nice and thin; and mothers and thin; and thin and thin and thin.'

JEAN RAFFERTY, *The Times*

'[Hornbacher] believes that she has a responsibility "to stay alive and do something with the life I've been given." Her book is that something...a remarkable gift. For not only is it a great read but it also provides the means to crack the magic circle of the eating disordered. Like the man who recently revealed David Copperfield's tricks, Marya lifts the curtain on a world of mystery and sleight of hand...Best of all she blows apart all the "little girl lost stuff" psychologists have been peddling and explains the allure of an eating disorder as it really is...Scott Fitzgerald said there were no second acts in American lives, but Marya's made it through to the final encore. Personally, I can't applaud her, or her book, enough.'

ROWENA O'CONNELL, *Ms London*

'Well read and eloquent, Hornbacher dissects her upbringing with acuity. Early on, the chasm between twinkling American glitter and her reality – between the literary Barbie dolls from *Sweet Valley High*, and Middle-America Minnesota – becomes very clear...Her descriptions gleam on the page (her scenes with her shrink, a typical Plathish 'Herr Doktor' are hilarious).'

TOBIAS JONES, *Frank*

'A raw and painfully honest book' *Cosmopolitan*

'I found [*Wasted*] compelling... dramatic and agonising... Hornbacher's passionate and urgent book should fascinate anyone who recognises in themselves or in those close to them an unbalanced attitude to food. JULIAN GIBBS, *Tablet*

'[Hornbacher's] accounts of the various treatment centres, of being asked politely to "deal with her issues", of her intermittent skirmishes and long distance calls to exasperated, incomprehending parents, of cruising all-night stores and gorging at Burger Kings are animated by her angry humour and an irony that suggested she knew what she was doing...However much of a literary success Marya may become, her prospects are bleak. Her body is wrecked, her life expectation is severely limited and her immune system doesn't work. But if she can prevent any girl from embarking on the same journey, she will have achieved something worthwhile out of her experience, and for that she deserves to be read.' KATIE CAMPBELL, *Evening Standard*

'Powerful and painfully honest...Hornbacher is fiercely intelligent and *Wasted* a precocious achievement.'
LISA ALLARDICE, *Literary Review*

'Unflinching in its descriptions of bingings and purgings, extraordinary deceit, incompetent doctors, through to Hornbacher's decision to brutally erase herself, *Wasted* is brutally honest, clear and utterly compelling.' *The List*

'*Wasted* is the personal testimony of a writer; an autobiographical account of a short and complicated life. Hornbacher's talent as an author makes this book more than just the record of an anorexic – she brings to bear considerable mordant wit as she casts a literary eye over her own experiences. Her responsibilities are those of a writer too. *Wasted* is not popular psychology, but the personal response of an intelligent and well researched individual to her own life...Hornbacher is a talented and fearless writer, and *Wasted* is consequently a shocking book. There is something deeply unnerving about occupying even a small part of the mind of someone who can exert such terrible control over herself, and when we start to consider the frighteningly large number of others who have experienced a similar personal hell, the book becomes all the more alarming...Marya is a compelling biographer of a particular private hell. I hope we get to read more from her, on any subject, very soon.'
HONOR WILSON-FLETCHER, *W*

'Hornbacher is articulate, clever and now that she has recovered has all the persuasive zeal of a convert, furious at the pressures that made her what she was. Paradoxically, however, her painful journey is also gripping and – dare one say it – entertaining in a way that no fiction could ever be. As she confesses her descent into "career anorexia" cultural criticism and memoir combine to make a compulsive read.' *Publishing News*

'Compelling' *Sunday Mirror*

'Hornbacher deliberately avoids using her own case-history to generalize about why so many women (predominantly) in the developed world, especially over the last thirty years, have chosen the rejection of food as a weapon...And, despite her good intentions, her story still reads like the prolonged wail of someone caught in the grip of a terrible compulsion, for whom the degree of control she has learned to exercise over it only makes life more difficult. A rational person might recommend deportation to a country where food is not so easy to refuse. But addictions are rarely cured by rational argument. All the love and tension and true-to-life existence of somebody coping with a recovering anorexic is in her husband's gentle admonition on the subject of dinner – "No, honey, let's *not* have rice cakes with jelly."' LIZ JOBEY, *TLS*

'A missive sent from inside a sickness; not just a description of what it is like to suffer from an eating disorder but an expression of that disorder... described with cinematic vividness. The strength of *Wasted* lies in its depictions of a life out of control, their urgency accentuated by the sense that Hornbacher has put less distance than might be comfortable between herself and the girl whom she describes.'

REBECCA MEAD, *London Review of Books*

'A haunting, harrowing true story.'

KATHERINE LACEY, *Oxford Times*

'Painful and horrendous reading – she doesn't stint on detail – and you will feel the utmost sympathy for [Hornbacher].'

MAGGIE O'FARRELL, *Independent on Sunday*

From the American reviews

'Telling her story with grace, sharp humor and candor, Hornbacher recalls her long struggle with the eating disorders that nearly killed her in *Wasted*, her scary but tentatively triumphant memoir...Hers is one of the wisest considerations in print of the baffling disease-obsession-addiction that turns woman (and some men) against themselves. She is more than a survivor, though; she is a writer of singular clarity and spirit.'

KATE REGAN, *San Francisco Chronicle*

'A compellingly written and very sad book' *Los Angeles Times*

'A startlingly frank, breathtakingly emotive account...remarkably wise' *Elle*

'A memoir written by a 23-year-old woman might sound like a contradiction in terms. Yet Marya Hornbacher's 14-year love-hate affair with food is stuffed with enough grit, drama, heart-break – and eventual triumph – to fill *several* life stories.'

MAGGIE HABERMAN, *New York Post*

'Had Sylvia Plath suffered from an eating disorder rather than manic depression, *The Bell Jar* might read a lot like *Wasted* – a primal scream of a story sure to resonate even with those who possess a healthy attitude toward food and weight.'

SARA NELSON, *Glamour*

'A riveting, startlingly assured account of her bout with anorexia and bulimia...Hornbacher's unblinking testimonial has the nuance and vividness of an accomplished novel. The fluent prose [of] her narrative supplies a wealth of information from varied psychologists and theorists and sensitively traces the crazy quilt of overlapping motivations and influences behind her disease.' *Publishers Weekly*

MARYA HORNBACHER

WASTED

A Memoir of Anorexia and Bulimia

Flamingo
An Imprint of HarperCollins*Publishers*

Flamingo
An Imprint of HarperCollins*Publishers*
77–85 Fulham Palace Road,
Hammersmith, London W6 8JB

This paperback edition 1999
3 5 7 9 8 6 4 2

First published in the UK by Flamingo 1998

ISBN 0 00 655089 4

Printed in Great Britain by
Bookmarque Ltd, Croydon, Surrey

To Brian

Introduction

Notes on the Netherworld

The awakened and knowing say: body I am entirely, and nothing else; and soul is only a word for something about the body.

—Nietzsche, *Thus Spoke Zarathustra*

It was a landmark event: We were having lunch. We were playing normal. After years in the underworld, we'd risen to the surface and were glancing around surreptitiously, taking tentative breaths of air. Jane, just out of the hospital, pale and shy-eyed, let her hair fall over her face, as though to keep from being seen as she committed this great sin of consumption, this confession of weakness, this admission of having a body, with all its impertinent demands. I was kicked back in my chair, extolling the virtues of health and staying alive, when she glanced up at me and whispered: "My heart feels funny."

I sat up and said, "What do you mean? Like, your physical heart?" She nodded and said, "It's skipping and stopping."

I took her pulse, then grabbed my keys with one hand and her with the other and hustled her to my car, head spinning with memory and statistics as we careened toward the emergency room: The first months of "health" are the most dangerous, the body reacting violently to the shock of being fed after years of starvation, the risk of heart attack high, especially just out of the hospital when anorexic behavior is likely to kick back in. Jane has her eyes closed and is breathing hard, she's twenty-one, I can't let her die, I know how this feels: the tightening of the chest, the panic, the what-have-I-done-wait-I-was-kidding. Eating disorders linger so long undetected, eroding the body in silence, and then they strike. The secret is out. You're dying.

In the emergency room, the doctor took her pulse again and ignored me—first in bemusement, then in irritation—as I asked him to please give her an EKG, take her blood pressure sitting and standing, check her electrolytes. He turned to me finally, after poking her here and there, and said, "Excuse me, miss, but *I'm* the doctor." I said yes, but— He waved me away and asked Jane how she felt. She looked at me. Asking an anoretic how she feels is an exercise in futility. I said, "Listen, she's got an eating disorder. Please just take the tests." The doctor, impatient, said, "What do you mean by *eating* disorder?"

I was floored. All I could see was Jane's heart monitor, ticking out her weak and erratic pulse, as this man stood here, peering down from on high, telling me that *he* was the doctor, that I, a mere young woman who had spent fourteen years in the hell of eating disorders, should keep quiet.

I did not keep quiet. I started to yell.

In the year that followed, as both she and I gained strength, weight, voice, Jane began to sit straighter in her chair, began to say, softly at first, then louder, those words so many millions of people cannot bear to say aloud: I'm hungry.

•

I became bulimic at the age of nine, anorexic at the age of fifteen. I couldn't decide between the two and veered back and forth from one to the other until I was twenty, and now, at twenty-three, I am an interesting creature, an Eating Disorder Not Otherwise Specified.[1] My weight has ranged over the past thirteen years from 135 pounds to 52, inching up and then plummeting back

[1] Throughout this book, I make a distinction between the words *anoretic* and *anorexic*. Though in common parlance the word *anorexic* is often used to describe a person ("she's an anorexic"), the technically correct usage of *anorexic* is as an adjective—i.e., it describes a type of behavior ("she's anorexic," meaning she displays some of the symptoms of anorexia), whereas *anoretic* is a noun, the medical term for a person diagnosed with anorexia ("she's anoretic" or "an anoretic"). For further clarification, *anorexia* is used to describe a set of behaviors, the foremost being voluntary self-starvation (the etymological

down. I have gotten "well," then "sick," then "well," then "sicker," and so on up to now; I am considered "moderately improved," "psychologically stabilized, behaviorally disordered," "prone to habitual relapse." I have been hospitalized six times, institutionalized once, had endless hours of therapy, been tested and observed and diagnosed and pigeonholed and poked and prodded and fed and weighed for so long that I have begun to feel like a laboratory rat.

The history of my life—one version of it, anyway—is contained in piles of paper and scrolls of microfiche scattered over this city in basement-level records rooms, guarded by suspicious-looking women who asked me why I wanted to see them, what I needed with the information contained in files labeled with my name and date of birth. I signed forms confirming that I was myself, and therefore had a legal right to view the documentation of me, and forms saying that I was not a lawyer and did not intend in any way to hold Such and Such Hospital responsible for (patient's name) myself (living or dead). I provided identification. I politely disagreed when I was informed, in a few of the hospitals, that I did not exist, because they could not find any files on—what was your name again?—no, no record of anyone by that name. Incomplete, out of order, nonexistent, I licked my finger and paged through my life, some two-thousand-plus pages of illegible notes.

I learned, among other things, that I am "chronic," a "hopeless case." I sat in my folding chair and perused the picture presented by these charts, a picture of an invalid, a delusional girl destined, if she lived, for a life of paper gowns and hospital beds.

That picture is a bit inaccurate. I am neither delusional nor an invalid. Contrary to the charts that slated me for imminent expiration, I have not, to the best of my knowledge, expired. I no longer perform surgery on the smallest of muffins, splicing it into infinitesimal bits and nibbling

---

meaning of the word is "loss of appetite," which is not accurate). *Bulimia* is a term used to describe a pattern of bingeing and purging (self-induced vomiting, compulsive exercise, laxative and/or diuretic abuse). A combination of the two disorders, which is probably the most common form of eating disorder (rivaled by compulsive overeating, now diagnostically known as BED or binge eating disorder), is commonly known as bulimirexia, though it is rare that the two diseases exist in their full-blown form simultaneously. Rather, a bulimirexic usually vacillates between periods of anorexic and bulimic behavior.

at it like a psychotic rabbit. I no longer leap from my chair at the end of the meal and bolt for the bathroom. I live in a house, not a hospital. I am able to live day to day regardless of whether or not, on a given morning, I feel that my butt has magically expanded overnight. This was not always the case. There was a time when I was unable to get out of bed because my body, its muscles eating themselves away, refused to sit up. There was a time when the lies rolled off my tongue with ease, when it was far more important to me to self-destruct than to admit I had a problem, let alone allow anyone to help. The piles of paper that I picked up and lugged to a table in the medical records rooms all over town sometimes weighed more than the annotated Case herself.

This is a different sort of time. I have an eating disorder, no question about it. It and I live in an uncomfortable state of mutual antagonism. That is, to me, a far cry better than once upon a time, when it and I shared a bed, a brain, a body, when my sense of worth was entirely contingent upon my ability to starve. A strange equation, and an altogether too-common belief: One's worth is exponentially increased with one's incremental disappearance.

I am not here to spill my guts and tell you about how awful it's been, that my daddy was mean and my mother was mean and some kid called me Fatso in the third grade, because none of the above is true. I am not going to repeat, at length, how eating disorders are "about control," because we've all heard it. It's a buzzword, reductive, categorical, a tidy way of herding people into a mental quarantine and saying: *There.* That's that. Eating disorders are "about": yes, control, and history, philosophy, society, personal strangeness, family fuck-ups, autoerotics, myth, mirrors, love and death and S&M, magazines and religion, the individual's blindfolded stumble-walk through an ever-stranger world. The question is really not *if* eating disorders are "neurotic" and indicate a glitch in the mind—even *I* would have a hard time justifying, rationally, the practice of starving oneself to death or feasting only to toss back the feast—but rather *why;* why this glitch, what flipped this switch, why so many of us? Why so easy a choice, this? Why now? Some toxin in the air? Some freak of nature that has turned women against their own bodies with a virulence unmatched in history, all of a sudden, with no cause? The individual does not exist outside of society. There are reasons why this is happening, and they do not lie in the mind alone.

This book is neither a tabloid tale of mysterious disease nor a testimony to a miracle cure. It's simply the story of one woman's travels to a darker side of reality, and her decision to make her way back. On her own terms.

My terms amount to cultural heresy. I had to say: I will eat what I want and look as I please and laugh as loud as I like and use the wrong fork and lick my knife. I had to learn strange and delicious lessons, lessons too few women learn: to love the thump of my steps, the implication of weight and presence and taking of space, to love my body's rebellious hungers, responses to touch, to understand myself as more than a brain attached to a bundle of bones. I have to ignore the cultural cacophony that singsongs all day long, Too much, too much, too much. As Abra Fortune Chernik writes, "Gaining weight and pulling my head out of the toilet was the most political act I ever committed."[2]

I wrote this book because I believe some people will recognize themselves in it—eating disordered or not—and because I believe, perhaps naively, that they might be willing to change their own behavior, get help if they need it, entertain the notion that their bodies are acceptable, that they themselves are neither insufficient nor in excess. I wrote it because I disagree with much of what is generally believed about eating disorders, and wanted to put in my two cents, for whatever it's worth. I wrote it because people often dismiss eating disorders as manifestations of vanity, immaturity, madness. It is, in some ways, all of these things. But it is also an addiction. It is a response, albeit a rather twisted one, to a culture, a family, a self. I wrote this because I want to dispel two common and contradictory myths about eating disorders: that they are an insignificant problem, solved by a little therapy and a little pill and a pat on the head, a "stage" that "girls" go through—I know a girl whose psychiatrist told her that her bulimia was just a part of "normal adolescent

[2] "The Body Politic," in *Listen Up: Voices from the Next Feminist Generation,* ed. Barbara Findlen, 75–84. A beautifully written, extremely insightful essay on the author's eating disorder.

development"—and, conversely, that they must belie true insanity, that they only happen to "those people" whose brains are incurably flawed, that "those people" are hopelessly "sick."

An eating disorder is not usually a phase, and it is not necessarily indicative of madness. It is quite maddening, granted, not only for the loved ones of the eating disordered person but also for the person herself. It is, at the most basic level, a bundle of deadly contradictions: a desire for power that strips you of all power. A gesture of strength that divests you of all strength. A wish to prove that you need nothing, that you have no human hungers, which turns on itself and becomes a searing need for the hunger itself. It is an attempt to find an identity, but ultimately it strips you of any sense of yourself, save the sorry identity of "sick." It is a grotesque mockery of cultural standards of beauty that winds up mocking no one more than you. It is a protest against cultural stereotypes of women that in the end makes you seem the weakest, the most needy and neurotic of all women. It is the thing you believe is keeping you safe, alive, contained—and in the end, of course, you find it's doing quite the opposite. These contradictions begin to split a person in two. Body and mind fall apart from each other, and it is in this fissure that an eating disorder may flourish, in the silence that surrounds this confusion that an eating disorder may fester and thrive.

An eating disorder is in many ways a rather logical elaboration on a cultural idea. While the personality of an eating-disordered person plays a huge role—we are often extreme people, highly competitive, incredibly self-critical, driven, perfectionistic, tending toward excess—and while the family of an eating-disordered person plays a fairly crucial part in creating an environment in which an eating disorder may grow like a hothouse flower, I do believe that the cultural environment is an equal, if not greater, culprit in the sheer *popularity* of eating disorders. There were numerous methods of self-destruction available to me, countless outlets that could have channeled my drive, perfectionism, ambition, and an excess of general intensity, millions of ways in which I could have responded to a culture that I found highly problematic. I did not choose those ways. I chose an eating disorder. I cannot help but think that, had I lived in a culture where "thinness" was not regarded as a strange state of grace, I might have sought out another means of attaining that grace, perhaps one that would not have so seriously damaged my body, and so radically distorted my sense of who I am.

I do not have all the answers. In fact, I have precious few. I will pose more questions in this book than I can respond to. I can offer little more than my perspective, my experience of having an eating disorder. It is not an unusual experience. I was sicker than some, not as sick as others. My eating disorder has neither exotic origins nor a religious-conversion conclusion. I am not a curiosity, nor is my life particularly curious. That's what bothers me—that my life is so common. That should not be the case. I would not wish my journey through a shimmery, fun house mirror-covered hell on anyone. I would not wish the bitter aftermath—that stage we can never foresee when we're sick, the damaged body, the constant temptation, the realizations of how we have failed to become ourselves, how afraid we were and are, and how we must start over from scratch, no matter how great that fear—on anyone. I don't think people realize, when they're just getting started on an eating disorder or even when they're in the grip of one, that it is not something that you just "get over." For the vast majority of eating-disordered people, it is something that will haunt you for the rest of your life. You may change your behavior, change your beliefs about yourself and your body, give up that particular way of coping in the world. You may learn, as I have, that you would rather be a human than a human's thin shell. You may get well. But you never forget.

I would do anything to keep people from going where I went. Writing this book was the only thing I could think of.

So I get to be the stereotype: female, white, young, middle-class. I can't tell the story for all of us. I wrote this because I object to the homogenizing, the inaccurate trend in the majority of eating disorders literature that tends to generalize from the part to the whole, from a person to a group. I am not a doctor or a professor or an expert or a pundit. I'm a writer. I have no college degree and I never graduated from high school. I do research. I read. I talk to people. I look around. I think.

Those aren't qualifications enough. My only qualification, in the end, is this: I live it.

> *If I bore you, that is that. If I am clumsy, that may indicate partly the difficulty of my subject, and the seriousness with which I am trying to take what hold I can of it; more certainly, it will indicate my youth, my lack of mastery of my so-called art or craft, my lack perhaps of talent. . . .*
>
> *A piece of the body torn out by the roots might be more to the point.*
>
> —James Agee

1 Childhood

1974–1982

"Well, it's no use *your* talking about waking him," said Tweedledum, "when you're only one of the things in his dream. You know very well you're not real."

"I *am* real!" said Alice, and began to cry.

"You won't make yourself a bit realer by crying," Tweedledee remarked: "there's nothing to cry about."

"If I wasn't real," Alice said—half laughing through her tears, it all seemed so ridiculous—"I shouldn't be able to cry."

"I hope you don't think those are *real* tears?" Tweedledee interrupted in a tone of great contempt.

—Lewis Carroll, *Alice's Adventures in Wonderland*

It was that simple: One minute I was your average nine-year-old, shorts and a T-shirt and long brown braids, sitting in the yellow kitchen, watching *Brady Bunch* reruns, munching on a bag of Fritos, scratching the dog with my foot. The next minute I was walking, in a surreal haze I would later compare to the hum induced by speed, out of the kitchen, down the stairs, into the bathroom, shutting the door, putting the toilet seat up, pulling my braids back with one hand, sticking my first two fingers down my throat, and throwing up until I spat blood.

Flushing the toilet, washing my hands and face, smoothing my hair, walking back up the stairs of the sunny, empty house, sitting down in front of the television, picking up my bag of Fritos, scratching the dog with my foot.

How did your eating disorder start? the therapists ask years later, watching me pick at my nails, curled up in a ball in an endless series of leather chairs. I shrug. Hell if I know, I say.

I just wanted to see what would happen. Curiosity, of course, killed the cat.

It wouldn't hit me, what I'd done, until the next day in school. I would be in the lunchroom of Concord Elementary, Edina, Minnesota, sitting among my prepubescent, gangly friends, hunched over painful nubs of breasts and staring at my lunch tray. I would realize that, having done it once, I'd have to keep doing it. I would panic. My head would throb, my heart do a little arrhythmic dance, my newly imbalanced chemistry making it seem as though the walls were tilting, the floor undulating beneath my penny-loafered feet. I'd push my tray away. Not hungry, I'd say. I did not say: I'd rather starve than spit blood.

And so I went through the looking glass, stepped into the netherworld, where up is down and food is greed, where convex mirrors cover the walls, where death is honor and flesh is weak. It is ever so easy to go. Harder to find your way back.

I look back on my life the way one watches a badly scripted action flick, sitting at the edge of the seat, bursting out, "No, no, don't open that door! The bad guy is in there and he'll grab you and put his hand over your mouth and tie you up and then you'll miss the train and everything will fall apart!" Except there is no bad guy in this tale. The person who jumped through the door and grabbed me and tied me up was, unfortunately, me. My double image, the evil skinny chick who hisses, *Don't eat. I'm not going to let you eat. I'll let you go as soon as you're thin, I swear I will. Everything will be okay when you're thin.*

Liar. She never let me go. And I've never quite been able to wriggle my way free.

California

Five years old. Gina Lucarelli and I are standing in my parents' kitchen, heads level with the countertops, searching for something to eat. Gina says, You guys don't have any normal food. I say apologetically, I know. My parents are weird about food. She asks, Do you have any chips? No. Cookies? No. We stand together, staring into the refrigerator. I announce, We have peanut butter. She pulls it out, sticks a grimy finger into it, licks it off. It's weird, she says. I know, I say. It's unsalted. She makes a face, says, Ick. I agree. We stare into the abyss of food that falls into two categories: Healthy Things and Things We Are Too Short to Cook—carrots, eggs, bread, nasty peanut butter, alfalfa sprouts, cucumbers, a six-pack of Diet Lipton Iced Tea in blue cans with a little yellow lemon above the word *Tea.* Tab in the pink can. I offer, We could have toast. She peers at the bread and declares, It's brown. We put the bread back. I say, inspired, We have cereal! We go to the cupboard, the one by the floor. We stare at the cereal. She says, It's weird. I say, I know. I pull out a box, look at the nutritional information, run my finger down the side and authoritatively note, It only has five grams of sugar in it. I stick my chin up and brag, We don't eat sugar cereals. They make you *fat.* Gina, competitive, says, I wouldn't even eat that. I wouldn't eat anything with more than *two* grams of sugar. I say, Me neither, put the cereal back, as if it's contaminated. I bounce up from the floor, stick my tongue out at Gina. *I'm* on a *diet,* I say. Me too, she says, face screwing up in a scowl. Nuh-uh, I say. Uh-huh, she retorts. I turn my back and say, Well, I wasn't hungry *anyway.* Me neither, she says. I go to the fridge, make a show of taking out a Diet Lipton Iced Tea with Little Yellow Lemon, pop it open, sip loudly, *tttthhhppptttt.* It tastes like sawdust, dries out my mouth. See? I say, pointing to *Diet,* I'm gonna be as thin as my mom when I grow up.

I think of Gina's mom, who I know for a *fact* buys sugar cereal. I know because every time I sleep over there we have Froot Loops for breakfast, the artificial colors turning the milk red. Gina and I suck it up with straws, seeing who can be louder.

Your mom, I say out of pure spite, is *fat.*

Gina says, At least my mom knows how to *cook.*

At least my mom has a *job,* I shout.

At least my mom is *nice,* she sneers.

I clock her. She cries. Baby, I say. I flounce out onto the deck, climb onto the picnic table, pull on my blue plastic Mickey Mouse sunglasses, imagining that I am the sophisticated bathing suit lady in the Diet Lipton Iced Tea commercials, tan and long and thin. I lean back casually, lift the can to my mouth. I begin to take a bitter sip and spill it all over my shirt.

That night, while my father is cooking dinner, I lean against his knees and announce, I'm not hungry. I'm on a diet. My father laughs. Feet dangling from my chair at the table, I stare at the food, push it around, glance surreptitiously at my mother's plate, her nervous little bites. The way she leans back in her chair, setting down her fork to gesture rapidly with her hands as she speaks. My father, bent over his plate, eating in huge bites. My mother shoves her dinner away, precisely half eaten. My father tells her she wastes food, that he hates the way she always wastes food. My mother snaps back defensively, I'm full, *dear.* Glares. I push my plate away, say loudly, I'm full.

And all eyes turn to me. Come on, Piglet, says my mother. A few more bites. Two more, she says.

Three, says my father. They glare at each other.

I eat a pea.

I was never normal about food, even as a baby. My mother was unable to breast-feed me because it made her feel as if she were being devoured. I was allergic to cow's milk, soy milk, rice milk. My parents had to feed me a vile concoction of ground lamb and goat's milk that made them both positively ill. Apparently I guzzled it up. Later they gave me orange juice in a bottle, which rotted my teeth. I suspect that I may not even have been normal about food in utero; my mother's eating habits verge on the bizarre. As a child, I had endless food allergies. Sugar, food coloring, and preservatives sent me into hyperactive orbit, sleepless and wild for days. My parents were usually good about making sure that we had dinner together, that I ate three meals a day, that I didn't eat too much junk food and ate my vegetables. They were also given to sudden fits of paranoid "healthy eating," or fast-food eating, or impulsive decisions to dine out at 11 P.M. (as I slid under the table, asleep).

I have had moments of appearing normal: eating pizza at girlhood slumber parties, a cream puff on Valentine's Day when I was nine, a grilled cheese sandwich as I hung upside down off the big black chair in the living room when I was four. It is only now, in context, that these things seem strange—the fact that I remember, in detail, the pepperoni pizza, the way we all ostentatiously blotted the grease with our paper napkins, and how many slices I ate (two), and how many slices every other girl ate (two, except for Leah, who ate one, and Joy, who ate four), and the frantic fear that followed, that my rear end had somehow expanded and now was busting out of my shortie pajamas. I remember begging my mother to make cream puffs. I remember that before the cream puffs we had steak and peas. I also recall my mother making grilled cheese sandwiches or scrambled eggs for me on Saturday afternoons when everything was quiet and calm. They were special because *she* made them, and so I have always associated grilled cheese sandwiches and scrambled eggs with quiet and my mother and calm. Some people who are obsessed with food become gourmet chefs. Others get eating disorders.

I have never been normal about my body. It has always seemed to me a strange and foreign entity. I don't know that there was ever a time when I was not conscious of it. As far back as I can think, I was aware of my corporeality, my physical imposition on space.

My first memory is of running away from home for no particular reason when I was three. I remember walking along Walnut Boulevard, in Walnut Creek, California, picking roses from other peoples' front yards. My father, furious and worried, caught me. I remember being carted home by the arm and spanked, for the first and last time in my life. I hollered like hell that he was mean and rotten, and then hid in the clothes hamper in my mother's closet. I remember being delighted that I was precisely the right *size* to fit in the clothes hamper so I could stay there forever and ever. I sat there in the dark like a mole, giggling. I remember the whole thing as if I were *watching* myself: I see me being spanked from across the room, I see me hiding in the hamper from above. It's as if a part of my brain had split off and was keeping an eye on me, making sure I knew how I looked at all times.

I feel as if a small camera was planted on my body, recording for posterity a child bent over a scraped knee, a child pushing her food around her plate, a child with her foot on the floor while her half-brother tied her shoe, a child leaning over her mother's chair as her mother did magic things with cotton and lace. Dresses, like angels, appeared and fluttered from a hanger on the door. A child in the bathtub, looking down at her body submerged in the water as if it were a separate thing inexplicably attached to her head.

My memory of early life veers back and forth from the sensate to the disembodied, from specific recall of the smell of my grandmother's perfume to one of slapping my own face because I thought it was fat and ugly, seeing the red print of my hand but not feeling the pain. I do not remember very many things from the inside out. I do not remember what it felt like to touch things, or how bathwater traveled over my skin. I did not like to be touched, but it was a strange dislike. I did not like to be touched because I craved it too much. I wanted to be held very tight so I would not break. Even now, when people lean down to touch me, or hug me, or put a hand on my shoulder, I hold my breath. I turn my face. I want to cry.

I remember the body from the outside in. It makes me sad when I think about it, to hate that body so much. It was just a typical little girl body, round and healthy, given to climbing, nakedness, the hungers of the flesh. I remember wanting. And I remember being at once afraid and ashamed that I wanted. I felt like yearning was specific to me, and the guilt that it brought was mine alone.

Somehow, I learned before I could articulate it that the body—my body—was dangerous. The body was dark and possibly dank, and maybe dirty. And silent, the body was silent, not to be spoken of. I did not trust it. It seemed treacherous. I watched it with a wary eye.

I will learn, later, that this is called "objectification consciousness." There will be copious research on the habit of women with eating disorders perceiving themselves through other eyes, as if there were some Great Observer looking over their shoulder. Looking, in particular, at their bodies and finding, more and more often as they get older, countless flaws.

I remember my entire life as a progression of mirrors. My world, as a child, was defined by mirrors, storefront windows, hoods of cars. My face always peered back at me, anxious, checking for a hair out of place, searching for anything that was different, shorts hiked up or shirt untucked, butt too round or thighs too soft, belly sucked in hard. I started holding my breath to keep my stomach concave when I was five, and at times, even now, I catch myself doing it. My mother, as I scuttled along sideways beside her like a crab, staring into every reflective surface, would sniff and say, Oh, Marya. You're so vain.

That, I think, was inaccurate. I was not seeking my image in the mirror out of vain pride. On the contrary, my vigilance was something else—both a need to see that I appeared, on the surface at least, acceptable, and a need for reassurance that I was still *there*.

I was about four when I first fell into the mirror. I sat in front of my mother's bathroom mirror singing and playing dress up by myself, digging through my mother's huge magical box of stage makeup that sighed a musty perfumed breath when you opened its brass latch. I painted my face with elaborate greens and blues on the eyes, bright streaks of red on the cheeks, garish orange lipstick, and then I stared at myself in the mirror for a long time. I suddenly felt a split in my brain: I didn't recognize her. I divided into two: the self in my head and the girl in the mirror. It was a strange, not unpleasant feeling of disorientation, dissociation. I began to return to the mirror often, to see if I could get that feeling back. If I sat very still and thought: Not me-not me-not me over and over, I could retrieve the feeling of being two girls, staring at each other through the glass of the mirror.

I didn't know then that I would eventually have that feeling all the time. Ego and image. Body and brain. The "mirror phase" of child development took on new meaning for me. "Mirror phase" essentially describes my life.

Mirrors began to appear everywhere. I was four, maybe five years old, in dance class. The studio, up above Main Street, was lined with mirrors that reflected Saturday morning sun, a hoard of dainty little girls in baby blue leotards, and me. I had on a brand-new blue leotard, not baby blue, but bright blue. I stuck out like an electric blue thumb, my ballet bun always coming undone. I was standing at the barre, looking at my body repeated and repeated and repeated, me in my blue leotard standing there, suddenly horrified, trapped in the many-mirrored room.

I am not a waif. Not now, not then. I'm solid. Athletic. A mesomorph: little fat, lot of muscle. I can kick a ball pretty casually from one end of a soccer field to the other, or bloody a guy's nose without really trying, and if you hit me real hard in the stomach you'd probably break your hand. In other words I am built for boxing, not ballet.[1] I came that way—even baby pictures show my solid diapered self tromping through the roses, tilted forward, headed for the gate. But at four I stood, a tiny Eve, choked with mortification at my body, the curve and plane of belly and thigh. At four I realized that I simply would not do. My body, being

[1] There are few classes for four-year-old female would-be boxers, and I think my parents were trying to get me to be slightly more graceful (bull-in-china-shop syndrome).

solid, was too much. I went home from dance class that day, put on one of my father's sweaters, curled up on my bed, and cried. I crept into the kitchen that evening as my parents were making dinner, the corner of the counter just above my head. I remember telling them, barely able to get the sour confession past my lips: I'm fat.

Since I was nothing of the sort, my parents had no good reason to think that I honest-to-god *believed* that. They both made the face, a face I would learn to despise, that *oh please Marya don't be ridiculous* face, and made the sound, a terrible sound, that dismissive sound, *ttch*. They kept making dinner. I slapped my little-kid belly hard, burst into tears. My mother's face, pinched in distaste, shot me a glance that I would later come to think of as the bug zapper face, as if by looking at me, she could zap me into disappearance. *Tzzzt*. I kicked the cupboards near my feet, and she warned: Watch it. I slunk to my room.

And I remember the women's gym that my mother carted me along to. In front of the gym, I seem to remember a plastic statue of Venus de Milo, missing half a breast and both arms. The inside foreshadowed the 1980s "fitness" craze: women bopping around, butt busting and doggie leg lifting, sweating, wearing that pinched, panicky expression that conveyed the sentiment best captured by Galway Kinnell: "as if there is a hell and they will find it." The club also had something called the Kiddie Koral. The Kiddie Koral was a cage. It had bars all the way up to the ceiling, and the sticky-fingered little varmints clung to the bars sobbing for Mommy. Mommy was wearing some stupid bathing suit contraption, lurching around on the floor with a bunch of skinny ladies, getting all bony and no fun to sit on anymore. All the little kiddies in the kiddie cage wept and argued over the one ball provided for our endless entertainment. I managed to unhook the door of the cage, a door of wrought iron bars, and stand on it, swinging back and forth as I watched my mother and the rest of these women hop and lurch after some state of grace.

I remember watching my mother and the rest of these women's bodies reflected in the mirrors that lined the walls. Many many mad-looking ladies. Organizing them in my head, mentally lining them up in order of prettiness, hair color, bathing suit contraption color, and the most entertaining, in order of thinness.

I would do a very similar thing, some ten years later, while vacationing at a little resort called the Methodist Hospital Eating Disorders Institute. Only this time the row of figures I lined up in my head included my own, and, bony as we were, none of us were bopping around. We were doing cross-stitch, or splayed on the floor playing solitaire, scrutinizing one another's bodies from the corners of our eyes, in a manner similar to the way women at a gym are wont to do, as they glance from one pair of hips to their own. Finding themselves, always, excessive. Taking more than their fair share of space.

I was born in Walnut Creek, California, to a pair of exceptionally intelligent, funny, wonderful people who were perhaps less than ideal candidates for parenthood. It must also be noted that I was not very well suited to childhood and should have probably been born fully formed, like Mork and Mindy's kid, who hatched from an egg an old man and grew progressively younger. I was accidental. My conception caused my mother to lock herself in her bedroom and cry for three weeks while my father chain-smoked in the backyard under the cherry tree. They seem to have gotten it together by the time I was born, because I was met with considerably more joy than one might have expected. I had a happy childhood. I was not, personally, a happy child, but at least things were exciting. Certainly dramatic.

I know there was a time when things were all right. I went climbing in the hills out back, slid down on paper bags over the gold-colored grass, played in the creek, climbed the cherry tree. I do not remember a childhood of chaos. Only in retrospect would I term it chaotic. I never knew where I stood with people, what they'd do next, whether they'd be there or gone, or mad or mean, or happy or warm. The colors in my mind of that time are green and gold—the trees and the hills—and the heat, the incredible heat. Tossing in bed those summer evenings, when the sun had not yet gone down. Through the open window, I could hear the clink of glasses and the music of voices and laughter out on the deck. I could smell the suffocating summer air, the dust, the garden, the glorious flowers, the narcotic spice of eucalyptus pouring into the lungs. Late-summer droughts, the wavering air above the road, out back behind the creek, the dapple-gray horse in the yard down the road, the chokecherries, sour, and lemon trees, walnut trees, women in white. The pink stone steps of somebody's pink stucco house, the oranges we ate with some lady. Perfume and cigarette smoke, late nights at parties when I fell asleep in the coats on the bed, the fleeting dreams of those sleeps, mingled with shadows and words. The three-footer's perspective on the world at butt level, searching for your mother's butt in the crowd, sensing the smell and glint of wine in glasses and men with beards and low belly laughs, tuxedos, some sense of an intricate dance of costumes and masks. It was a world that I, through the keyhole of years, watched and reached a small hand out and tried to touch.

It was not an unhappy childhood. It was uneasy. I felt as if I were both living my life and watching my life simultaneously, longing for access and yet fearing the thing that I longed for. In fact, my whole life has been this, moving in and out of the day-to-day world, both fascinated by and afraid of its sheer voluptuousness. The parallels in my approach to food and my body are striking: bulimia, feasting on food and then throwing it back; anorexia, refusing food and feasting on hunger itself.

As a child, I was always vaguely nervous, as if something was looming, something dark and threatening, some deeper place in the water, a place that was silent and cold. I was afraid that the shah of Iran was under my bed waiting to snatch me up and take me away. I was terribly, terribly afraid of the dark, and of my dreams of the horrible goat-man who kidnapped me at night as I slept. People made me nervous. I preferred to stay in my bedroom with the door shut tight, dresser shoved up against it (it was a very lightweight dresser), and curl into the corner of my bed with a book.

Therapy charts ten years later, will note:

> Marya wants to live in a private world . . . is not open to trusting people . . . tends to shut people out if they try to get too close.

The therapists will scribble down:

> Hypervigilant. Massive fear of abandonment. Controls fear of loss through fear of food.

The world outside my room seemed a seductive, fascinating, but very dangerous place to me. That sense of danger may have come in part from my father's near-paranoid overprotectiveness. My own sense of inadequacy in the face of a threatening world may have come also in part from my mother's attempts to knock me down a notch or two. I misread her advice. She tells me now that she was worried I would dream too big and get hurt. What I saw, though, were her skeptical eyebrows lifted as I regaled her with babbled tales of flying just that afternoon, her narrow, ramrod back swishing about the house as I trotted after her, trying to cut through her selective deafness: Mom. *Mom.* MOM! *What?* she'd finally say, Don't *shout*. I remember her as she tried to read in the living room when I was four, hand to her ear as I randomly banged away on the piano, crowing, "Mom, listen! Mom, listen!" "What *is* it, Marya?" she asked. "I'm playing Bach! Mom!" She lifted herself from the couch and left the room, voice and the scent of Chanel No. 5 trailing behind her: "Oh, Marya," she said. "That isn't Bach."

I stopped banging. I thought, I know *that*.

In the therapy charts, my parents are quoted as saying that they felt a need to "scale down my expectations." They apparently mentioned, not once but four times in a single session, plans I made when I was *three* for a birthday party that was, admittedly, a bit elaborate. Their "scaling down" of my expectations, which seemed to me more like an abiding doubt in my ability to do so much as blow my nose properly, would continue from early childhood until, oh, last year. It had an interesting effect: My behavior became ever more grandiose, while I myself became progressively less certain that I could accomplish even simple tasks, let alone achieve any significant success.[2] My parents, I sense, thought I was a few sandwiches short of a picnic. Who knows? Maybe they were right. They say, in the charts: *fears, nightmares, too much fantasy.*

The scream in the night, the sobbing as I fumbled my dark run across

---

[2] Whatever success is. For further musings on the mutable meaning of *success*, see also chapter 5. My own uncertainty about achievement and success, combined with my agitated certainty of its importance, would lead to frenetic workaholism by the time I was sixteen, and would also feed into my idea that an eating disorder—or "thinness"—was the only success that I would ever fully achieve.

the endless house to the door of my parents' bedroom, the incoherent rambling about monsters that were stealing pennies from my penny jar, the desperate weeping: I won't know how many I *have* now, I howled. My father, stubbled and striped-pajamaed, sitting sleepily up in bed, carting me back to my room, sitting by my bed, singing me songs in the dark until I fell asleep. The tape recorder playing books-on-tape that I placed under my pillow. I would lay my head on it, listening to the story over and over as the night wore on, sure that if I kept listening long enough, morning would come, but if I did not, the horrible prayer would come true: If I should die before I wake—

The shrinks scrawl these words on their notepads: *Magical thinking.* Their books call it "a disposition to regard the metaphoric as the concrete" and "to attribute primitive magical powers" to objects.[3] One might, for example, attribute magical powers to food. For example, if I am three years old and standing on a chair making myself an apple sandwich, and if I eat this apple sandwich in precisely *twenty bites,* no more no less, then I will be happy. If I eat it in more than twenty bites, I will be sad. If I am nineteen years old, sixty pounds, and eating a carton of yogurt a day, and it takes me precisely two hours to eat this carton of yogurt, and I smoke a cigarette every fifteen minutes to prove that I can stop eating, then I will be safe, retaining my dictatorial grip on my body, my life, my world. By contrast, if I so much as taste a bit of unsafe food on my tongue, it will not travel through my body in the usual biological fashion but will magically make me grow, like Alice taking a bite of the wrong cake.

It is not uncommon for young children to develop elaborate self-protective systems to give themselves a sense of control over their surroundings: imaginary friends, particular arrangements of stuffed animals in their arms in bed. Eventually, they will loosen their grip on these systems as they develop an understanding of security in themselves and in the world. My systems—precise arrangements of the knickknacks on my dresser, of stuffed animals imbued with "primitive magical powers," exact ways of walking down the street, and weird ritualistic eating behaviors, even in my earliest years (num-

[3] Noelle Casky, "Interpreting Anorexia," in *The Female Body in Western Culture,* ed. Susan Suleiman, 183.

ber of bites, size of bites, order of bites, number of chews)—were systems that acted as a buffer between me and the world. My focus on minutiae calmed me. It was a simple refusal to look up at the larger world, which always seemed to dilate my pupils, making me squint and shy from the glare.

An eating disorder is just such a system. And it indicated, in me at least, an inability to believe I was secure in myself or in my world.

The trouble, looking back, is that there were a bunch of contradictory things going on at once. I lived in a perfect little family of three, we three against the world, a team. And we really were very close, most of the time. It was the mutability of things that disturbed us all. Everything kept turning upside down and backward, the perfect little family blown apart by the slightest touch, the team splitting into multiple teams, players switching sides without warning. My father, a brilliant and severely depressed man, was by turns adoring and unstable. My mother, a brilliant and severely repressed woman, was by turns tender and icy. My childhood home may as well have been a bumper car rink. We each drove wildly around, crashing into one another and bouncing off again. I personally did not care for this. I usually retreated to my bedroom, or to the bath, where things were quiet and consistent from minute to minute. The white curtains were always the same. The bedspread with small purple flowers was always the same, as were the curios of my infinite collections—rocks and boxes and feathers and knickknacks and ceramic ducks, carefully arranged and rearranged on my dresser, over and over, obsessive-compulsively organized and dusted and arranged. The books and the corner into which I tucked myself were always the same.

My parents were never the same. Opening my bedroom door, I could not guess who I would find: my father, loving and cheerful and wanting to play? My father, red-faced and screaming at my mother? Kicking the dog? My mother, cheerful and wanting to chat? My mother, stone-faced and hissing at my father? Swishing out the door in a rustle of silk? My parents, a unit, glamorous and reeking of perfume and Scotch, wanting to go out to dinner at 11 P.M.? My parents, a unit, rushing over to me with terribly worried parental looks on their faces, wanting to know why I was crumpling up in a pile of tears?

Or would I find an empty house? The baby-sitter sitting in front of the television, watching *Love Boat*, offering me untoasted English muffins with honey. No, thank you, I said. I waited in my room, under a blanket in my closet, with flashlight in one hand and book in the other, until I heard the car pull up, heard the muffled screaming discussions, the slammed doors. Then I could dash to my bed, yank the covers over my head, turn my face into the pillow, screw my eyes shut, pretend to sleep.

If you are bulimic, it is assumed that you come from a chaotic family. If you are an anoretic, it is assumed you come from a rigid and controlling family. As it happens, mine was both.

In childhood, all of us go through a process of discovering how to self-regulate—to calm down, to stop the flood of tears, to release fears. It's a necessary process. Usually, children look to their parents to set an example and emulate them. You run into a bit of trouble if your parents' means of self-regulation are a little weird.

My father ate like a horse, drank like a fish, smoked like a chimney, and screamed. My mother stopped eating, grew thinner, sharper, more silent. I looked at each and settled on both: eat, throw up, starve, scream, skip town, disappear, reappear screaming and skinny, smoke and smoke and smoke. Of course there were other, numerous, factors that helped create my eating disorder, but I took the prototype of my family dinner table and elaborated on it. While my relationship to my parents has always been very complex, there is also the simple fact that both of them used food—one to excess, one to absence—as a means of communication, or comfort, or quest. Food was a problem in my family. A big problem. The shrinks say that two common elements in an anoretic's family are a focus on food and diet, and a significant degree of personality disturbance in one or both parents.[4] My father was a periodic heavy drinker, ate constantly, and was forever obsessing about his weight—he would diet, berate himself for falling off his diet, call himself a pig.[5] My mother was a

[4] Casky, 186.

[5] Friendly nicknames probably being fairly benign, it is still worth noting that my father calls himself Mr. Pig, calls my mother Dr. Pig, and (before my eating disorder came out of the closet) called me Piglet. None of us is, or ever has been, fat, and I have no idea where this came from.

former—or was it closet?—bulimic with strange eating habits. She'd eat normally for a while, then go on a diet, pick at her food, push it away, stare at her butt in the mirror.

Watching the two of them eat played out like this: My father, voracious, tried to gobble up my mother. My mother, haughty and stiff-backed, left my father untouched on her plate. They might as well have screamed aloud: I need you/I do not need you.

And there I sat in my chair—two, three, four years old—refusing to eat, which created a fine little distraction from the palpable tension that hummed between them. I became their common ground: Piglet, they said, please eat.

This, the shrinks tell us later, is called being the "symptom bearer." You get to do a little pantomime of the family's problems, playing all the parts, and everyone claps and you bow. What really happens is everyone gets into a big fuss over you and stops fighting for a while. This only works for one or two hospitalizations. After that they think you're crazy, so you have to come up with a new reason to starve yourself to death, which you always do.

"The parents of the anorexic person are often preoccupied with themselves but overtly appear worried or concerned about other family members."[6] I was my parents' only child, which is unfortunate, because you are their pride and joy and the bane of their existence all at once. You get way too much hyper-invested attention and become very manipulative. My father had adoptive twin sons from a previous marriage who spent some time with us, and whom I adored. When they were not there, there was no mitigating factor, no other focus of attention. My parents' fury with each other was somehow always related to, or channeled through, or deflected onto, me.

You do a little tap dance all the time to try to make what is very obviously not working, work. You, imagining yourself a small Hercules, hoist your bickering parents onto your shoulders and carry them around. You also begin to tire of it, so it is not so surprising that one day you will up and quit. Weaken yourself. Drop them, oops. Take

[6] Zerbe, 131–32.

up residence in a hospital bed, where everyone is taking care of you. Where you, vindictive and infantile, can turn your sunken eyes on them and say, *J'accuse*.

Whereupon they promptly begin blaming each other for the mess that you've become.

Let it be noted here that it is decidedly not their "fault." If someone tells you to jump off a bridge, you don't have to jump. But if you jump, you can always blame them for pushing you. It would be very easy to blame this all on my parents, if I weren't so painfully aware that I was also very curious about how it would feel to fall.

The shrinks call it "enmeshment," they call it "triangulation." They talk about a "confusion of pronouns" in families like mine, a situation where each person seems to pay more attention to the ideas, the perceptions, the needs, of the other people than to his/her own. They say that "anorexics [sic] have from an early age learned to be more responsive to others' perceptions of their needs than to the needs themselves."[7] It becomes ventriloquism on a grand scale: Dad thinks Mom is being cruel to him, so Dad takes Marya for ice cream. Marya is grateful and lovey-dovey, so Dad is happy and Mom is jealous. Mom thinks Dad is shoving her out of the family, so Mom buys Marya new books, which Dad thinks are too old for Marya, and they argue in the kitchen while Dad is making dinner.[8] Grandma Donna, Mom's mom, comes to visit, tells Marya she wouldn't be so fat if her father didn't feed her so much (Grandma Donna is stone blind, and Marya is not fat). Grandma Ellen, Dad's mom, comes to visit, feeds Marya nonstop for days, and comments spitefully on how skinny Mom is.

I was not what my parents expected. My father expected, or at least

---

[7] Hilde Bruch, cit. Casky, 178.

[8] Studies indicate that conflict at mealtime can exacerbate eating-disordered behavior. On the cultural front, there is some evidence that the specifically modern trend of solitary eating in general leads to *weird* eating, food choices that would not be made in a family or social eating situation: people eating alone tend to eat what one might call "comfort foods," or in my case "binge foods": high in carbohydrates, high in salt and fat, low in their capacity to satiate actual physical hunger and likely to cause eating well past the point of fullness. While my own family ate dinner together every night, as I got older, I ate alone more often—and ate more carbohydrates, sugar, and fat.

hoped for, a child who would adore him and make him feel needed, one who also would remain a child, world without end, amen. My mother, by contrast, expected a miniature adult. Quit acting like a child, she'd say. That always confused me. I *was* a child, but I got the point. Quit *acting* like a child. Be whatever you want, but don't let anyone see. Perfect the surface. Learn your lines. Sit up straight. Use the right fork, put your napkin on your lap, say excuse me, say please, smile for chrissakes, smile, stop crying, quit whining, quit asking why, because I said so, dammit, don't talk back to me, watch your mouth, missy, behave yourself, control yourself. I always had this mental image of me, spilling out of the shell of my skin, flooding the room with tears. I bit my lip until it bled and furrowed my brow in a scowl.

By the time I was five or so, I began to believe in some inarticulate way that if I could only contain my body, if I could keep it from spilling out so far into space, then I could, by extension, contain myself. If I could be a slip of a thing, a dainty, tidy, bony little happy thing, then the crashing tide of self within the skin would subside, refrain from excess, be still. I locked myself in the bathroom, stood on the sink, stared at the body before me, and cried. And then pinched myself hard, telling myself to quit being a baby. Crybaby, I thought. Fat little pig.

The patterns in eating-disordered families are, in some senses, as varied and unpredictable as an image in a kaleidoscope. In other ways, they are as predictable as the rising and setting of the sun. In earlier research, the shrinks seemed absolutely convinced that there would be these necessary ingredients: one overbearing, invasive, needy mother; one absent and emotionally inaccessible father; one materially spoiled but emotionally neglected, regressive, passive, immature child. This particular configuration is so far from my own family that I was not, theoretically, allowed to have an eating disorder. To adjust the above pattern for my own family picture: one absent and emotionally closed-off mother; one overbearing, invasive, needy father; one strange, anxiety-ridden, hyperactive, aggressive child trying very hard to be an adult.

I was too small to understand how significantly my parents' marital problems caused each of them to respond not to me but to each other through me. My father felt my mother did not need him, and so he turned to me because I did. My mother felt my father was too needy, and so she turned away from me. My father's all-encompassing needs scared her, she's claimed, and my needs seemed to her only an extension of his. She's commented since on her very strong need to protect herself. My father, in what seems to me a bid for a monopoly on my attentions, told her early on that she was a bad mother. She believed him. There is such a thing as a self-fulfilling prophecy.

My parents did not, to the best of my knowledge, like each other very much, though I do know that they loved each other. They're still married. They honk and bite and flap their wings at each other like cranky old geese, but they're married. They, like a lot of parents of eating-disordered people, were notably unsupportive of each other when I was a kid. Jealous of each other's successes, bitterly sarcastic toward each other. The shrinks note that a couple who cannot nurture each other cannot consistently nurture a child either. Shrinks also note that, lacking a marital alliance, each parent will try to ally him/herself with the child. The child becomes a pawn, a bartering piece, as each parent competes to be the best, most nurturing parent, as determined by whom the child loves more. It was my job to act like I loved them both best—when the other one wasn't around.

And so, with one parent at a time, I ate. Each had special foods, foods that only he/she was allowed to give me, all comfort foods, each food a statement of nurturance, a statement about the other parent's lack thereof. My father's dominion was school days and afterschool snacks, good midwestern stick-to-your-ribs breakfasts, the basics, the day-to-day must-haves, my balanced-meal lunch in its brown bag. My mother was queen of Special Treats, our afternoon truffle teas, scrambled eggs for dinner when my father was gone, fudge we made in the dark when the electricity went out, croissants after shopping, secret trips to Burger King for fries, cottage cheese and cucumber sandwiches for breakfast in the summertime out on the deck.

I do not remember a time when I was ever certain what the word *hungry* signified, or a time when I recall eating because I was *physically* hungry. "Hungry" did not necessarily connote a growling belly. Rather, "hungry" was begging my mother to bake bread, thus securing a proximity to the scent of her perfume, standing on a chair with her hands on my hands as we kneaded the dough. "Hungry" was wheedling my father into taking me for rainbow sherbet, thus securing his jokes and funny voices and solid shoulder to lean my head on and watch pigeons in the park. "Hungry" was the same as lonely, and not-hungry was the same as scared.

My memories of childhood are almost all related to food. Food is, quoth the shrinks, "a reasonably consistent and available source of nurturance."[9] This is not to say my parents were not nurturing—they were, my mother primarily through special books and foods, my father in his ever-present profferings of food and hugs and games. I was my father's darling, and the way he showed love was through food. I would give away my lunch at school, then hop in my father's car, and we'd drive to a fast-food place and, essentially, binge. He'd take me out of school on "date days," where we'd go to McDonald's, get cheeseburgers, fries, and shakes, sit in a park to eat and chat. We'd go to A's games and stuff ourselves on popcorn and licorice. When he quit smoking, we ate peanut M&M's all the time.

My mother was another story altogether. She ate, some. She would pick at cottage cheese, nibble at cucumbers, scarf down See's Candies. But she, like my father, and like me, associated food with love, and love with need. Whereas my father was painfully aware of his needs, my mother did her damndest to prove that she had none. Hence the distance she forced between herself and my father and me, her exaggerated distaste for food, the tidy bits left over on the plate, precisely the same size every time. Hence her lumping me with my father, as if we were another breed of people, those who were excessive, needy, hungry, in stark opposition to herself.

Food has two salient qualities for all humans. First, it stirs a sense of nurturance. The physical food transubstantiates in our minds into something more ethereal, of human and emotional nurturance, a sense that our hungers are being sated. Even if you are just stuffing handfuls of fries into your mouth on a binge, you still feel that some emptiness, if briefly,

---

[9] Zerbe, 131–32.

is being filled. Second, food has a simple, chemical effect of calming the brain. Food gave me a sense that things were going to be all right. That if I just ate things in a precise fashion, if I just ate special foods—mushroom soup, toast, tortillas with cheese, scrambled eggs—my brain would stay still, the world would stop spinning, and I would have a focal point for my eyes: the book beside the plate, the food, the project at hand. Things would remain calm.

I went to school some days. The rest of the days, I stayed in bed, claiming grave illness. I doubt that either of my parents believed me. They let me stay because, I believe, they were trying to de-escalate my borderline hysterical anxiety level about school. My mother had spent most of her own childhood at home in bed with her books. I stayed at home to read and eat, or more accurately, to be fed—passive tense—and to disappear into the world in my head, the world I read of in books.

Mostly I read fairy tales, plays, Ramona Quimby books, *Anne of Green Gables*. Italo Calvino's nine-hundred-page tome *Italian Folk Tales*. I would read it through and then start over. It was my favorite. It seemed such a thing of might, such a *weighty* book (and indeed it was—I began reading it when I was five), such an *endless* sort of diversion, the kind of book that might stave off the world at large a bit longer than the others. I was perpetually grief-stricken when I finished a book, and would slide down from my sitting position on the bed, put my cheek on the pillow and sigh for a long time. It seemed there would never be another book. It was all over, the book was dead. It lay in its bent cover by my hand. What was the use? Why bother dragging the weight of my small body down to dinner? Why move? Why breathe? The book had left me, and there was no reason to go on.

You can, perhaps, foresee a series of terrifically dramatic relationships in my future, all ending with me in an Ophelian heap in my quilt. I had a love affair with books, with the characters and their worlds. Books kept me company. When the voices of the book faded, as with the last long chord of a record, the back cover crinkling closed, I could swear I heard a door click shut.

But books were better than school by far, and if one read very fast, and without pause to so much as patter down the hall to pee, if one kept a *stack* of books right by the bed, and rested one's right hand on the top of the stack while reading another, it was even better. You finished one book, closed it, picked up the next, read the inside front cover, took a sip of water, opened to the first page. No break in the fantasy, no fissure into which reality might seep. So I stayed home and periodically yelled: Daddy! And sometimes again, more urgently: Daddy! And Daddy came and said: Whaddaya need, Piglet? I'd answer: Soup. And ginger ale. *Please.* And lo! it arrived, in its bowl, with crackers that one mashed up with a spoon. I ate the mushroom soup in bed, the two of us sitting and chatting. And he would take the bowl away, close the blinds, while I slid down into my sheets and let the sound of the afternoon breeze wash me to sleep.

When I woke, there was always panic. What now? Where are things, what day is it, what time, do I have to go to school, where's Daddy, has everyone left? Are they gone? I'd strain my ears for the sound of a chair scraping back, or a sigh. No sound. Surely they're gone. But there were the books and the glass of water. All things in their place. No need to worry. Just read.

Climb down from the bed, creep to the bedroom door, peek out. Look around, check for monsters. Call out, Daddy?

No answer. Run to the kitchen, open the fridge, look for something to eat. Fast. Before you have time to get sad.

An important fact: I grew up in the theater. My parents were actors and directors, and I myself began performing when I was four.[10] There is no place on earth that fosters narcissism like the theater, but by the same token, nowhere is it easier to believe that you are essentially empty, that you must constantly reinvent yourself in order to hold your audience in thrall. I became fascinated with transformations, with mirage and smoke and mirrors. I hung at my mother's elbow in front of the mirror as she took out her makeup case, pulled back her hair, painted herself into someone else. I held very still as

---

[10] I played Want in Charles Dickens's *A Christmas Carol*. I was the little girl dressed in rags and dusted with white baby powder, yowling with hands outstretched as I emerged from the Ghost of Christmas Present's cloak. An impassioned performance.

she dabbed powder on my nose and curled my hair. I grew up standing in the wings of the theater, wrapping myself in the velveteen curtains as I watched my parents onstage, disappearing into blackouts and going up in smoke.

I loved the dressing room. Mirrors bordered by blinding lights, costumes, bustling, nets, wigs, masks, boxes, hats, women, the room buzzing with loud voices and laughter and snatches of song, a blur of fabric and skin. I put on my costume and someone zipped me up and tied my sash. I smelled the smells, listened to the chatter, sat down at the long wall of mirrors to apply my lipstick. I was five. A woman turned to me and offered: Oh, honey, here, let me do that. My lipstick wasn't exactly painted inside the lines, and it was a bit too red. I remember the scent of her perfume and hair spray, that musty smell of velvet. She rustled. She leaned close and showed me how to pout my lips: soft, like this, she demonstrated. And she pulled my hair down, brushed it out and curled it: the heat of a curling iron at the nape of my neck, the soft feel of curls on my cheek. She pulled it back, clipping it with a taffeta bow, and turned me toward the mirror: See? You're all pretty now. I stared at the new, distant girl in the mirror, pleased with how grown-up I looked. Not the anxious, wide-eyed little *baby* I saw in the mirror at home. All pretty, now. A New Me.

The women all blended into one nice-smelling creature back then. They sat me on their laps, and I fell asleep when rehearsals ran late. These women were particularly warm. I remember the flutter of my eyelids, their hands holding a soft brush close to the eye, painting on lines and shadows and mascara: Hold still, they would say. I'm almost done. I listened to everything. I made mental notes. People gave me candy bars and laughed when I stood on my head. I ate the candy bars like this: Eat the chocolate off, then eat the middle. Nibble first at the flat part on the bottom. Then eat each side, then the top, then, fingers sticky with chocolate, eat the carmelly middle part, making a big mess. If you eat it wrong, something bad will happen.

My father was a fierce director. He was also a fantastic director, as it happens. One night, I was upset. I scuttled around after him, hiding my face in the back of his knees. He kept saying, Dammit! I was crying and put my fists in my eyes, smearing my makeup. Finally he turned to me, picking me up by the shoulders, shaking me, and advised: "Child, when you come here, check your problems at the door."

It was a maxim I'd heard before, usually thrown at some cast member who was whining or weeping or wailing about something or other. My father's voice would shoot through the room. Cut the crap, he'd bark. When you come to rehearsal, check your problems at the door. Everything would go quiet for a minute, and I would hold very still, blushing and wanting to apologize for him and make everything better again. Some nights when he did this, I would hide in a cupboard. But he'd never turned those words on me before.

I stopped crying. I wiped my nose with the back of my hand. He stood me on a chair, fixed my makeup, and said: "See? There. The show must go on."

My family and I took the theater metaphor a little too far. I have had the working assumption, since I was very small, that nothing was as it appeared. Appearances were not to be trusted. In fact, nothing was to be trusted. Things existed in layers, and under the layer lay another layer, like my little Russian Petrushka dolls, which came apart at the waist to reveal another doll, and another, and another. Everything was about context. Everything was costume and makeup, and the role that one played. When one of us went on too long with our monologue, someone would start to clap a slow, sarcastic clap, and would say, flatly, "Wonderful, wonderful." Everyone's favorite insult was, "Oh, get off the stage." But no one ever did.

Somewhere in the back of my brain there exists this certainty: The body is no more than a costume, and can be changed at will. That the changing of bodies, like costumes, would make me into a different character, a character who might, finally, be all right.

I learned very early to choose my lines carefully. I still have a terrible habit, when people pause too long between words, of feeding them their line. I know my lines in advance. I dress for occasions, for personae. There are women in my closet, hanging on my hangers, a different woman for each suit, each dress, each pair of shoes. I hoard clothes. My makeup spills from the bathroom drawers, and there are different women for different lipsticks. I learned this very young. I was not as I appeared. I liked that. I was a magician. No one could see what I hid underneath, and I didn't want them to, because what I hid seemed raw. Excessively hot and red.

We took our places and played our roles. I was the crazy child, uncontrollable and ticking like a small bomb. My mother was the woman trapped in a family she didn't want, bitter and resentful. My father was the misunderstood sensitive guy, given to outbursts of uncontrollable rage. It was darling. We were all incredibly melodramatic. But of course, in all that, we were also simply three people who loved one another and didn't know how to negotiate living together.

When I was between the ages of five and seven, my parents' marriage deteriorated faster, as did the vacillation between calm and chaos. My mother went back to school to complete her license in educational administration. This done, she began working days in the school district office, performing and rehearsing at night. She directed several shows and won awards for them. My father was becoming increasingly annoyed by her absence, more still by her success. He was also entrenched in a massive war with the people at his theater. There was talk of separation, of divorce. There were screaming fights in the kitchen about who would go to the grocery store, who was a bigger martyr. There were also cozy outings together, hands held, pictures of big smiles. And then there were dinners where we all chattered happily, making each other laugh as I fell asleep in my soup. There were impromptu trips taken by one or both of my parents, out of town for inscrutable reasons. Occasionally I would be shipped off to the grandparents. I had a small plaid suitcase.

I dimly recall a war in the living room as I sat on the piano bench, swinging my legs. Apparently my mother and I were headed for Portland. My father screamed at my mother, begging her not to leave him. My mother loudly retorted that we were going and he couldn't stop us. I was humming Sunday school songs in my head, wishing they would kiss and make up. When the decibel level made it impossible to properly hum, I sprang up, shouted over them, told them I loved them, demanded that they be quiet, and announced that everything was going to be okay. My father cried and picked me up and hugged me, and then my mother and I left. My mother remembers that fight, that trip. My father does not. Over the phone, he sighs, and says, "There were lots of those." We took a train. I remember laughing at the Murphy bed that came out of the wall of our room on the train, and the nap I took, the trees outside flying past the window. I remember my grandmother giving me toast and tea when we got there. My grandmother then told me I'd get fat and whisked the toast out of reach.

In the boxes of old papers, I find strange things from this era: letters, drawings, report cards, newspaper clippings, and a sign that I must have hung on my bedroom door that read: IF YOU ARE THINKING ABOUT COMING IN HERE, TURN YOUR MIND AROUND FAST! I DON'T WANT TO SEE YOU. Among these papers, two things made me curious. One, a card from me to my mother, written when I was in preschool, judging by spelling and punctuation: On the cover, a stick-figure sad girl in purple pen, with the words: "to mom." Inside, the lines slant sharply downward: "DeAr mom./I do Not Liek [scribble]./It wen You Are/awae. I want You Back!/I can not sleep wen/Out you! love, marya." At the bottom of the card, there is a purple heart. I hated drawing hearts. My hearts always seemed lopsided and skinny, never the round, symmetrical hearts that the other girls drew. This particular disfigured heart is crying purple tears.

I asked my mother—via E-mail, as is our way—if she remembered this card. She did not. She wrote back, saying: "It could've been that trip to London. It could also have been nights I was in plays. . . . argggghhhh . . . Did I ever get the card? If not, why not? If so, where was my head? Obviously up my ass." My father doesn't remember it, either. They also can't explain the odd letter my father sent to me when I was six. It was written during the summer when he was directing at a theater in Scottsdale, Arizona. It repeatedly mentions his sudden realization that he couldn't stand to be away from us, that he missed us horribly and needed us around. After finding this, I called him to ask if he had been planning to stay in Arizona without us. "I don't think so," he said. He paused. "Maybe I was. In the back of my mind."

He later explained that the following year, when I was seven, the shit hit the fan. This may explain why I do not have any recollection of that year, save for vague memories of late-night screaming matches and crashings about in the dining room, when my parents returned from the theater. I was usually reading under the covers, and one night a strange stench of alcohol came from the kitchen, which I followed to find my mother pouring a number of bottles of booze down the sink. That year is a blank, aside from my seventh birthday party (I got a splinter in my nose). The next thing I remember comes a year later, when I was abruptly informed that we were moving, without apparent reason, to Minnesota.

Here is what I don't remember: My parents went, as my father put it, "completely out of control." My mother had a midlife crisis. My father had a professional and an identity crisis at once. My mother was turning forty. My father's whistle-blowing on some corrupt professional politics at his theater wound up getting him smeared and blackballed. He says that he came to a painful realization that he would never be what he had dreamed of being ("great"). He says he suddenly saw himself as just "some guy schlepping his way through the best he can, but I couldn't respect that for what it is. All I could see was that I was a failure. And I went crazy." He was drinking way too much, "mostly to dull the pain," he says. I remember his rages. My mother became further obsessed with her appearance, worried about losing her looks. She began dyeing her hair, wearing inch-long porcelain nails (those I also remember), spending more money on clothes, losing weight, and in my father's eyes, flirting a lot (I remember some very low-cut blouses). My father was, as he put it, "mad with jealousy, on her case all the time." Though she was not involved with anyone else, my mother was drifting away from him. He believed she was thinking about leaving. "Of course, I was driving her away," he says. "But I felt like she was seeing me going through mental crisis and saying, 'I have nothing to do with this.' Everything I did that year was hyperemotional. I was a raw nerve. I had no skin."

I ask him if he was suicidal. He laughs. "Probably, all the time, you know? Without really thinking about acting on it. I had to take care of you.

"You and your needs," he says, "held me together that year. You were the only stable thing in my life." He pauses. "It was like I said, 'Okay, now you're going to be my stability. I realize you're only seven years old, but—'"

I cut in, "But do the best you can."

"Yes." He sighs. "It was too much to ask."

Me and my needs kept my father stable. Me and my needs were driving my mother away. Me and my needs retreated to my closet, disappeared into fairy tales. I started making up a world where my needs would not exist at all.

All of us carry around countless bags of dusty old knickknacks dated from childhood: collected resentments, long lists of wounds of greater or lesser significance, glorified memories, absolute certainties that later turn out to be wrong. Humans are emotional pack rats. These bags define us. My baggage made me someone I did not want to be: a cringing girl, a sensitive plant, a needy greedy sort of thing. I began, at an early age, to try to rid myself of my bags. I began to construct a new role. I made a plan. When I was six, I wrote it down with my green calligraphy pen and buried it in the backyard. My plan: To get thin. To be great. To get out.

I believed, even then, that once I got thin, left home, became great at whatever, once I was more like my mother, I would finally have something of my own—something, though I could not have articulated this then, resembling an identity. Only when I look back can I say that I was trying to escape what seemed my fate: to be a replica of one of my parents, thus inciting the other's wrath. Each of them, by turns, spat out: Oh, you're just like your father/mother, and then exulted when I did something they liked, saying, Oh, you're just like me.

When I was eight years old, the war between my parents reached its apogee, unbeknownst to me. My father informed my mother that he was leaving her and taking me with him to Minnesota, where he had been raised. My mother said she was coming, too. He retorted nastily that he didn't recall having invited her. She was, I hear, afraid that he would keep me away from her, a worry not entirely without basis. He says, in retrospect, that he is "grateful for her wisdom." They told me that we were moving. On July 4, 1982, my family moved to Minnesota. One year and three months later, I was eating my Fritos, scratching the dog with my foot, and then suddenly heading downstairs.

2 Bulimia

Minnesota, 1982–1989

But, when the Rabbit actually *took a watch out of its waistcoat pocket,* and looked at it, and then hurried on, Alice started to her feet, for it flashed across her mind that she had never before seen a rabbit with either a waistcoat-pocket, or a watch to take out of it, and burning with curiosity, she ran across the field after it, and was just in time to see it pop down a large rabbit-hole under the hedge.

In another moment down went Alice after it, never once considering how in the world she was to get out again.

We got in a big moving truck—it was a sunny day, the pictures of us show us squinting, shading our eyes with our hands—and headed east for Edina, a smallish, very wealthy suburb on the outskirts of Minneapolis.

My most salient memories of the trip cross-country—my father driving an eighteen-wheel Hertz truck for the first time in his life, my mother driving the old Ford—are as follows: my father choking on a chicken bone in Reno, almost dying (food, death). The view from the cab of the truck in the Rockies, looking over an unrailed cliff that descended into endlessness. I pulled my stuffed animals around me and put their ears over their eyes so they wouldn't see (death). I recall the baked Alaska my half-brothers ate in Yellowstone on their fifteenth birthday (food). There's a memory of standing in front of the mirror in a Wyoming hotel room, panicking about my hair, looking down at my body and "realizing" that I was fat, fat, fat. My thighs and belly and face were fat (body, food). I burst into tears. The picture in my parents' photo album of that day—me in a flowered jumpsuit, my hair wet from its eighth trip to the sink as I obsessively tried to get it right—shows me half-smiling, hunching into myself, face swollen from tears.

The year we moved to Minnesota, my family's tenuous grasp on stability slipped. My parents were together solely because each of them wanted to parent me. Period. In addition, neither had a job lined up. They were a bit stressed.

Eventually, after the turmoil of moving settled down, the two of them pulled it together and began to like each other again. I, on the other hand, became completely neurotic. My neurosis surprised even me. All of a sudden, I was a mess. It's quite possible that I had some preexisting depression and/or anxiety disorder and/or mania, and the confusion simply gave it a chance to surface. And it did surface. Almost immediately upon our arrival, I developed an acute, bizarre fear of everything. I was a walking bundle of anxiety, crying easily and afraid of the dark, the kids at school, the teachers, the sun, the moon, the stars. I got it in my head that prayer would work. I began to pray constantly, frantically, as I peered around me to see if anyone was watching. I dropped to my knees, pressing my nails into the palms of my hands, praying wildly for God to forgive me, muttering manic prayers that would've made little sense to any god: Please God I'm sorry don't let me get fat I'm sorry forgive me Father for I have sinned bless my mother and my father and the dog and my friends and I'm sorry and thank you for books and forgive me and don't let me get fat I'm sorry I watered my plant with 7UP—.

Suddenly all inanimate objects were imbued with aforementioned "primitive magical powers," from stairs to chairs, books to forks, curtains to lamps. Everything had to have an extremely precise order: the bed made a particular way, the clock watched so that things happened on time. I remember lying on my parents' bed watching the old digital clock flip its numbers like cards: 5:21. 5:22. 5:23. I made sure time didn't stop, that dinner happened when they said it would happen. "It's been forty-five minutes!" I'd yell down the stairs, bursting into tears when dinner wasn't ready yet. Time had failed me. Nothing was happening in the right order. I talked to myself all the time, in bed, in the bath, in the park, in the yard. I made lists, a primitive form of a day planner scrawled on my mouse stationery, each day carefully planned. The days that said "nothing" sent me into manic turmoil; what would I do? who would I play with? who would keep me company and help me pass the time? I saved our California license plates so they wouldn't be sad when we threw them away. I lay on my bed with a harlequin doll, a gift from California friends, winding it up to make it play "Send in the Clowns" time and again. The doll's terribly sad tinkling, the silver painted tear on its cheek, made me cry. I talked to it, neatly propped it up against the pillows, told it not to be so sad. Everything would be okay.

> In a study of [anorectic] patients, most had suffered from childhood anxiety disorders approximately five years prior to onset.[1]

The first year in Edina, we lived in a horribly ugly, brown, flat-roofed rented duplex on a busy street. The carpet in my bedroom was puke green. I got new school clothes. I did not wear slim-sized jeans, I wore "regulars," and my cousin, whom I trotted after like a puppy and whom I aspired to emulate in all ways, wore "slims," a fact that was, as I recall, discussed at length between my mother and aunt. I developed a deep, abiding fear of jeans, which I still have. I hold my breath and shut my eyes when I pull on a pair in the dressing room, afraid they will now, as then, get stuck at my hips and there I will stand, absurd, staring at the excess of hips that should, if I were a good person, be "slim." *Slim* is such a strange, grinning sort of word, sliding out of the mouth, ending in the labial hum of "immm." It's the sound of the girl in 1980s Chic jeans commercials, slipping snakelike into her slim chic jeans. Slimmmmmm.

I wasn't. I was regular. I had a gray dress that my mother said was "darling." I didn't want to be darling. I was sick of being darling. I wanted to be Slim. Or Chic. The dress was a shapeless square of gray fleece with two yellow stripes around the hips. I put it on when she brought it home for me, stood on the toilet, and bellowed, "I LOOK LIKE AN ELEPHANT!" I bawled. She said, No, honey, you look darling. I wept profusely as she braided my hair. I undid it because it wasn't perfect. There were lumps, I said. She lifted her hands in bewilderment and left the room, shaking her head. I stood back up on the toilet, lifted my dress, staring at myself from all sides.

It might have occurred to someone that I was on the brink of

[1] *International Journal of Eating Disorders (IJED)*, April 1995, v. 17, n. 3: 291.

puberty. I'd reached it awfully early, so I suppose no one was really looking for it. I was caught by surprise more than anyone, having never even had *sex* explained to me in anything but the most abstract terms. Still, I would have appreciated some insight as to why, at the ripe old age of eight, I found three completely uncalled-for hairs at a most inappropriate spot on my theretofore smooth self while perched on the toilet. I got the tweezers, plucked them out, wondering if I was turning into some sort of ape. The more I plucked each day, the more hair would appear, weird, wiry little hairs, until I had what could only be described as a small beard between my legs. Eventually, realizing it was a hopeless effort, I surrendered the plucking. A few years later, when at slumber parties the other girls, in shortie pajamas and ponytails, were confessing during red-cheeked games of truth or dare that they had counted their pubic hairs, I was thinking to myself: Count them? Where would one begin? At eight years old, I stood on the edge of the tub so I could see in the mirror and watched my hips suddenly widen, my wrists, my bones and lower belly growing heavier. My vague surprise at my arms and legs *being* there, my tendency to crash full force into things like a mini–Mack truck, became a virulent hatred for my body. I had bruises on the nubs of hips that jutted where they'd never jutted before. I had a spatial relations crisis, becoming increasingly disoriented in my skin and annoyed at my own height and width and elbows and knees. I turned into Alice on 'shrooms.

The years I spent at my Edina elementary school are a blur of mortification. In third grade I began fooling around with the neighborhood girls in the basement, under the stairs, fueling my furious, nightly self-flagellation for infinite sins. Sex was a taboo topic in my house. No one had ever even explained where babies came from, though of course I'd figured it out—and as kids are wont to do, I'd become very interested in the whole affair. This interest, however, seriously conflicted with my truly crazed anxiety, and suddenly the rather innocent rubbings and gigglings I was engaged in took on the sharp tang of bad-wrong-dirty-evil, leaving me lying silently on my bed, my hands pressed into my temples to beat back the headache, the racing thoughts. In my chest, a great hole sighed open, wide as the sad sunny sky at which I stared.

It is commonly assumed that women with eating disorders have a neurotic fear of sex, and that this fear manifests itself in a desperate attempt, at puberty, to stave off the increasingly visible sexual signs of their bodies. Some women do have this fear, but in some cases the reasons are perhaps less related to an individual's own fear of sex—I personally was not *afraid* of sex, merely ashamed that it so fascinated me—than to a fear that other people will see them, and *judge* them, as sexual. Eating-disordered people are often far more concerned with other people's perceptions than with their own feelings. Fear of sexuality may well have something to do with a culture that has a highly ambiguous, conflicted view of female sexuality, as well as a family that shares this perception. My parents' response to my general craziness—the reports from school that I was talking dirty to other girls, their sense that my girlfriends and I were up to something nasty in the basement—was not to sit me down and tell me that sexual feelings were normal but something I might want to keep to myself. They stared at me, bewildered and angry, and told me to stop using "sewer words."

Fourth grade, and I was terribly worried about the strange and painful swellings on my chest, nubs of prenipple. I pulled my mother into my room, yanked up my shirt and said: Look! Something's wrong! I have cancer! I said. She peered at them and took me to the doctor. The doctor, who was very nice about the whole affair, said, She's just starting to develop. Oh, my mother said. Oh, I concurred. We got into the car and drove home. After a while I asked, What does that mean? It means you're going to get breasts, she answered. *Oh,* I said. Oh, dear. I looked out the window of the car, watched the McDonald's go by, the Bridgemann's Ice Cream Parlor, the Poppin' Fresh Pies. It was a sunny day and the seat belt hurt my chest. I kept shifting around. Dear God I'm sorry for everything. Counting the driveways, the cars, my breaths, counting, counting, counting the even, steady throbs in my head.

I am aware that puberty is not an occurrence that's particularly *uncommon,* but I was (a) not prepared, and (b) not interested. My body, which I felt unruly to begin with, suddenly did what I had always feared it would do: It defected. Without my permission, and without warning, my body began to "bloom." I woke up one morning with a body that seemed to fill the room. Long since having decided I was fat, it was a complete crisis when my body, like all girls' bodies, acquired a significantly greater number of actual fat cells than it had ever possessed. At puberty, what had been a nagging, underlying discomfort with my body became a full-blown, constant obsession.

With fourth grade, along with a steadily swelling, repulsive body, came a new house, a redoubled anxiety, insomnia, nightmares, compulsive eating, headaches, and a desperate fear of being alone. Because I am a masochist, I begged my parents to let me stay home alone after school. They were both working a lot, and I usually had baby-sitters. I wasn't a baby (I howled) and didn't need to be sat upon. It was a matter of principle. I wanted them to think I was responsible, I wanted them to trust me. Eventually they agreed that I was old enough.

In truth, the last thing I wanted was to be alone. As I turned the corner down Nancy Lane, the house's blank eyes stared back at me. I began picturing the inside: the mirror in my bedroom, in my bathroom, in the downstairs bathroom, in the laundry room. I began thinking of what to eat once I got inside. Was I hungry? Not terribly. I was overwhelmed by time, all that blank space in front of me, a few hours stretching out into silent eons, the house as bare and full of sad light as my chest. As I walked the block toward the house, the panic mounted. I ran the rest of the block, opened the door, dropped my book bag on the floor, and sought solace in front of the refrigerator, heart pounding in my chest. I melted cheese on toast and ate. And more cheese, more toast. Cereal. Mushrooms fried in butter and brandy. Filling the mouth, the hole in my heart, the endless hours with the numb stupor of food.

Predictably, these afternoons spent watching *Three's Company* and reruns of *Gilligan's Island*, hand to mouth, put a few pounds on me. My time in front of the mirror, at night, found me pinching my thighs hard, harder, until welts rose, slapping my ass to see if it jiggled, so I could say, Fat bitch. Turning around and around like a music box doll in front of the mirror, face pinched.

And so it came to pass that one day, stuffed full of Fritos, I took a little trip downstairs to the bathroom. No one gave me the idea. It just seemed obvious that if you put it in, you could take it out.

When I returned, everything was different. Everything was calm, and I felt very clean. Everything was in order. Everything was as it should be.

I had a secret. It was a guilty secret, certainly. But it was *my* secret. I had something to hold on to. It was company. It kept me calm. It filled me up and emptied me out.

But, as is always the case with bulimia, it is at once tempting, seductive, and terrifying. It divides the brain in half: you take in, you reject; you need, you do not need. It is not a comfortable split, even early on. But early on, its pros seem to outweigh its cons. You have a specific focus, your thoughts do not race as much. They stay in an orderly row: go home, eat, throw up. The problem in your life is your body. It is defined and has a beginning and an end. The problem will be solved by shrinking the body. Contain yourself.

You no longer face the threat, upon opening the door, of falling headfirst into the white light of silent hours and wild worries, as you pace up and down the hall, sit on the couch while staring out the window at the light coming off the lake. Getting lost in the light and the lack of boundary, sitting there listening to words whistle through your ears, listening to your breath or the wind or the light banging around in the echoing hole in your chest. Forgetting who you are and where you are and if you're there. Getting lost in the thought that you might be imagining everything, you might be dreaming your life. You look at your hand in front of your face, surrounded by light, and your heart thrums as you think: I'm dreaming, I'm not even here, I don't exist. It is too fascinating, the thought that you *aren't*. The thought that if you watch the lake long enough you might disappear into the white flames of light on the blue, which seem to be just inches from your face. It sucks you in, and you stare, only a little afraid. And then you scream, startled, when your mother comes through the door. You crash back to earth. It's dark. It's evening. You're here and your mother is looking at you and asking, What?

No more of that. Crazy girl. You're losing your marbles. Come in the door, eat. Fill up the space. Keep yourself on the ground.

> May experience the world as strange and depersonalized. . . . For the bulimic person, what is outside or inside the body is often quite confusing . . . bingeing is an attempt to experience containing by exerting control over what goes in. . . . Purging defines the

> body by keeping certain contents out. . . . The quest to feel alive and full by taking in . . . substances . . . is fueled by experiencing one's self—and one's body—as inherently empty or dead.[2]

Shortly after I became bulimic, I went to the library one day to check out a book on anorexia nervosa called *The Best Little Girl in the World.*[3] I wanted to be her: withdrawn, reserved, cold, wholly absorbed in her own obsession, perfectly pure. Shutting everything out. It is in fact a rather romanticized account, written by a doctor intent upon demonstrating not the experience of having an eating disorder but rather his own genius in curing them. The book said you could die of an eating disorder. That didn't bother me. What it did *not* say was that if it did not kill you right away, it would live with you the rest of your life, and *then* kill you. I wish I would've known that. I decided that if I did nothing else with my life, I would be an anoretic when I grew up. Bulimia seemed a good place to start.

As it turned out, I was very good at it.

My nighttime baby-sitter Kelly would watch me and laugh as I boasted, I bet you I can eat this entire loaf of bread. No you can't, she'd say. Determined, I'd start popping bread in the toaster, heart pumping. I remember the toast, the butter I spread on it, the crunch of toast against teeth and the caress of butter on tongue. I remember devouring piece after piece, my raging, insatiable hunger, the absolute absence of fullness. I remember cheerfully heading off for my bath. Night, I said. Locking the bathroom door, turning the water on, leaning over the toilet, throwing up in a heave of delight.

But the delight did not last long. The daily bingeing was making me heavier, and though I did not make the connection, it was also making me increasingly volatile. Though the purging was initially rare—maybe

[2] Zerbe, 155–56.

[3] The TV movie based on this book, which details the brief stint in anorexia of a girl in her early teens (and which therefore is not overly representative of the eating-disordered population), is often shown on eating-disorder units and never fails to bring a great many patients into a tizzy over how skinny the actress (who starved herself to play the part) is, and how they need now to be as thin as her.

once or twice a week—it was right about this time that I began to get in trouble at school. With frequency. I got into fights. My grades fluctuated, notes were sent home about my disruptive behavior: talking back, being sarcastic, causing a stir. I began to spend more time alone in my room when my parents were home, drawing pictures of skeleton-thin women. My parents and I began to fight. An uncalled-for level of anger on my part began to surface, only to escalate over the next few years until I seemed, to my father, "a ticking bomb."

At nine, ten, eleven years old, I paged through the teen magazines at Clancy's Drug Store. While my friends were standing in front of the 99-cent Wet 'n Wild lipstick displays, I was poring over Diet Tips for Teens, staring at the paper doll figures of clean, hairless, grinning girls ("Mandi is wearing Shell Pink Lipgloss" and her smooth toothpick legs are doing chorus line kicks. My legs in their regulars are too big, too hairy). I slapped the magazine shut, caught sight of my face in the makeup mirror: round cheeks, round freckled cheeks, cow eyes. At night, I would lie on my bedroom floor practicing their Tight Thighs! leg lifts. I would lick my finger and turn the pages, looking at their faces. There were Mandi and Sandi and Kari and Shelli with their Shell Pink skin and Toned Tushes, glancing sexily at the camera, flouncing boyish bodies about. I practiced the looks in the mirror, casting bedroom eyes at my reflection, thrusting my hips to the side and tossing my hair. My body was wrong—breasts poking through my shirt, butt jutting, all curvaceous and terribly wrong. Everything was wrong.

During my grade school years, I'd wake with a jolt at 6:30 A.M., when the alarm started blaring awful 1980s pop music. Into the shower, out of the shower, climb up on the toilet with a hand mirror: look, peer, examine, critique. Frontal view first. Legs too short, too round, thighs touch. *Seventeen* magazine advises that thighs should not touch. Mine touch. I suck. It's all over. How can I hide it? How can I stand so I'm not so swaybacked? How can I curve myself inward, as if preparing to implode? Left side: butt too round, juts out, major gross, ohmigod, the butt, the horrible butt, the butt that is so undeniably a butt. Rear view: hips curve out from the waist. Are those saddlebags already? Butt, the butt! Two hand spans wide. Oh, fuck it all! Right side: the fucking butt! Who said I wanted a butt? Why can't I have a *flat* butt, the kind that seems to sink right into the pocket of Guess jeans when the leg goes back? I don't *want* this thing, not this round, imperious, proud little *butt.*

I get up in the morning. I'm maybe nine or ten. I sit down on the couch and pick up the newspaper. There is a story on the front page of the metro section: a girl from my town, Edina, has committed suicide.

Let's take this a little deeper. Here's what I know: There is a girl, sixteen years old, from the town where I live, who has imploded. She has gotten into her mother's car, driven to a peak (there are no peaks in Minnesota, I only picture it this way, a James Dean–esque peak). She has parked the car. She is wearing jeans (did the story say that? Why would it say that? Did I picture her in jeans? With long brown hair). She has poured a circle of gasoline around her. (The gasoline was in the trunk? Lighter or matches?) She has lit the gasoline on fire. She has burned herself to death.

I know that she was an anoretic. I know that she left a note saying she couldn't go on because she couldn't stand to live inside her body anymore. Too heavy a weight to bear.

My first thought: I can understand that.

I read the story, then the comics, the horoscope, the weather, the national news, the arts section. I rose when my father called me for breakfast, ate breakfast, bye Daddy, took a left turn out of Nancy Lane, took a right turn down the embankment of the pond at the end of the road, walked into a grove of trees, held my ponytail back, stuck my fingers down my throat, kicked leaves over the mess, spat, put two pieces of gum in my mouth. Walked out of the grove, down St. John's Avenue toward Concord Elementary School, thinking of weight, unbearable weight, and understood. I felt sad for the girl. I felt sad that she would never marry or have babies. I also understood, sadly, and apologized to God for not having thought: Oh no! How awful! How could she do that? How could it happen? Such a waste! Such a shame! Instead I thought: I could do that.

I could do that. That is the shock. It stops me in my tracks. Narcissist. Attention grabber. Always thinking of myself. Pray for the girl!

But I can't. I'm thinking of unbearable weight. I'm thinking of where to get gasoline.

The town I lived in operated on money. Money—class, really—and eating disorders share a direct relationship with each other. In our culture, thinness is associated with wealth, upward mobility, success. I may not even need to point out that these things are associated with self-control and discipline: the yuppification of the body and soul, perfect people with high-powered jobs and personal trainers, perfect-toothed smiles and happy-happy lives. Conversely, fat is associated with weakness, laziness, and poverty. Thinness has become "an ideal symbolizing self-discipline, control, sexual liberation, assertiveness, competitiveness, and affiliation with a higher socio-economic class."[4] To put a finer point on it, the very recent trend of "working out," the necessity of being "toned," not merely thin, expresses sexuality—but "a controlled, managed sexuality that is not about to erupt in unwanted and embarrassing display."[5] Taking part in the fitness craze requires time and money, a privilege available to those only with the means. The "perfect body" becomes a public display of those means. The body as costly bauble.

My generation was raised on popular media, television, teen magazines, billboards that bellowed "If you could choose your body, which would you choose?" with pictures of hard bodies getting yet harder at a very chic gym. Well, what the hell do you think I'd choose? The perfect body, of course. Our magazines were stuffed with ways to achieve it. "Lose That Baby Fat!" "Nose Job for Your Sweet Sixteen!" We read the endlessly boring series of *Sweet Valley High* pulp novels like Bibles, with their terribly chipper stories of twin sisters who were, of course, the most popular girls in their Southern California high school. They were smart and nice and always getting the guy. As every single book in the series reminded us, they were also blond, blue-eyed, tan, and a "perfect size six." A pair of literary Barbie dolls. We read the books in class, hidden behind our math books. We stood in the school bathrooms dis-

---

[4] Horesh, Stein, et al. "Abnormal Psychosocial Situations and Eating Disorders in Adolescents," *Journal of the American Academy of Child and Adolescent Psychiatry,* July 1996, v. 35, n. 7: 921. See also Becky Thompson's *A Hunger So Deep and So Wide.*
[5] Bordo, *Unbearable Weight,* 195.

cussing the plots as we compared our thighs. Look at this, we'd say, slapping our bodies so hard we left white welts. Look how my fat jiggles. But you—we'd say, turning to another girl—you've got, like, the *perfect* body.

It is crucial to notice the language we use when we talk about bodies. We speak as if there was one collective perfect body, a singular entity that we're all after. The trouble is, I think we *are* after that one body. We grew up with the impression that underneath all this normal flesh, buried deep in the excessive recesses of our healthy bodies, there was a Perfect Body just waiting to break out. It would look exactly like everyone else's perfect body. A clone of the shapeless, androgynous models, the hairless, silicone-implanted porn stars. Somehow we, in defiance of nature, would have toothpick thighs and burgeoning bosoms, buns of steel and dainty firm delts. As Andy Warhol wrote, "The more you look at the same exact thing . . . the better and emptier you feel."

I grew up in a world of children who seemed unnaturally *clean*, dressed in matching outfits bought from the same line at the same store. They were playing grown-up—there were miniature trophy wives and their miniature lawyer husbands prancing around the playground with perfect teeth and hair and tans from Mazatlán vacations or wintertime tanning booth sessions. There were perfectly folded notes and psycho-soap-opera grade school dramas. I was an indeterminate quantity. I was liked but not particularly cool. I was too quirky to be cool, too loud-mouthed and quick tempered, smart enough to verge on nerd, too wild.

There was a social caste system at my school. I was from the wrong side of town, where the houses were plainer, smaller, 1950s-style ramblers. I lived on the side of town by the public pool, where the mothers worked and the kids were latch-keyed. On the other side, by the country club, the houses were old Victorian para-mansions with housekeepers and gardeners, huge stone walks and grand oak trees and BMWs in the three-car garage. Mothers went shopping and decorated obsessively. Their lanky children were clad in Ralph Lauren and Laura Ashley. The fathers seemed to be hidden in the attic, appearing only to pat their daughters on the fanny at dinnertime. Girls got manicures in the fifth grade, did not swear, ate white bread at lunch in the horrible lunchroom, and laughed a very dainty sort of laugh that matched their dainty Keds decorated with ballpoint-pen scrawlings that said "I luv (name)."

When we first arrived in Minnesota, I went on a desperate crusade to get my parents to buy all the stuff that "everyone else" had: microwaves, VCRs, reproductions of bad art in gilded frames, plush couches, sports cars, expensive clothes that I would surely outgrow within weeks. They refused. I gave up my cause and settled, for good, on the goal of getting thin.

The year is 1984. It is fall and I am in Mrs. Novakowski's fifth-grade class. I am living in the land of the Pretty Blond Girl in White. I am not a pretty blond girl. I am short, solid, brown haired, freckled, snub-nosed, and loud. I can't help it. I try to be dainty and pleasant and sweet. It works for about five minutes at a time, when suddenly I laugh too loud, or shout out in class, or get in a fight. Every time this happens, in the embarrassed aftermath, I am suddenly, horribly fat. I pull my sweater down over my butt because it is too big. My thighs are also too big, and my boobs poke out through my shirt. I cross my arms over my chest and put my hand over my mouth to shut myself up. I am too much. There's too much of me. My parents are weird, and I wear Lee jeans, not Guess. Plus, I puke in the bathroom during recess, and that is definitely not dainty. Definitely gross. *Eeew*, say the blond girls during sex ed class as we watch the screen showing the weird cross-sectioned female lower body. The body is outlined in pink, and it suddenly starts to bleed as the motherly voice-over tells the blond girls that they, too, will bleed, and that they should watch what they eat as they go on their Journey to Womanhood, or else they'll break out in zits. Meanwhile, under the desk, I am surreptitiously bleeding. I picture myself cross-sectioned. I fold my arms over my chest and say, overvigorously, *Eeew*.

That year, I began posting letters to my mother: a note in the sewing room, an eleven-page missive on my best stationery folded neatly in her jewelry box. It was at about this point that my poor dad told me that I needed to get a bra because, in a white T-shirt (he stood, staring at his shoes) I was a little (he rubbed the stubble on his chin), I looked a bit (he twitched and pulled at his ear), well, *busty*. There was no reply to my mother-bound letters, which formally requested some data on the female body and what, *theoretically*, might be happening to mine. The only response was from my father. He freaked out. He was jealous that letters, marked PRIVATE, were circulating. He began to avoid me. My mother averted her eyes when I asked: Did you read my letter? Yes. Well? I'll talk to you later.

Something had to be done. I finally accosted her in the living room and demanded that she take me to buy a bra. I HAVE TO HAVE A BRA, I declared. Why? she asked. I burst into tears because she couldn't see that I was wiggling and jiggling everywhichway and what I really wanted was a good butcher knife to chop 'em right off, which I actually threatened to do once, as I sat sullenly in the car with my father. He believed me. But my mother, sighing heavily, said, well all right. Everything was silent: our drive to the mall, our walk through the shops, our perusal through the children's department of Dayton's, where, of course, none of the damn things fit. But we bought them anyway, ugly white training bra contraptions that itched and pinched. They were too tight. My mother was inexplicably furious, so I thought I'd best shut the hell up.

When I was ten, I also got my first period. I took a five-dollar bill from my stash of run-away savings and tromped up to Valley View Drug Store. I plunked a box of tampons on the counter, stared at the ceiling, and paid. Back home, I locked myself in the bathroom and read the directions very carefully. I hated the diagrams; more cross-sectioned half-bodies. But, truth be told, I was glad. For some reason, I had an innate sense that menstruation was a good thing. All the literature on eating disorders claims that anoretics hate menstruation. I loved it. I thought it meant I was that much closer to being grown-up and getting out of the house. I missed it a great deal when it stopped two years later.[6] At this point in my life, nothing had validity until my mother confirmed it with praise. This was really the wrong place to look for praise. I kept my perverse enjoyment of bleeding to myself. In fact, I kept my bleeding to myself and didn't tell my mother about it for more than a year, when I ran out of cash and had to confess. I muttered that I'd just gotten my

[6] "Amenorrhea," which is the loss of menstruation due to a lack of nutrition and/or body fat. It causes deterioration of bone mass because of insufficient calcium retention. A broken hip is a common primary cause of death in anoretics.

period for the first time and could she, um, get me some, um, things. She got me pads and, naturally, did not pursue the issue further.

I find out, nearly twelve years later, that she thinks menstruation is, at best, a major nuisance, hardly a thing to celebrate. So in the fifth grade, bleeding like a stuck pig and with only one pad on my way to school, I casually asked her if she thought one pad was enough. Of course, she said, tsking at my sheer stupidity. That day, wearing a new pair of white Guess pants and a T-shirt that I'd bought with my own money, I stood in the front row of choir, in the school gym. Some idiot yelled out: Hey Marya, what'd ya sit on? I turned around and looked at my backside: blood from my waist to my knees. I walked what seemed a million miles from the choir to the door with my chin up and went to the nurse, who informed me that they had no pads, because (stupid child) this is an elementary school. Oops! Excuse me, I thought I was in college. She picked up the phone to call my mother. I said my mother wasn't home. Where is she? At work. *Oh*. (*That* kind of mother.) Well, who's home? My father. *OH*, I see. *Well*. She called my father, who rushed into the school wild-eyed and offered to take me to the doctor, and then offered to take me for ice cream. He receded as I slammed into my room. I crawled into bed, drew the blinds, and didn't come out for a week. I could hear whispered voices through the wall: What's wrong with her? whisper whisper. whisper crazy. whisper.

The following summer I was eleven and took a solo trip to the West Coast. I stayed with my grandfather and stepgrandmother, who both drank nonstop and literally never ate. I remember eating an appetizer (they told me I didn't need to order an entrée, that was too much food) of mussels in white wine while they got bombed and hobnobbed with the owner. I excused myself to go to the bathroom, bought a tampon from the machine. It was a dime. I remember looking in the mirror, my pink striped dress bought specially for the trip, thinking how grown up I looked. I lost weight at their house, subsisting primarily on mints and Shirley Temples, as I held drinking competitions with my grandfather (martinis). A letter to my parents, in my downward-slanting scrawl, ends: "P.S. I'm not gaining any weight!!!!!"

Back home, my parents and I snapped at one another. I cried without cause and stormed around. I got "sick" more and more often, stayed home eating, curled up on the couch watching soap operas and game shows. When the food I was eating was gone, I'd throw up, go upstairs and get more food. And throw up. Etc. My bulimia developed in tandem with my body. I was soon throwing up almost every day. When I was home "sick," I threw up several times a day. By the time I was eleven, I met the full diagnostic criteria for bulimia nervosa (severe and uncontrolled); and by the time I was eleven, my body was fully developed.

"Fully" was the key word here, much to the delight of the older boys at school who snapped my bra in the halls or came up to me during lunch, leering, saying, "Marya, do you wear a bra?" No, I said, staring at my lunch, the sticky ball of mashed potatoes, the gray peas, the beef stroganoff that lay in a vomitous pile on my tray. "Yes, you do. Admit it," they taunted, grinning. One would trace the line of my bra across my back, his finger gentle, almost seductive, then snap it hard. "What's that?" they'd say. "Huh? Huh? Is that a *bra*? Are you developing *breasts*? Say it!" they'd say, getting louder. "Say, 'I'm getting titties.'" They laughed. I was flushed with fury from my forehead down to my toes, "Oooo, she's blushing! Are your titties blushing, Marya? What size bra is that?" Looking up at the one across from me, blond sonofabitch in an Edina hockey jacket, or the brown-haired, rat-faced skinny kid whose little pecker poked through his jeans even though he kept a hand in his pocket to cover it up. It didn't matter. They were all the same horrible creature. I searched my brain for some witty response, but before I could stop myself I blurted out, "Fuck off." Ooooo, they said, and told the lunch lady, who grabbed my arm hard and hauled me out of the lunchroom. I glanced back and watched them laugh at me. One of them put two fingers up to his mouth in a vee and wiggled his tongue between them. I had no idea what that meant. I took my bra off in the bathroom, stuffed it into my locker, and crossed my arms over my chest.

There is a plethora of recent data focusing on the relationship between puberty and eating problems. Researchers are finally turning away from the long-held assumption that eating disorders are the result solely of innate neurosis and are now looking at culture and family. The first of these, culture, is relatively self-evident: When a prepubescent shape is held up as an ideal to (impressionable, pubescent) girls, they may balk at their own bodies' sudden mute refusal to adhere to cultural requirements. They might, if their personal chemistry is right, go head-to-head with nature and bust their asses in a campaign to defeat their own biology. A body that begins to look exactly opposite of what it's "supposed" to look like is an uncomfortable body indeed. Rather than take a feminist delight in your Cycles and Curves, you're probably going to freak.

Puberty is a perverse rite of passage in contemporary culture. The nice school nurse comes to talk to your class, telling you how you're going to Become a Woman. You want to scream with horror as visions of cellulite dance in your head. Girls, Becoming Women, begin to emulate the older women in their lives: They diet. They borrow their mothers' vocabulary, expressions, mannerisms. Between poring over the mysteries of long division and playing kickball at recess, they also discuss, in weirdly adult voices, "keeping their weight down," with that regretful, knowing smile. They pinch their bellies, announcing, "I'm not eating lunch today, oh, no, I really shouldn't." Becoming a Woman means becoming someone dissociated from, and spiteful toward, her body. Someone who finds herself always wanting.

Even the *timing* of puberty is important. Extensive data supports the assertion that early-onset puberty may significantly predispose some young women to eating problems, whereas girls who develop closer to or later than their same-age peers have a more positive body image and fewer eating problems. I was not the only one who felt painfully aware of my suddenly sexual body in the midst of a bunch of gangly girls, nor was I the only one who tried to beat my body back. My body was visible evidence of all that was wrong with me: I had hips, ass, boobs, the whole nine yards, and was therefore a person who clearly ate food. I was a human-type person as opposed to an ethereal pale mannequin type, or a tall, thin, blond, blue-eyed, Scandinavian, future Bikini-Team type, with whom my little school-hall-size world was primarily populated. Worse, I was sexually developed and therefore obviously a sexual being at a time when boys were still known to punch your shoulder and holler, "Cooties!"

Added to the slush pile of mental contradictions was the association of female sexuality with sexual voracity, weakness, an inability to control one's physical *appetites,* one's *hungers,* one's *needs.* It has been argued that food and eating have replaced sex as our foremost cultural taboo.[7] To some extent I agree with this but would point out that the taboo is not against food, or sex, or flesh, but against a loss of control. Our most hallowed virtue in modern society is self-control, personal "power" (also the most hallowed virtue in my own family). If you thumb through the cannon of philosophy, you find Augustine and Co. speaking of women with the same fear and virulence that we now use to speak of food, as something "sinful," something that "tempts," something that causes a loss of control. "The slimy desires of the flesh," Augustine writes. Note: not the flesh itself, but its *desires,* arising from the flesh, dismantling our control.[8]

That is to say, *my* control, what little I had. Sexual maturation was terrifying to me, not for the reasons shrinks often cite, but because I was already utterly terrified of my needs, my passions, and, admittedly, my derriere. The last thing I wanted was *more* of any of the above. Believing that I was already perceived as uncontrollable, I was most alarmed to find my body going out of control, internally and externally—and also alarmed by the response it was causing. It was as if people could *see,* just by the very presence of my breasts, that I was bad and sexual and needy. I shrank back from my body as if it were going to devour me.

The cacophony in my head was not only cultural. My family, always skittish about the topic of sex, grew increasingly bizarre during my pubertal years, from eight to twelve. They seemed as surprised, and annoyed, by its advent as I was. My father said, years later, that I became "something of a foreign animal" to him during that time. My mother simply did not know what to do. This is not uncommon. Fathers are often uncomfortable with their daughter's maturation, and my father was perhaps overly so. My physical development scared the hell out of my mother and sent her into a

---

[7] See Jeremy Iggers, *The Garden of Eating: Food, Sex, and the Hunger for Meaning.* A food critic for the Minneapolis *StarTribune* with a Ph.D. in philosophy, he provides an excellent discussion of the translation of cultural taboos into issues of food and body.

[8] Susan Bordo, "Psychopathology as the Crystalization of Culture," *The Philosophical Forum,* Winter 1985–86, v. 17, n. 2: 79.

frenzy of reading up on the Gifted Child and the Child Who Grows Up Too Fast. The closeness I had shared with my family, as strange and tentative as it was, disappeared altogether—and I saw my impending sexual maturity as the culprit. That is to say, I blamed my body itself.[9]

My physical and intellectual development were careening far ahead of my emotional development. My mother was concerned, and rightly so, for I did not have the emotional tools to negotiate the new confusion of both sexual and intellectual possibilities. Chock-full of hormones, I babbled maniacally at the dinner table about my test scores and how, after I finished high school at fifteen, I was going to Columbia Medical School to be a neurological surgeon and was going to figure out how to cure all the ills of the world by the time I was twenty. My parents stared at me and suggested I be a little more realistic. I threw a rather age-appropriate temper tantrum.

Recent research suggests that an extremely strong desire for academic achievement may be as significant as sexual maturation, if not more so, in the development of eating disorders in young women.[10] There is a combination of issues at work here: a family that has high expectations of achievement (as distinguished from genuine encouragement and prompting of a child to develop her intellectual skills); a child who is prone to excessive self-imposed pressure; and a child who exhibits unusual levels of academic ability and intelligence. The combination often results in mental paralysis. The child may defect from expectations—her own above all else—and take refuge in an entirely antirational set of behaviors that have, in fact, a highly organized structure.

This is my own experience: I was suddenly, deeply, passionately interested in everything. I couldn't stop thinking. I woke up in the night, heart pounding and head spinning with thoughts. I turned on my light and began to plot things out on notepads. Plotting was—and in fact still

---

[9] In a family with an absence of "healthy dependency," a situation in which needs are stated, accepted, and met when appropriate, a daughter may interpret relationships in a very unhealthy manner: "dependency will equal slavery; intimacy will mean surrendering integrity; and *sexuality will mean a loss of control over her own appetites*." (Zerbe, 132; italics added).

[10] Casky, 182; Zerbe, 338.

is—the only way to get the thoughts to slow down, planning my life out step-by-step, how I would get everything done in time, how it would all be okay. I plotted, mostly, careers—doctor, actor, politician, writer, geologist, singer, violinist, soccer player, Olympic swimmer, professor. Everything seemed possible. Everything also seemed deeply *necessary,* and, of course, I had to start preparing for every possible career *right now* or it would be too late. Essentially I worked myself into a tizzy. I was going to too many rehearsals, sports practices, music lessons, reading under the covers late into the night, reading in class, reading in the bathtub, asking my parents over and over, Do you think I could do this? This? This? Sure, they said. Why not? When I was about twelve, I developed an obsession with time, always sure that I would run out of time, time was awastin' and I wasn't Great yet. I started reading college catalogs and began badgering my parents to let me go away to boarding school, in hopes that it would get me Somewhere faster.

Faced with what seemed a staggering number of possibilities, I quit. The ever-expanding sea of thoughts that wash over one at a particular point of mental development is, in fact, a bit overwhelming to a person who is still trying to figure out tampons and the etiquette of writing love notes in grade school. I wanted to be a surgeon and I wanted Chad to give me a Valentine. I wanted my mother to let me sit on her lap and I wanted her to send me to college, *immediately.* The dissonance in the brain is extreme at this point. Some children have the capacity to bore through it. I didn't. The idea of my future simultaneously thrilled and terrified me, like standing at the lip of a very sheer cliff—I could fly, or fall. I didn't know how to fly, and I didn't want to fall. So I backed away from the cliff and went in search of something that had a clear, solid trajectory for me to follow, like hopscotch. Like a diet.

> [Young women] can experience [professional liberation] as a demand and feel that they *have* to do something outstanding. Many of my patients have expressed the feeling that there were too many choices and they had been afraid of not choosing correctly.[11]

---

[11] Hilde Bruch (1978), viii–ix.

In sixth grade, I began to "take days off" from eating, to "cleanse my system." I tossed my lunch in the lunchroom trash can, keeping only the carrot sticks or the apple. When I think about it now, I can see how I began to withdraw into myself, away from the laughter and noise of my friends, focusing instead on the sensations of hunger, the lovely spinning feeling in my head, the way I would veer in and out of conversations. While my mouth jabbered, my eyes wandered off into space as my thoughts returned to the ache in the pit of my stomach, the heart-pounding feeling of absolute power.

Eventually I'd break down and eat. And eat and eat and eat. I'd stop off at the neighborhood market on my way home from school to buy jars of hot fudge, caramel, marshmallow cream, eating each jar with a spoon. The binge provided a perfectly reasonable excuse to stop eating again. Or I'd walk home with two neighborhood friends and go to Sarah's house, to sit in her cozy kitchen. There, we'd have a small communion of hysterical laughter, followed by sudden silence and food. As we talked over homework, or lay sprawled on the white couch in front of the television, we'd eat: little white buttered buns, ice cream with chocolate syrup, potato chips, Double Stuf Oreos, microwaved frozen hamburger patties, Fruit Roll-Ups, Flintstones vitamins. Eventually, the two of them would stop eating. I wouldn't. Just before dinnertime we'd part ways. I'd go home, throw up, eat dinner with my parents, fight with one or the other, do homework, snack, bathe (throw up), and off to bed.

I lay sleepless. Tossing. Head pounding. Fingers swollen, throat puffed up like a bullfrog. The light flipped off, the dark and the racing thoughts flooded in. The fears. The prayers.

> After purging, the bulimic individual will sometimes retain fluid . . . causing edema of the hands and legs. . . . Electrolyte disturbances cause a constellation of symptoms that patients must guard against, including generalized weakness, confusion, memory and thinking impairment, and emotional lability.[12]

[12] Zerbe, 261.

I was friends with some amazing girls, most of them a little quirky, all of them strikingly intelligent and imaginative. And sad. There was a clique of girls that grew over the years, fumbled our way through a doll-house-size world, told secrets and had sleep-overs and maybe once or twice touched. Girls who laid out select pieces of the family's dirty laundry in careful, hushed voices. The families of our group had secrets that none of us ever really knew for certain: a mad mother, an incestual father, money that caused more pain than joy, a little virulent Catholicism, a dash of this and that. My own family was a mystery to them, as theirs were to me. They knew I fought with my father and spoke little of my mother. They knew that I hated my body. They knew, about five years into it, that I had an eating disorder. But what's a girl to do? We turned our heads and wished there were something we could say, but there never was. We lay close together on beds and spoke of the usual topics of teenage angst: boys, school, future, sex, bodies, life. They helped me maintain relative sanity for a very long time.

Childhood, such as it was, ended, and with it, the immediate experience of fear. Fear, looking back with perfect hindsight, was sublimated, swallowed, puked, starved away. The summer between grade school and junior high, I metamorphosed into a young woman and became Impossible. I don't remember what happened that summer. But my first-day-of-school photo from sixth grade shows me standing in a knee-length blue skirt and a plaid shirt, bobby socks and tennis shoes, pony-tail, ribbon, smiling for the infernal camera. One year later, I am leaning against the house, my hair down, wearing a long black skirt and a tank top, unsmiling, face thinner, lipstick, morning light. I am twelve years old. I look about twenty-two.

During my transition from grade school to junior high, I remember seeping into the mirror. My mother told me I looked like a tramp, my father vacillated between anger and worry and silence. My face was fading from that of a child into something narrower, more defined. My bones were twisting into something almost pretty, my body losing the snub awkwardness of breasts on a childish frame as I stretched taller. I stood for hours in front of the mirror, putting my hair up and letting it fall, trying on dress after dress. Watching the infinitesimal motion of skin tighten on a leaner frame, listening to the strange hiss of a silk blouse on the bare skin of a back. I saw all this and said it was good.

My parents did not think it was good. In retrospect, this is understandable—when your child is growing up way too fast, you get scared—but at the time, I did not understand. All my life, my parents had acted as if childhood should be a state of constantly acting older. When I finally and irrevocably began to, in fact, be older, their response was one that I read as disgust. They seemed to avoid looking at me. I feinted and jostled for a spot in their line of vision, I argued with them, LOOK! I said, LOOK, I'm growing up, why is that so awful? Where have you gone? Why won't anybody look at me? Just as I had always feared my body would defect (and it had), my fear that my parents would one day disappear without warning came true.

One day I went into the bathroom, pulled open my mother's makeup drawer, pulled my hair back, and did a strange revival of what I had done as a very small child: I painted myself. Black eyeliner applied Cleopatra-style, green eye shadow, brilliantly red lipstick, thick mascara. I stood back and surveyed my work in the mirror. I licked my lips. On my way out the door to school, my father looked at me and said, Are you wearing makeup? Yes, I said. Take it off, he ordered. I walked out the door and sashayed away while he stood on the front step in his pajamas, hollering after me.

They sniffed me as I came in the door. Is that perfume? What are you wearing? My mother would repeat her own grandmother's phrase: You may be dressed, but your butt don't know it. I stood in my bedroom, piles of clothes on the floor, on the bed, on the chair, trying on this and that, every possible combination of clothes, anything to make me look older, anything to speed up this interminable lag time between here and there.

Looking back, I can understand my parents' fear. They will tell me later that they were worried I was on drugs, that they weren't sure where the normal mood swings and rebellions of adolescence ended and real disturbance began. They kept stretching the boundaries of normal, my mother tells me, wanting to believe that I was really all right. In truth, I *was* too young to look as I looked and talk as I did. When I think about this now, I feel torn between an adult's prissy disapproval of a child in heels and teased hair (slut), and my own memory of that time. I did not look or feel like a child. Something else was going on, some poison had crept into my blood. In my mind, things go dark: The colors of this time are deep and pervasive, blood reds and shadows, dark rooms, dark halls, a very dark desire.

I stood in the kitchen after school, scarfing down food without tasting it, staring at the television without seeing it. I would go through the perfunctory motions: washing my dishes, going into the bathroom, puking. In the bedroom, I'd stare at the mirror. When I entered junior high, at twelve, I'd been throwing up almost daily for three years. In seventh grade, it increased to two or three times a day. I began to do it whenever I got the chance.

Until I was twelve, I was probably still afraid of bulimia, though my bulimia became increasingly serious, to the point where I was bingeing and purging every day after school in the morbid silence of my parents' home. My mind pulls away from the early years, doesn't want to watch. My brain says: This is still the warm-up. Still prep school. Things were okay. I had the usual crushes, school yard catfights and melodramatic crises. I had plenty of friends, tight friends whom I loved very much and eventually lost. Nothing was *so* bad, I kept telling myself. Nothing that losing weight couldn't cure.

But I became less afraid, and there's the rub. One really ought to be afraid of self-torture. But it tempted me. It begged. The dark place that my mind was fast becoming blends, in my memory, with the dark womb of church: the chant, the fugue of prayer, the strange erotic energy that carving a very small cross into my thigh with a nail had brought.

In the garish glaring picture book sun of that small town, I was carefully constructing my own private hell.

Here is where the film begins to heat and melt, white absent spaces on the screen. Chronology ends—time and language twist upon themselves and become something else. Tenses, past, present, and future, lose their meaning. Here my life became a living theater of the absurd: the mistaken identities, the terrible coincidences, the exaggerated gestures, inane arguments, two plots circling each other, missing contact by the theatrical split second. There was self by day and self by night. There was life, within the four flowered walls of my childhood bedroom, and life in the echoing, spotless, white hallways of my parents' home, in school, at church. Backstage and onstage. Behind the velveteen curtains of the wings, I sat facing my mirror, took the cold white cream and tissues, first wiping away the dark black of the eyes, then the rose blush and white powder of cheeks, then the blood red of the lips. I sat staring, in silence, at the blank white nothing that remained. The oval absence, framed by wild black hair.

Something changed the year I entered junior high. For one thing, bulimia took over my life. It stopped being a moonlighting gig, something I just happened to feel like doing when things in my head were particularly crazy, or when I was angry or lonely or sad or flat. It began to have a force and took on a life of its own. From this point on, there are no memories that are not related to food or my body or barfing. It became a centripetal force that sucked me in, something I knew and needed. Badly. All the time. I did not put a bite of food in my mouth without considering if, when, and where I would throw up. I did not ever look in the mirror without thinking, *Fat*.

Consider, for instance, junior high parties. They started at seven and ended at ten. If you were lucky, they ended a little bit later. You wore a dress that made you look thin. You tried on every single piece of clothing you or your mother owned in search of the thing that would make you look thin. Fifteen-odd kids gather awkwardly in the basement of someone's gorgeous, enormous house. You all start eating. This is relatively normal, this is what people do at parties. They eat the Doritos and pretzels and Ruffles and nobody eats the veggies. You nibble on cookies and Hershey's kisses that somebody's mother has put in a cut-crystal bowl. Somebody's mother is hovering in the doorway, nervously glancing at the mixture of boys and girls. A pizza is ordered. Someone puts a movie in the VCR.

However. If you are bulimic, when the lights go out and cute kiddie couples pair off, slurpily kissing and fumbling on the couches, you will walk up the plush-carpeted stairs, heart pounding, face flushed with fear that the food is going to be digested before you can get it out. You will ask the sweet perfectly-made-up hovering mother where the bathroom is. She will point it out to you, smiling sweetly. You will go into the bathroom, take note of the brass fixtures on the sink, the Laura Ashley print wallpaper, the fresh flowers in a Waterford vase, the wicker magazine rack holding *Condé Nast Traveler* and *Forbes*. You will take a mental inventory of all of these things and scrutinize your face in the mirror.

You will beg God to keep your face normal after you puke as you turn on the water full force to drown out the retching and splashing, hoping to hell that the walls are thick so nobody hears. You will lift the toilet seat, carefully slide your fingers inside your mouth and down your throat, and puke until you see orange. The Doritos. You ate them first because you, like most bulimics, have developed a system of "markers," eating brightly colored food first so you can tell when it's all out, and it all comes out, in reverse order: the pizza, cookies, Ruffles, pretzels, Doritos, all swimming in dark swirls of Coke.

You straighten, flush. You turn the water down, put your hands under it, scrub with the Softsoap in a special matching Softsoap cover. You scrub hard, sniffing your hands and forearms. You look at your face. Thank you, God. No puffiness, eyes a little watery, but not red or bulging. You rinse your mouth with water, then look under the sink for mouthwash, find it, slosh it around. Redo your lipstick. Smile at the mirror, eyes bright and wide. Open the door, go downstairs.

Your friends turn and say, laughing, "Why was the water on?" In Minnesota houses, water pipes run downward through the center of the house and end in the basement. Three floors away, you can hear water running. You laugh, and say, "I'm paranoid about people hearing me pee." Everyone laughs. Your boyfriend, teasing, says, "We heard anyway."

You freeze, still smiling.

"No, I'm kidding," he says. You laugh nervously, take your place beside him, sit on your hands to hide the shaking, the nicks on the knuckles of the first two fingers of your right hand.

> Self-induced vomiting . . . causes abrasions on the back of the dominant hand or knuckles. Calluses form, creating what in medical parlance is called "Russell's sign."[13]

My boyfriend was sweet. We had a little puppy love. My parents and his parents panicked. You are too young for all this, they said. "All this" amounted to teddy bears at Valentine's Day, Saturday afternoons spent

---

[13] Ibid., 263.

sitting on the couch holding hands, watching movies while my father found countless excuses to traipse through the room, peering at us suspiciously. Kissing when he left, whispering dramatic things in long late-night phone calls, passing love notes in the halls. All was very chaste. I began to feel like I was wearing a sign on my forehead that said FUCKED UP in big neon letters. There was no visible reason for his parents to distrust me, nor for my parents to distrust my involvement with him. I had the feeling they knew something was wrong with me, some reason why I was problematic, but they couldn't pinpoint it.

The same held true at school. Rumors about me—that I was pregnant, I was easy, I was doing drugs—flew during seventh grade, which infuriated me, because none of these were true, yet. School was hell. My grades fell from As to Cs and Ds, the occasional F. I was in trouble all of the time. I was talking back, sitting in the back of the room with my head on the desk, reading a novel in my lap, whispering, passing notes, getting into screaming fights with boys who pissed me off. I developed a severe intolerance for any sort of irritant, especially the "in-crowd" boys, who were the main sources of those whispered rumors. These were boys who had money, played hockey, pinched girls' asses, told dirty jokes to make people blush, and never failed to solicit a loud string of obscenities from me. I spent a fair amount of time in detention, in-school suspension, or just plain kicked out.

Sitting in detention one day after school, I was reading and eating a bag of chips. The teacher didn't know it was the first thing I'd eaten that day, and would also be the last. She didn't know I was bulimic. She was a nice person who encouraged my writing, often calling me into her classroom to say, in a very concerned voice, that I wasn't living up to my Potential. There was nothing wrong with her, so I don't blame her for this. She said, wagging her finger at me as I munched away on my bag of chips, "A moment on the lips, forever on the hips."

I stopped midchew. Looked at her hips. She had big hips. She smiled at me. I smiled back. On my way out the door, I dropped my bag of chips in the garbage can, headed straight for the bathroom, threw up in the stall farthest from the door. Got dizzy as hell as I walked down the hall, footsteps echoing weirdly. I stumbled as I went down the stairs, hitting my head on the wall. I rubbed the bump and watched the patterns in the tile floor as they seemed to slide closer to my face, then veer away.

It was about then that I began to have regular, severe migraine headaches that knocked me into bed and left me shivering in the artificial night of drawn blinds and cold cloths. I began to have massive menstrual cramps, to complain of dizzy spells during gym class. I'd retreat to the locker room where I could barf and lie down in peace. I began to leave classes, dizzy and with black spots swimming before my eyes, and go to the school nurse, who had me lie down. It was very quiet in her office. She shuffled papers. I began to have stunning backaches. My mother gave me back rubs, knuckling knots the size of her fist. My parents took me to doctors. I spent the next several years discussing things with neurologists, biofeedback specialists, orthopedists, orthodontists, gynecologists, pediatricians, back specialists. I sat in waiting rooms paging through women's magazines, reading diet articles and ads for liposuction. People gave me pills and tried to worry out a possible cause, but none was available. Rare and mysterious illness. Psychosomatic complaints.

> [Bulimic] patients tend to somatize to other body systems. These patients are often referred to various medical subspecialists, because they complain of headaches, back pain, breathing difficulties, abdominal cramping and nausea, muscle and joint pain, and the like. . . . No doubt the pain is real but misplaced. Raging internal emotions erupt in the body . . . [the patient] would much rather have a concrete and treatable condition than a diffuse, potentially untreatable and shameful psychological one.[14]

I appeared at dinner one night, sat down, looked at my mother, and watched her open her mouth and scream. What the hell? I said, and apologized. Jesus, my father said, staring at me as if I'd grown horns. WHAT? I said. Honey, what's wrong with your eyes? He reached toward me. I jerked away and toward the mirror that hung above the buffet. I looked: The lower half of the white of my eyes was deep red. My eyes

[14] Ibid., 267–68.

looked as if they were welling with tears of blood. In fact, I had popped all the blood vessels while vomiting that afternoon, and the liquid red lay below the shimmery skin. I screamed and ran to my room.

Looking back, I can say: There. My life split in half, finally and definitively, right there, seventh grade. The outside world began to fade into the middle distance, and then to the background. Right there, I began to run toward the vanishing point with cold sweat running down my face. It did not seem that way at the time. It felt more like a bad day, an embarrassing event, a too-close call—I almost got caught. I sometimes think about how different my life might have been if I'd done what I should have that day: I should have confessed. I should have been scared off. I should have taken my cue from the universe that this was only going to get worse.

I did not. I threw up again that night, half-afraid that my eyeballs would explode. But it was, by far, more important that I get rid of dinner. Of course, by then, throwing up was the only way I knew to deal with fear. That paradox would begin to run my life: to know that what you are doing is hurting you, maybe killing you, and to be afraid of that fact—but to cling to the idea that this will save you, it will, in the end, make things okay.

At a certain point, an eating disorder ceases to be "about" any one thing. It stops being about your family, or your culture. Very simply, it becomes an addiction not only emotionally but also chemically. And it becomes a crusade. If you are honest with yourself, you stop believing that anyone could "make" you do such a thing—who, your parents? They want you to starve to death? Not likely. Your environment? It couldn't care less. You are also doing it for yourself. It is a shortcut to something many women without an eating disorder have gotten: respect and power. It is a visual temper tantrum. You are making an ineffective statement about this and that, a grotesque, self-defeating mockery of cultural standards of beauty, societal misogyny. It is a blow to your parents, at whom you are pissed.

And it is so very seductive. It is so reassuring, so all-consuming, so entertaining.

At first.

"Well!" thought Alice to herself. "After such a fall as this, I shall think nothing of tumbling down-stairs! How brave they'll all think me

at home! Why, I wouldn't say anything about it, even if I fell off the top of the house!" . . .

Down, down, down. Would the fall never come to an end?

Junior high is an unpleasant experience for many people. It was certainly not pleasant for me. The family was a raging mess. My parents were, as usual, not getting on very well, and I was not getting on very well with anyone. My father and mother were extremely volatile. My mother, when I ask her about it now, says she felt she was unwelcome in the family. That makes, by my count, three of us. We flitted in and out of the house. We perched on couches, plodded through the farcical ritual of the family dinner, silver pinging on the plates. My mother, like me, is a workaholic of astounding proportions, and she disappeared into the abyss of meetings and conferences. My father worked strange hours and was home more often than she. But my father and I were engaged in an undeclared war over everything. Nothing was too inane for us to get into a red-faced screaming match over. I discovered that breaking things, including but not limited to door frames, which suffered unduly from my endless door slamming, was very cathartic, as was my projectile launch from the door to the bed, face buried in the pillows, kicking and pounding the walls.

Years later, as we screamed at each other in family therapy, it would be none-too-gently pointed out to us that we fought so hard and so often for a very simple reason: It was the only mode of connection that we could agree upon. We baited and bit, taunted and tore at each other—but there was a point of contact, there was an assurance that the other one was *there,* that they knew *we* were there, that we were all being given our due moment of attention, that *we are all here together,* even if we are all here for the sole purpose of picking on each other. In the absence of tenderness, battle was preferred to the slow backward walk away from one another that silence would bring. Hatred is much closer to love than indifference. As I got older, the fighting grew more and more intense, as if we were all afraid of the inevitable moment when our cozy little war zone would fall silent, the small city of our family reduced to the razed fields and burnt-out buildings of separate lives.

One might wonder what, precisely, was the problem. This is an interesting and perhaps unanswerable question. There was no articulated problem. Nothing, the party line went, was wrong. People at church saw us as the perfect family. Friends thought my parents were darling. My parents' friends thought I was a dear, if a little hyperactive, a little mouthy. Later, a therapist would say, "Your family was very carefully constructed to say: We are a good, solid family. Nothing wrong here." And I think we were desperate to believe that. We did not discuss my mother's emotional absence, biting sarcasm, caustic comments about what I was wearing ("you look like a tart" was my personal favorite), sneering remarks about my adolescent angst, melodramatic mimicries of my tears ("Don't MOCK me, Mom," I'd scream, and in a high-pitched whine, imitating my Minnesota accent, she'd reply, "Don't MAAHK me, *Mahhm")*, irritated sighs at the slightest request—or utter silence. We did not discuss my father's unbelievable panic about my catapult into womanhood, nor did we mention his inarticulate and misdirected emotional needs, nor his causeless rages. We did, from the time I was thirteen until I left home at fifteen, discuss, at incredible length, my: melodrama, demands, moodiness, temper, bad behavior, irresponsibility, childishness, excessive precocity, attitude, mouthiness, craziness, etc. *I* was the problem. But we never wondered why I was the problem.

And we did not mention, or perhaps we did not notice, that not only *was* I the problem, but that I *had* a problem. I knew, by then, that I had a problem. I knew it the way alcoholics know in the back of their brain that they have a problem. They know, but they don't believe it's out of control. The convenience in having an eating disorder is that you believe, by definition, that your eating disorder cannot *get* out of control, because it *is* control. It is, you believe, your only means of control, so how could it possibly control you?

You know, for example, that making yourself an entire box of macaroni for dinner one night, drowning it in butter, and shoveling it into your mouth is being out of control. But it's really okay, you say to yourself, because you're going to puke, you're going to be overcome by an uncontrollable-oops-urge to throw up, thereby taking back control. You'll breathe easier, your stomach will no longer be distended or your face bloated. Your soul will be at ease. You'll get the bright idea to have a drink. You'll go into the kitchen, drink bad red wine until you're bombed and happy as a pig in clover, and walk up and down the hall juggling oranges, and then remember that wine has calories. You'll return to the bathroom, throw it up, and go to sleep. A problem? Yes, eating is definitely a problem. Got to stop eating.

I have to answer the obvious question: How could my parents *not* notice? They noticed that something was wrong with me—my anger was completely out of control, I was getting more and more batty by the day—but bulimia, especially in someone so young, is not the first thing that comes to a parent's mind when their thirteen-year-old kid is running wild. I did it when they weren't home, when I was out, or when I had the bathroom door locked and the tub running. I was becoming increasingly aware that I was an exceptionally good liar. My eating disorder was for me, as it is for many of us, one of the only things that I could call my own, something that I could keep private. My father was extremely intrusive at the time. It was his way of dealing with his own fears of my physical maturity and what myriad troubles that might bring. To be fair, I was indeed acting a little strange, and my parents were wondering what the hell was going on. He grilled me with inappropriate questions. He went digging through my drawers, my garbage, read my notes, grounded me for truly minor infractions. He was scared that I was in serious trouble and scared of losing his little girl. I can understand this. But it backfired.

The shrinks call it "emotional incest." Personally I find the term to be a little excessive, a little shrill. My father, like many fathers, freaked out when I hit puberty, and he began suspecting vast licentiousness on my part. I think if he had just told me he was worried about me, it might have gone over better. As it was, he acted like a jilted lover. He became more overprotective, more anxious, more rageful. As most adolescents do, I rejected his involvement in my life. He took it too personally and did his damnedest to show me who was boss. We fed on each other's escalating mania to such a degree that I'm surprised we're both still alive, let alone friends.

An environment that supports autonomy, quoth the shrinks, will foster a greater sense of self-esteem, of self-determination, of separateness from other people—in short, if your family assumes that you are capable of doing things yourself, you will internalize that assumption and act accordingly. You will develop a firm sense of self, a belief in your own capability. Whereas if you grow up in a controlling environment, where your ability to make decisions and act independently is constantly being undermined, you are likely to internalize a deep level of self-doubt and "develop a sense of self-worth contingent upon extrinsic rewards and the evaluation of others."[15]

Too often the shrinks assume an eating disorder is a way of avoiding womanhood, sexuality, responsibility, by arresting your physical growth at a prepubescent state. But more recently, some insightful people have noticed that some of us may be after something quite different, like breathing room, or, crazy as it sounds, *less* attention, or a different *kind* of attention. Something like power. An eating disorder appears to be a perfect response to a lack of autonomy. By controlling the amount of food that goes into and out of you, you imagine that you are controlling the extent to which other people can access your brain, your heart. You also throw the family into turmoil, neatly distracting them from their endless bickering, focusing their worry on your "craziness" while you yourself saunter off stage left. The shrinks have been paying way too much attention to the end result of eating disorders—that is, they look at you when you've become utterly powerless, delusional, the center of attention, regressed to a passive, infantile state—and they treat you as a passive, infantile creature, thus defeating their own purpose. This end result is *not* your intention at the outset. Your intention was to become superhuman, skin thick as steel, unflinching in the face of adversity, out of the grasping reach of others. "Anorexia develops when a bid for independence on the part of the child has failed."[16] It is not a scramble to get back *into* the nest. It's a flying leap *out*.

And no, it doesn't work. But it seemed like a good idea at the time.

Anorexia was my Big Idea, my bid for independence, identity, free-

[15] Frederick and Grow, "A Mediational Model of Autonomy, Self-Esteem, and Eating Disordered Behaviors and Attitudes," *Psychology of Women Quarterly*, v. 20 (1996): 218–19.
[16] Casky, 180.

dom, savior, etc. etc. It's astonishing how many eggs you can put in one basket, how much symbolic and emotional interest you can vest in one little disease. Anorexia—not just a "diet," not just losing a little weight, but a full-blown, all-out big bang die-of-starvation Problem—looked like the path to my salvation. This is relatively common in bulimics who jump the fence. Bulimia disgusted me, and I was disgusted enough with myself as it was. When I was thirteen, I began inching my way toward anorexia.

You don't just *get* it, the way you just *get* a cold; you take it into your head, consider it as an idea first, play with the behaviors awhile, see if they take root. Most people develop anorexia more abruptly than I do, but a lot of people travel seamlessly between bulimia and anorexia, torn between two lovers. This is what I did. I wanted to be an anoretic, but I was already seriously addicted to bulimia and couldn't just up and leave it. I felt like I was going out of my mind. My head was never quiet. Quiet is an in-between point, implying a balance between noise and silence, between the strange blackouts I began to have—pure silence, not sleeplike but deathlike—and the hellish shrieking jumble of my own thoughts and the voices of the world.

And the sharp hiss of one voice that started out softly, as though below layers of moss, or flesh, and gradually became so loud it drowned out everything else: *Thinner*, it said. *You've got to get thinner.*

But you know, even then, that word was wrong. It is more than Thinness, per se, that you crave. It is the implication of Thin. The tacit threat of Thin. The Houdini-esque-ness of Thin, walking on hot coals without a flinch, sleeping on a bed of nails. You wish to carry Thinness on your arm, with her cool smile. You wish for that invisible, vibrating wire that hums between lovers, implying a private touch. You wish for such a wire, humming between you and Thinness, at a party, on the street, humming softly between you and death.

In the lag time between now and thinner, I went looking for something else to fill the void. In the summer of 1987, I lost my loose grasp on a sort of self-respect, and with it fell the last of my caution. I stopped caring about much of anything at all, save for self-destruction. That interested me plenty.

In eighth grade, I grew tired of vacillating between dual personae—good student/troublemaker, nice girl/mean bitch—and I threw in the towel. I dove into sluthood with vigor. I dyed my hair a darker black, bought new lipstick, pleaded no contest to the rumors at school. My eighth-grade class picture shows me glassy-eyed, glossy-lipped, black hair curly and falling sexily over one eye. I was thirteen. Over the summer, my boyfriend and I had broken up over the fact that I'd been messing around with (fucking, though no one knew that) a true jackass while I was away at camp. My new persona forced up my chin in the halls when my ex-boyfriend's friends called me a whore. I swished by. I got stuck in a revolving door of crushes and fucks. The crushes my friends knew about. They were junior high crushes, the cute new kid with cool glasses and a funky name. The fucks I didn't mention. They were extracurricular. They were skanky morons from the city or from neighboring suburbs who wore duck-tailed hair and obscene pubic mustaches. I met them in malls or movie theaters. They skulk over to the suburbs looking for jailbait. The conversation always goes like this: Hey/Hey. Routine flirtation occurs and you stand there batting your eyes thinking how butt-ugly they are. Phone numbers are exchanged. Meetings are arranged. They say, Hi, you look nice. Then they stick their tongue down your throat and the rest is history.

Choices, choices. So many means of self-destruction, so little time. I branched out. I expanded my horizons. Why be just bulimic when you can be fucked up every day in school without anyone ever noticing? Why not carry vodka in a mineral water bottle into choir and drink it between songs? Why not, since everyone seems to think you're a slut anyway, just prove them right? Why not flirt and fuck around with strangers? Why not sleep with strangers who deal drugs, or who have a friend of a friend who deals drugs, and ask, pouting sexily (you've been practicing "sexy" in the mirror), if you can have some? Why not whine, Fair's fair—? Brighten up happily when you get a Baggie full of pills or powder, pocket it, flounce out of the car, say, sweetly, "Thanks." Walk the rest of the way home, running your hand over your rumpled hair, thinking, I need a shower.

I did not stop bingeing and purging. I kept right on doing it, usually twice a day I simply entertained myself with the delusion that bulimia was not as interesting as some other things. It came to seem tangential, a part of the day as basic and predictable as breathing. I had better things to do than waste my time with such petty distractions as food. The year is a blur to me. I can only recall, with utmost clarity, the bathrooms at school (downstairs, upstairs, locker room), the bathrooms at home, the bathrooms at church. The solitary drinking of whatever booze I could sneak, the drugs. The feeling of the back of my head bumping against the handle of a backseat door, the sound of the breath of the body above me. My report cards show a steady string of D's. I was kicked out of the Gifted and Talented program at school and called, with sad sighs and deep sympathy for my parents, an Underachiever. There were terribly concerned parent-teacher conferences. I stared upward, counting the little dots in the panels on the ceiling while everyone talked about how I was not living up to my Potential. Notes were sent home saying: Talks too much. Work lacks effort. Disruptive behavior. Work incomplete. My favorite one, a midterm notice with a big obscene-looking F on it, says: "Marya . . . just seems to dissociate herself. . . . Her work quality has gone down. She gives the impression of being 'indifferent' to the situation."

I was indifferent. I remember zoning off during classes, staring out the window, writing stories in my head, fixing my gaze on the particular shape of a particular tree's branch outside. Sound stopped. I stared. Class ended. I wandered out, down to lunch, ate a little minipizza and an ice cream bar, stopped in the bathroom to puke, went to the next class. Sometimes I wandered out of school, down the road, alone. Just floated off. Came back for musical rehearsals or newspaper after school. Finished that, stopped at the community center next door, got a candy bar, chips, Mr. Pibb. Ate in the bathroom stall of the empty building, then barfed.

While I danced and sang with a big happy smile in school musicals and wrote ridiculous smart-assed editorials for the school newspaper, while I told my parents, "I'm going to the mall with friends," my shadow slipped away, shut the bedroom door, opened the bedside drawer, reached a hand behind it, untaped the small plastic bag of cocaine, stuck a long pinkie nail up the nose, and breathed in hard: infinitesimal slivers of glass flying into the gray matter of my brain.

> At least 30% and perhaps as many as 50% of patients with bulimia nervosa also have a history of current or prior substance abuse. . . . Substance abuse often is not restricted to street drugs . . . Valium, Librium, Dalmane, Xanax, and Halcion can also be abused by these patients, because [of] their propensity toward insomnia.[17]

Shivering, I lay in the dark in a field of scratch grass and nettles, watching the stars spin like pinwheels, biting the left side of my lower lip so as not to scream. I have always disliked needles. My skirt hiked up, the dry dirt and weeds were itching my thighs, the ragged strip of tire around my right arm pinched the skin. I leaned back, tense, into the awkward cradle of elbows and knees of some boy, who crooned to me. I remember thinking he would make a good nurse. I laughed a jerky laugh and he said Shhh. His thumb ran up and down the inside crook of my arm. In the blue light, the joint looked off somehow, looked broken, sadly removed from my body, and I began to cry for the loss of my arm. He, his thumb thudding softly over the bump of the vein, said, Shhh. The needle bit my arm. I felt the sharp sting of liquid in the vein, imagined I could feel it tracking its way to my brain, a maze like they have on kiddie paper place mats in midwestern restaurants. I got up, swayed off, sat down by a swamp. He came and sat beside me. I watched the murky reflection of our faces in the slag water, pale moonish faces. He said: Amazing, isn't it? I said: Amazing.

He was anyboy. Their hands are what I remember. Or not so much their hands, but my body under their hands. The way I slid my body under their hands, as one might slide a note under the door. Wanting their hands, the clutching hands of boys who do not know the weight of their bodies, or the weight of their words, so they drop these things carelessly, and bruise, wanting only to touch.

I wanted them to bruise. I wanted to know I was there. I wanted to

---

[17] Zerbe, 224, 265.

touch and be touched, if only for the intense explosion of nerve endings that said *I'm here he's here we're here.* And I wanted to feel used. Or at least feel useful. And, the eternal masochist, I wanted to go home afterward, look at my thighs, my ass, eyes narrowed at myself, mouthing names at myself in the mirror.

> Sex, like bingeing, is an attempt to fill a void . . . bulimic patients tend to have more past and current sexual involvements [than anoretics] . . . tend to be more sexually active than individuals who do not have eating disorders . . . not looking so much for a compatible and complementary partner as she is attempting to experience herself as more whole and alive . . . alleviates terrifying anxiety and brings the other person close . . . to such a degree that the patient loses sight of any boundaries between herself and her partner . . . terrifying experience . . . temporary loss of identity . . . body begins . . . ends . . . fragmentation. . . .[18]

I spent my nights up late: towel pressed against the crack below the door to block the thin knife of light, one light on the bedside table. I lay on my side on the green carpet of my bedroom floor, in front of the mirror, watching my legs move up and down, and up and down, in endless calisthenics, a precise number of each. Even if the muscles, weakened, began to tremble, I kept lifting, thinking *lazy bitch.* Left side first, then right side, then standing, then on my back, then on my belly. I watched each inch of my flesh as it flexed and relaxed, got lost in the repetition, got off on the image, pictured myself smaller, and smaller, and smaller, until I was no more than a slip of a thing. I pulled my thighs apart to see how they'd look when I got skinny, pinched hard at the excess, tried to smother the wellspring of terror that rose in my chest when I thought: *I'm fat.* If the terror would not go down, I'd promise myself: no food tomorrow. None. That let me breathe a little easier. The punishment seemed just, seemed as if it might make things better, more organized, the calming twist of hunger in the chest might remind me

[18] Ibid., 183.

that things were all right. I'd lie down on the bed, open my bedside table drawer.

Inside the drawer, pills for night and powders for day, my little bag of tricks, my expansion of mind, my great experiment, my Mr. Hyde. The glass-eyed grin that spread across my face each morning, isn't life exciting, what shall we play today, isn't everything just so traumatic, so dramatic, just so high and shrill, the sound of this blurred whir of the cogs and wheels inside my head.

My friends looked at me, perhaps wondered once or twice about the manic extremes of my voice, my mood, my laughter and screams, barely a breath apart. I was vivacious, rebellious, obnoxious, often sick, sometimes cruel, and sometimes falling apart on the locker room floor, usually seething at something, running away from my house in the night. Slipping out the back door, over the frozen white still of the lake behind my parents' house, over the white-lit-blue calm of snow-washed lawns, through the crunching lamplit streets, shivering. Standing sometimes on the icy walkway over the freeway, gloveless hands gripping the chain-link fence, watching the cars drive by.

My parents wondered, later, where I got the drugs. They wondered who, and how. They wanted to know when. They sat on the therapist's couch, staring at me, bewildered, disbelieving, wanting to know how the rose-cheeked, snub-nosed little girl they remembered could play this fantastic trick under their roof. My actor parents in my theater of a house sat looking out separate windows, wanting, absurdly, to know where I learned to lie so well. They decided they didn't believe me. Fair enough.

I learned about sex the way you learn about reporting: you just do it. No one ever explained it to me. Sex ed class was actually menstruation class. No one ever mentioned birth control in my presence. The shrinks say, by the way, that there is a strong connection between early interaction with the opposite sex and concerns about weight. In my experience, there was a strong connection between sex, a temporary adrenaline rush, and a flooding sense of being fat and needing to throw up. Despite my level of not only sexual behavior but also sexual fascination, I knew precious little about its technicalities. When I was nine, and indisputably a virgin, I stood in front of the mirror sticking my little belly out, wondering in panic if I might have gotten pregnant from playing doctor with a little boy when I was five, and if I was still pregnant, how would I explain it to my parents? What would they say?

Five years later, at fourteen, I stood in front of the mirror and realized I *was* pregnant.

How would I explain it to my parents? What would they say?

I asked my friends what they would do if I got pregnant. My friends were used to my weird, morbid, hypothetical questions. I asked them with some regularity what they would do if I died. No, seriously, I said. What would you do? I casually fished for opinions on abortion: a unanimous no, ringing with the righteous certainty of Catholic girls who've never had sex. Abortion is Wrong, we all agreed. I asked my mother what she would tell me to do if I was pregnant. She said, clearly uncomfortable with such a topic, that she would want me to get an abortion.

Then one night at dinner while I was building small cities out of mashed potatoes and peas, I felt something somehow *snap.* It was a funny sort of snap, not like cracking your knuckles. It was more like the smallish snap of a thread, more of a *snip*. Suddenly I felt very pale and sick to my stomach. I said excuse me. I went to the bathroom, running my hand along the wall. I locked the door, sat down on the toilet, and doubled over. I turned on the bathwater tap with difficulty. I could not get my hands to stop shaking. I saw my face, an ugly gray, in the mirror. I felt a dullish, carving, strange sort of feeling inside. Then it turned sharp and stabbed. I remember thinking, very clearly, Well. That was easy. I remember standing up on the toilet when it was over, lifting my skirt up, and looking at the blood coating the inside of my thighs. And then I remember getting distracted. I turned to one side and scrutinized at my butt. Fat ass, I thought. Pig.

Things move in fast-forward from here on out. To get drugs I was sleeping with some boyfriend-of-a-friend-of-a-friend when I could. I woke up in the morning, took uppers that I washed down with lukewarm water on my bedside table, took downers at lunch in the bathroom stalls after throwing up. I opened the refrigerator door after school, the most dreaded part of the day. Drank a little wine, nips from the rarely used bottles in the liquor cabinet, went to sleep or read, ate dinner, threw up, took downers, slept. In the whirl of things, somewhere along the line, there are these flashes: a boy in the back of a car, hand laid on my belly, saying, Such a pretty belly, such a pretty little body. And the thought through my mind: get rid of the belly. The damp feel of the concrete wall in the locker room bathroom stalls, the sweaty palm groping upward for something to hang on to, head spinning, lunch and blood spinning away. These flashes, which somehow, even now, knowing they took place, do not line up with who I was, or who I thought I was, or who I seemed to be, or the mundane sunny halls of Southview Junior High, where I was just another teenage girl gone wrong.

My parents thought I was going out of my mind. Off to the psychiatrist I went.

> *The Caterpillar and Alice looked at each other for some time in silence: at last the Caterpillar took the hookah out of its mouth, and addressed her in a languid, sleepy voice.*
>
> *"Who are you?" said the Caterpillar.*
>
> *This was not an encouraging opening for a conversation. Alice replied, rather shyly, "I-I hardly know, Sir, just at present—at least I know who I was when I got up this morning, but I think I must have been changed several times since then."*
>
> *"What do you mean by that?" said the Caterpillar, sternly. "Explain yourself!"*
>
> *"I can't explain myself, I'm afraid, Sir," said Alice, "because I'm not myself, you see."*
>
> *"I don't see," said the Caterpillar.*
>
> *"I'm afraid I can't put it any more clearly," Alice replied, very politely, "for I can't understand it myself, to begin with; and being so many different sizes in a day is very confusing."*
>
> *"It isn't," said the Caterpillar. . . .*
>
> *"Well, perhaps your feelings may be different," said Alice: "all I know is, it would feel very queer to me."*
>
> *"You!" said the Caterpillar contemptuously. "Who are you?" . . .*
>
> *As the Caterpillar seemed to be in a very unpleasant state of mind, she turned away.*

"Come back!" the Caterpillar called after her. "I've something important to say!"

This sounded promising, certainly. Alice turned and came back again.

"Keep your temper," said the Caterpillar.

"Is that all?" said Alice.

The psychiatrist, who hated me because I called him Dokter Freud, or possibly for other reasons, was a very small, gray sort of man who wore fine suits and black shoes spit-polished to a leering gleam. I was not entirely sure why I was seeing him. He was my mother's psychiatrist, so I guess it was just easier to take me to him than to anyone else. My headaches were still a mystery, as were my occasional trips to the school nurse for blackouts. The problem, I thought, wasn't medical. I wondered if I was being sent to a shrink because of my grades, but I couldn't figure out how he would help with that. I went, amiably enough, because I got to miss school to go.

On the first visit, he opened the door, swung his arm toward the room, and told me to come in. I stood stiffly, going nowhere. He pointed to a chair. It was very quiet and the circulated air made my nose burn. I sat down in the chair. It was black leather, and I think it had wheels. It faced his desk. There was one plant, I think, by the windows to my right, which looked out on the parking lot of the business complex we were in, the manicured park, the freeway overpass, and America's first shopping mall, Southdale, built in 1958, an important fact we learned repeatedly in grade school.

On the wall facing me there were bookshelves: mostly Freud, or about Freud, or taking a Freudian approach to something. Some Jung, the DSM criteria manuals, abnormal psychology books. One book I recognized with horror, *The Gifted Child,* which my mother was reading and I had stolen, read, and dismissed as completely ridiculous, mostly because I was sure she was reading it because something was wrong with me. A lot of books with titles that were hard to see, so I craned my neck in an effort to read them.

"What are you doing?" he said.

I jumped. He'd been sitting in his chair, watching me. "I'm looking at the books," I said. He had big square black 1950s glasses that made him look a bit mean and excessively paternal.

"Why?" he asked.

I was at a loss. "Why not?" I said.

He made a note. He wrote on lined yellow legal-size paper and used a black pen with a wide tip. I craned my neck to see what he was writing. He moved the pad away. There were perhaps eight feet between us, and I needed glasses but hadn't told anyone. His writing was very small, very square, block printing, all caps. I could tell the shape from where I sat but not what he was writing. He wrote, I would later note, on only one side of the paper, flipping each used page upward with a slightly over-dramatic flourish and beginning again at a mad pace. I would remark that he was wasting paper. He would peer at me and make a note.

To my left was a black leather couch. I said, half-joking, "Will I have to lie on the couch?"

He looked at me, furry gray eyebrows arched. "Do you want to?" he asked.

I was mortified. "No," I said. "Why would I want to lie on the couch?"

He peered. "I don't know," he said. "Why *would* you want to lie on the couch?"

"I DON'T," I said, glaring at him. We sat in silence for a few minutes. I looked at the parking lot.

"Do you want to leave?" he asked.

"Excuse me?"

"Do you want to leave?"

"I don't really care," I said, which was true. We sat. He made notes.

"What are you writing?" I asked.

"Notes."

"Thank you," I said, like a mouthy little rat. "That's very helpful. Notes on what?"

"Observations."

"Observations of me?"

He stopped writing and looked at me. "Is it important to you, how people observe you?"

"Not particularly," I said, which was a bald-faced lie, "but I'm just wondering, since I haven't said anything yet."

He didn't answer. I picked up a magazine and started thumbing through it. *National Geographic*. Giraffes.

He leaned back in his chair. It creaked. "Mayra," he said, contemplatively.

"Marya."

"Pardon?"

"Marya. My name is Marya. Not Mayra. *M-A-R-Y-A*."

"Ah," he said. "Maria—"

"MARYA. MAR-YA. Two syllables. Not Maria. Not Myra, not Mayra, not Mara. Marya."

"Does it bother you when people mispronounce your name?"

"YES."

He made a note. I started sliding downward in my chair.

Things proceeded in this fashion for the first few visits: I came in. He looked at me. I glowered at him. I looked out the window. He asked what I would later learn in journalism school were very leading questions. ("So, you're afraid of snakes, aren't you?") I'd counterquestion. Then I began to get bored and, having nothing better to do for an hour, began to tell him, rather abruptly, the truth.

"What do you want to talk about today?" he said.

"Well, I think I have an eating disorder." I pulled my knees up into the black leather chair and picked at the fraying gray canvas of my Keds.

"Oh?"

"Yes. I think so. I read some books."

He took notes.

"And also I drink a lot. At least, like, a lot, for like, I guess, my age, or something."

Pause.

"And also I'm sleeping with people and also I'm sometimes doing drugs."

Long pause.

"Like, heroin."

He peered at me over his glasses.

"And?" he said, bemused.

"Um. Well, I don't know." I pulled at the place where the soles were coming loose from my shoes. I tossed my hair arrogantly. "I guess it's like, fine. I mean, whatever. I mean, who cares? It's like, not a big deal."

He took notes. The rest of the sessions, I did talk. I told him everything that came into my head, jabbered cheerfully, swearing like a sailor for kicks. Pulled up my shirtsleeves to show him the bruises on my arms, opened up my mouth as far as I could to show him the raw patch on the back of my throat that burned like hell when I drank orange juice. Rubbed the even row of scabs, little dash marks, teeth marks made in haste, on the first and second knuckles of my right hand. Then fell silent, slouched back in my chair, chin up, daring him to call my bluff.

But it was not a bluff.

He never said a thing—that is, until the last day, when I was shouting, as I often did, that he never said anything. Why didn't he ever say anything? It made me fucking NERVOUS, like, what are you writing there, anyway? Aren't you like, going to fix it? This is like, NOT HELPING, you ASSHOLE, and like, WHY are you CHARGING my PARENTS all this fucking MONEY so you can SIT there and like LAUGH AT ME?

"Do you think people laugh at you, Maria?"

"MARYA! MY NAME IS MARYA, you FUCK! Are you like, going to tell me what my PROBLEM IS, or WHAT? Tell me! Just TELL me what is WRONG with me!" I hollered, red-faced and shaking and furious at this bastard's interminable poise.

"I think," he said calmly, leaning back in his chair with a smile on his face, "that you," he said, clicking the pen cap back on his fancy pen, "are a very angry young lady."

I, halfway out the door, swung back around and started laughing like a hyena, horrible rasping laughs. "That's it?" I said. "It took you all this time to figure THAT out? Brilliant! You're fucking brilliant! Oh, my GOD!" and I slammed the door, hoping it would fall off the hinges. It didn't. But I never went back.

In fact, I didn't go back into therapy for another three years, not until I was put into the hospital for the first time.

Years are important here. The research shows that one of the major factors in "chronic" eating disorders is duration. By the time I got professional help, at the age of sixteen, I was well past the five-year mark, the mark where the doctors will look at your charts, raise their eyebrows, shake their heads, and say, "Since you were nine, huh?" You will nod and look at the scale, cold and waiting to bruise the soles of your scaly feet. "Do you want to get well?" they'll ask. You'll shrug and look at the scale, wondering how off it is, whether it will lie and tell them you weigh three pounds more than you actually do. You will be obliged to correct it, on principle, to save your soul, and for your pains you will find yourself with a new address, Eating Disorders Unit, Eighth Floor, having confirmed their suspicions, because who, with a pulse of forty-three and a systolic pressure careening in vertical swoops, gives a flying fuck if the scale is three pounds off? An anoretic, that's who. Does she care that she's dying? Hell, no.

Toward the end of eighth grade, a friend from church ratted on me. I'd known her a long time. We weren't exactly close, but through confirmation class she'd come to know me better than most of my closest friends. She told the school counselor that I was throwing up. As mad as I said I was at the time, I had never been so grateful for anything in my life. I was called into the counselor's office. As I sat there, staring over her shoulder out the window, I was not ashamed. I was not even afraid. I was flattered. And, God help me, I was proud. Something had been confirmed: I was worth giving a shit about; I was getting to be a successful sick person. *Sick* is when they say something. Of course, I'd been sick for five years. But now, now maybe I was really sick. Maybe I was getting good at this, good enough to scare people. Maybe I would almost die, and balance just there, at the edge of the cliff, wavering while they gasped and clutched one another's arms, and win acclaim for my death-defying stunts.

But who the hell were they? Just what was I trying to prove, and to whom? This is one of the terrible, banal truths of eating disorders: when a woman is thin in this culture, she proves her worth, in a way that no great accomplishment, no stellar career, nothing at all can match. We believe she has done what centuries of a collective unconscious insist that no woman can do—control herself. A woman who can control herself is almost as good as a man. A thin woman can Have It All. At the mirror, I pulled the skin of my face tight and grinned a garish, bone-protruding grin.

The counselor was very concerned in that way people who haven't the faintest idea what to do, or even what the problem is, always are. She said one of us would have to tell my parents that I'd been throwing up, me or her. I thought it over. I said that I would tell them, guessing they would take it less seriously if I told them. I guessed right.

That night, at dinner, I said MomandDadIhavesomethingtotellyou. Staring at my plate, I said, I've been making myself throw up.

There was a long pause and low light. The window to my left looked out on the night. The mirror to my right reflected the stone wall. Dinner sat on my plate, waiting. The fork in my hand shook and dinged against the glass.

My mother said, "I used to do that."

My father said, "I knew it!"

I sat blankly. My father said, "See?" and tapped his temple. "Mr. Pig knows," he said. "Remember the other day, when I came into your room, and I asked if you were getting obsessive about your weight?"

I said yes. I said, um, you were right.

I cried. I said I had stopped. We all, for some reason, had a good laugh.

I had not stopped. My eating disorder had taken a sharp turn for the worse. I was bingeing, alone, whenever I could, with whatever money I had. Fast-food restaurants, diners, food from home, food from other people's houses. I was doing hours of calisthenics in my room, wondering if, at the age of fourteen, I could get a plastic surgeon to do liposuction on every inch of my body, suck each molecule of fat out, leaving me with nothing more than a gleeful clattering set of bones. I lay in bed each night and stared at my body with a hate that even now brings bile to my tongue. My hatred of the bulimia, as well, steadily grew. That hatred became, with a little time, an absolute commitment to becoming an anoretic. I ate less normally, began "dieting," lying to friends who were asking me about why I wasn't eating, whether I was throwing up, what the hell was going on. I began passing out in school. Flu, I said.

Headache. Allergy to MSG, on the rag, not enough sleep, bad cold, bronchitis.

Bulimia is hard to see, because it doesn't necessarily change your body size. It is also more immediately dangerous. I ditched one boy for another boy, phone fucking until all hours of the night. Making out in movie theaters. I had begun to be objectively good-looking, older looking. I'd lost the baby fat and was steady at my natural weight, a nice hour-glassy sort of shape I draped with low-cut sweaters and short skirts.

My life had begun to revolve around men, as many women's lives do. We sat—a few girls whose reticence about sex was, by necessity, fast disappearing—discussing dicks. To an extent, I feigned ignorance, but to a greater extent, I simply was ignorant. I knew how to give passable head and make noises at the right time, but I probably could not have defined *testicle* if I'd been called to, nor could I have explained the biological basis for the bizarre phenomenon of a hard-on. The nature of dicks was a mystery to us—the mechanics of dicks, the tremble of a belly as your tentative, spidery hands crept down. We discussed the direction of dicks: Peter, up to the right, David, straight to the left, Brian, a hard line down, an arrow. We were certain that they were supposed to point *up*. We laughed and laughed. We discussed: Was it possible to get pregnant from giving head? One girl said yes; one girl said no, not if you didn't swallow. I adamantly insisted that it would only be possible if you had an ulcer, and the cum somehow *got out*, and we pictured all those blind tadpoles wiggling their way through our innards, heads bonking against liver and spleen, taking the long way around. Leslie offered, on the matter of dick direction, that they pointed toward you. They did, she said, nodding. Her mother had said so. Their dicks would point straight at you. I wondered aloud: So what if you stood up, and walked back and forth in front of them, would they follow you? A little radar? I pictured my dog, following the teasing bone above her head.

The very idea that you could control a man's body was intoxicating; that you could make his head turn, follow your passing steps, that you could lean just so, or speak just so, or simply glance and toss your head, and he would be caught. The wonder of the female body, in all of its impossible secrecy, is understood in some innate sense but is not easily articulated. You cannot explain, with the limitations of language and inexperience, why your body can cause such a sudden, fumbling response in someone else, nor can you put into exact words what *you* feel about your body, explain the thrum it feels in proximity to another warm-skinned form. What you feel is a tangle of contradictions: power, pleasure, fear, shame, exultation, some strange wish to make noise. You cannot say how those things knit themselves together somewhere in the lower abdomen and pulse.

We knew what we could do and feel, but we could not say why. I do not think we understood then that the female body is more than the sum of its mute parts. We misunderstood the power we sensed, the scent and shape of ourselves. What we were discovering, flopped across one another's warm laps, was physical, sensual, sexual, material, and it was power. Why must the power of the female body cancel the power of the female mind? Are we so afraid of having both? What would it mean for women to have both? It's fine for a woman to be smart, so long as she is mousy, bespectacled, shy, because she is then no longer the obvious object of desire. It's okay for a woman to be sexual, tits bouncing and ass-presenting, because she is no longer obvious competition for intellectual glory. What if she is both? We complained that the double standard just wasn't fair: if a girl has sex, she's a slut; if a guy has sex, he's a stud. But we probably believed that to some extent.

I was light-years away from reading the first word of feminist literature, let alone developing my own understanding of feminism, sexuality, intellect, and ultimately, health. I loudly called myself a feminist, but it was mostly by principle. I had no idea what feminism actually meant, beyond the fact that I thought it was bullshit that all the boys in Gifted and Talented were drooled over for their grubby little pages of Fabulous Scientific Inventions while my friends' footnoted analyses of the American judicial systems, their artwork, their poetry, my stories, were smiled at, given Creativity awards, and then ignored. Where I come from, "feminist" is an insult. My friends—several of whom would go into feminist academia as adults—occasionally took me aside and told me that I was getting, like, a little militant about this whole "feminism" thing. I'd already landed myself in detention more than once for calling the psycho art teacher a sexist, and also for punching Jeff Seick when he insisted upon calling me a women's libber. To tell you the truth, *libber* sounded like *blubber* to me, so I didn't care for the term.

My body, for no reason I could understand, was an object of considerable interest to the lewd and obnoxious boys of my school, to the skanky sons of bitches I picked up like crusty green pennies from the gutters of neighboring towns. I believed that my power—it was a general sort of idea—would be incrementally increased with each pound lost. There is plenty of research to suggest that I was not alone in that belief. Studies of girls show that they associate thinness with both academic and social success.[19] I saw it more as a prerequisite to success of any sort. I saw it as the ticket out of my suffocating suburban life, out of the torrent of untoward thoughts in my head, out of the self that was simply not good enough.

The anorexic body seems to say: I do not need. It says: Power over the self. And our culture, in such a startlingly brief period of time, has come to take literally the idea that power over the body has a ripple effect: power over the body, over the life, over the people around you, power over a world gone berserk.

We are about to watch one person's systematic, total loss of any power at all.

Fourteen years old at the end of eighth grade. A surreal and hot-as-hell summer ensued. I listened to maudlin love songs by the Beatles and Simon and Garfunkel as I lay on the couch in the basement, cooling off in the long, blindingly bright afternoons. I wandered into the kitchen, ate, barfed, lay back down. Lay in the sun in the yard reading a book. Days melted into one another, a progression of meals and bathrooms and naps. Ninth grade began, the last year of junior high, and I began plotting, in earnest, to get out. I hated Edina and had no interest whatsoever in going to the high school there. I begged my parents to let me go to boarding school, to move into my own apartment, to let me go somewhere, anywhere but there. I wanted to cut my ties to where I'd been and who I was, and make up someone new.

---

[19] Ibid., 119.

The girl gets up each day and creates herself out of cloth and paint. She writes at night about men who looked, and boys who touched, and weight. She writes of the great weakness that drove her to the cupboard and made her eat. The writing is never enough. Confession is insufficient. Absolution never comes in the articulation, only in the penance. She thinks of the saints: their flagellums, their beds of nails, their centuries-late apologies for Eve who doomed all women to the pains of the flesh by giving in to the pleasures of that flesh. They lacerate their own flesh in penance for Eve, for the sins of the world, which they shoulder as their own. They wear hair shirts, or razors next to their skin.

She reads books on the saints. The sainted anoretics, who, in their holy asceticism, insisted that God was telling them to starve. She considers God. She determines he, if they were on speaking terms, would tell her to starve for general sins. The hair shirt is her own skin, rasping on the rawness of what lies beneath. She wills herself to rise above the flesh: not food, not sex, not touch, not sleep. She snorts cocaine in her flowered room to keep from giving in to sleep, a weakness, and she, already too weak, refuses to give in. The bulimia and the drugs give rise to insomnia and chemical imbalance. The insomnia gives rise to mania, a racing of thoughts and sadistically vivid images flashing in the brain—"the atrocious lucidity of insomnia," Borges called it—the thoughts spiral upward, whistling shrill as a teakettle screaming inside the brain.

She goes too long without sleep and freaks.

She doesn't remember when it begins. She becomes violently afraid of the dark again. She is too old for this, her parents remind her. Each night, she makes her father check every lock, every window and door, scour the basement for the man she is sure has come to get her, the man with the knife. She lies in her bed, stiff as a corpse, waiting for the footstep on the stair. She cannot sleep. Each twitch and sigh of the house, each wind tapping the walls and trees, bolt her upright, screaming for Dad. Dad comes running and tries very hard to understand. She cannot stay home alone. She has been staying home alone since she was nine years old. At fourteen, it becomes impossible. She sits on the front steps of the house when she gets home from school and waits for someone to come home. The shaking: She remembers mostly the shaking, her whole body, tense and trembling, waiting for the man who will corner her in her room, with his knife, and slice her apart.

She thinks, looking back, that this was a premonition. This is the last year she lives at home. She wants her mother and father to save her. She says this, and Dad asks in earnest: From what?

From myself.

My night fears ended as suddenly as they began. I began applying to art high schools. I had won several writing awards during my three years in junior high, had played leading roles in plays. Everyone said I could sing, everyone said I was headed for Broadway blah blah blah. I just wanted to get the fuck out, and "talent" was as good an excuse as any. By that point, I was as firmly convinced as anyone that I was not particularly intelligent. As I recall, I thought I was a fuck-up with good tits, useful for sex and laughs.

In the winter of ninth grade, I carefully typed my poems and stories, put them into a blue three-ring binder, and prepared two monologues. My father blocked the scenes. It was the first time I'd solicited my father's advice since I was a little girl. In March, I sent my application to Interlochen Arts Academy, a small school in northern Michigan, and arrived to audition. I fell in love with the place: the loud, theatrical voices, the trees, the dorms, the students, the classrooms, the theaters. On my first night there, accompanied by my mother, I turned to her and said urgently: I love it. I have to get in. I have to.

I did.

3 The Actor's Part

Michigan, 1989–1990

Watch out for games, the actor's part,
the speech planned, known, given,
for they will give you away
and you will stand like a naked little boy,
pissing on your own child-bed.

—Anne Sexton, "Admonitions to a Special Person," 1974

Summer, 1989. I was fifteen years old and feeling terribly mature. It was a sticky, sweaty Minnesota summer. I'd stumbled high and drunk through and out of ninth grade. I was finally, I said to friends in all-night diners, drinking coffee, tossing my hair back and blowing smoke in boys' faces, getting the hell out of Dodge. I was preparing to leave for boarding school, with no intention of ever, ever coming back. I spent lazy summer nights riding around in somebody's daddy's car with the windows down, shouting over the music, watching my reflection in the rearview mirror, trying out new faces, faces more suited to a girl-of-the-world, a girl-on-her-way, a girl-on-her-own: sleepy-eyed, casual glances, slow smiles. I imagined calling my parents from school, casually telling them of my grand accomplishments. I thought about returning to Edina in a swish of perfume, all cheekbones and eyes. Everyone would stare at this new creature with wonder—you've lost so much weight! I could already hear them say it—and I would wave my hand and speak in casual tones of this lecture and that writer and the absolute superfluity of food to the artist, who feeds only on her thoughts. I was fifteen, sad, in search of balance, and trying very hard to become someone other than me. Not uncommon in teenagers. Teenagers like me, desperately hitting the gas to get from zero to sixty in seconds flat will plow down anything in their path on their way out of Norman Rockwell hell, including their past. Including themselves. Teenagers do not know that both past and self will rise up like flattened cartoons on the road, unflatten themselves, and follow them everywhere they go. A shadow, or ghost.

That summer I had a job at McDonald's. I liked standing at the counter, having men from the Jiffy Lube shop next door flirt with me. I lived for the speed of it, the eight hours neatly bracketing my day. It felt tidy. I liked the break room, the bawdy talk through a fog of menthol smoke, and the early shift, old men in black coats and bowlers shuffling in on their canes, ordering coffee two creams and a water, dear, and they'd wink. They called me Polly Green Eyes. I liked being one of the guys, forcing a loud laugh when some ferret-looking kid said, real loud, "Snatches are ugly as sin." All the women blushed except me. No more girly blushing for me. My eyes hardened that summer. I watched them in the mirror, watched my practiced sneer. Splashed water on my face, rinsed the residue of vomit from my mouth, felt my glands for swelling, redid my lipstick, smiled coolly at the mirror. Wrapped my fingers around my wrists as I walked down the hall, out the door, to feel the bones.

I was Grown Up. I was going away to school. I had a job. I was leaving everyone. There was a twinge of sadness. A pretty big twinge, more like a knife twisting between two ribs. I was bummed about leaving my friends, in the back of my head knowing the friendships would end when summer did, when I left. Forks in the road, etc. We promised to write. They'd been the only thing that had kept me marginally sane for all those years, and I loved them a whole hell of a lot. Of course I was sad about leaving my parents, though less so—they would still be my parents when the summer ended—and of course I was scared of what would happen when the safety net fell away. I had the usual fears people have when going into the world. Alongside the sadness and fear, there was a rush of necessity. A need to leave. A need so fierce that it has been matched, in my life, only by two other needs: to eat and to throw up.

It seemed to me that two things were of the essence in proving my worth and my control, and one without the other was not enough: "Success," that meaningless term, and weight loss. A cutting loose from that which seemed to weigh me down: my father's worries, my mother's doubt, my small town, and my body itself. I would prove them wrong, that Great They for whom I have always lived. I would prove there was no child here, no weepy and weak little creature, no bouncy smiley smart-but-lazy rah-rah teen, no crazy kid, none of the things that they saw. I would disappear, only to come home reinvented. I would be unrecognizable upon my fleeting returns.

This fantasy was realized, but not quite the way I had intended. In deciding to remake myself, I managed to avoid the fact that I would also, by definition, have to erase what self there was to begin with. I began to wonder, many years later, if total erasure had been my intent all along.

I felt weightless at night, untethered from my white bed. I would jerk upright from a half-sleep dream of stepping off a curb, foot feeling for the ground and finding nothing but space beneath my shoe. I'd wake up just before I fell, feeling around on the nightstand for the glass of lukewarm water, drinking. Pressing myself into the bed, clutching the pillow, a solid thing, reminding myself, Just a dream. That's the nice thing about dreams, the way you wake up before you fall.

It was a period of waiting. Waiting in the limbo of childhood's end and the advent of Life. On a level I sensed but could not articulate, these were the last dangling hours of a time when I could still turn back. I planned to stop eating as soon as I crossed the Minnesota state line. I had had enough of bulimia. It seemed so crass, so gauche, so unlike the person I wanted to become: a woman, dark and mysterious, regal. Like my mother. I wanted to turn heads not with lecherous leers of bemusement but with awe. I wanted to become untouchable, cruel, glittery, sleek and haughty as a cat. I wanted to take a running leap, jump over adolescence, land cleanly in the world of adults, where, at last, I would be good enough.

There was a woman I worked with at McD's, much older than I, two kids and a missing husband, blue eye shadow, overweight. She and I sat eating together, talking about diet and weight. Now that I think of it, most of the women I worked with talked about diet and weight. But this particular woman, who was probably fifty or sixty pounds heavier than I and the same height, said to me one day, "You're kind of chubby. But you're a *cute* chubby. It looks good on you. You look like me."

It is not uncommon for people who are overweight to tell thinner people that they're overweight, too. I didn't know that then. I have since associated *cute* with *chubby*. When people tell me I'm "cute," I hear "chubby," no matter how far from either I may be. I hear them telling me that I'm still a snub-nosed little girl with big tits and a round ass who's too loud and too intense and entirely too much. That summer, I had decided that "cute" was the last thing I wanted to be.

At my lunch break, I would eat a quarter-pounder with cheese, large fries, and a cherry pie. Then I would throw up in the antiseptic-scented bathroom, wash my face, and go back on the floor, glassy-eyed and hyper. After work, I would buy a quarter-pounder with cheese, large fries, and a cherry pie, eat it on the way home from work, throw up at home with the bathtub running, eat dinner, throw up, go out with friends, eat, throw up, go home, pass out.

My parents watched me transform that summer, the constant purging thinning me quickly. Bulimics often vacillate between eating "normally" with other people and bingeing and purging in solitude, which keeps them at an average weight. I'd already stopped the "normal" part. I was doing drugs that put a weird sheen on my eyes and having backseat sex with young men dumb as sticks, flushing my cheeks and making me perpetually nauseated. I ignored my parents, full of a delusional certainty that one day soon I would walk back into the house, tall as a magazine model, cool and collected, a new woman, you've come a long way, baby, and *then* they would see. *Then* they'd know they'd had me all wrong, I would sweep into their perfect white living room and sit down on the couch, crossing my (magically long) legs and give them a bored stare. *Then* they'd be impressed.

Fat chance.

I fell for the great American dream, female version, hook, line, and sinker. I, as many young women do, honest-to-god believed that once I Just Lost a Few Pounds, somehow I would suddenly be a New You, I would have Ken-doll men chasing my thin legs down with bouquets of flowers on the street, I would become rich and famous and glamorous and lose my freckles and become blond and five foot ten. I would wear cool quasi-intellectual glasses and a man's oxford shirt in a sunny New

York flat and sip coffee and say Mmmm and fold my paper neatly and He would come up behind me and look at me with an adoring gaze. I would swing sexily into my red coupe, and the wind would blow through my hair as I drove into some great big city, stepping off the elevator and striding (with a feminine but authoritative step) into my office where everyone would be impressed with my every feminine but authoritative word. In the evenings I would go home and make magical gourmet meals and eat three bites, and He would look at me in the candlelight and I would be a superwoman 1980s goddess, yes indeed. As soon as I left my hometown and lost a few pounds.

Somehow I managed to believe this schlock (lying on my side on the green fuzzy carpet of my suburban bedroom reading *Seventeen* magazine diet articles and doing incessant, endless leg lifts), even though I was well aware of two facts: (1) All I really wanted to do was write poems, and (2) I'd met this clean-cut He of my just-before-sleep fantasies, and he bored the hell out of me. Not to mention the fact that I was at that time five feet tall in shoes, and had no immediate future as a calm, cool, and collected woman, given my basic personality. But no matter. In America, you can have anything if you just work for it, dammit, and I was bloody well ready to work.

Children, or so the literature goes, separate from their parents gradually. Not painlessly, but the small rips in the heart reknit themselves in time. I stood up abruptly and tore myself out at the roots. This has left me rootless, of course. But for my parents, I think, it must have been worse. The what-has-gone-wrong, what-is-happening, the gut knowledge that *there is something wrong with my daughter* is something I can only vaguely imagine. I do not have a child, I do not know what it would mean to watch that part of yourself begin to fester, shrivel, and die.

I was somewhat aware that my parents were worried. I try to imagine the conversations in my parents' room, in their minds, during the year that preceded my departure. Perhaps they went like this: She sits in the dark all day like a vampire. I come in, saying, Open the blinds, open the windows, you need light. She says: I hate light. Leave me alone. The room reeks of sickness and sweat. She lies on the bed, lank, her face to the wall. She shuffles in the night. There are pills in her purse. What is she on? What is she taking? What's wrong? Why? Why? Why? There is something wrong with her eyes, what is it? She screams and cries at the slightest thing. She's lying. I see that she's lying. *But what is she lying about?*

I come from a family of divine liars. There is always the smell of a lie, a smell of things unspoken. I have never understood what it was, but that summer, I was the lie, the walking lie, the elephant in the living room that no one mentioned because it would have been gauche. I was throwing up three to four times a day. I was on some stomach-twisting combination of drugs, and I was drinking. I began to be rather ostentatious about my "diet." My parents were not entirely unsupportive of this diet, given my running commentary about how I felt so Healthy now, given the fact that my father had been on one diet or another for most of my life (slapping his belly, saying Gotta get rid of this thing), and given that my mother had always, if only in an implied way, been worried about my weight, and hers, and everyone else's. Lunch in a café with my mother one summer day went like this: I order the dieter's plate, cottage cheese on a "nest" of wilted lettuce, two slices of canned peaches. I remember saying, Mom, it's so cool, I can eat a little healthy meal like this and be, like, totally full! She nodded, Yes, you can, she said. Bulimia, now that I was too good for it, was being phased out. This was my last hurrah on the roller coaster of intake and output.

What I am about to say is tricky, and it is a statement about my own relationship with bulimia and anorexia. Bulimia is linked, in my life, to periods of intense passion, passion of all kinds, but most specifically emotional passion. Bulimia acknowledges the body explicitly, violently. It attacks the body, but it does not *deny*. It is an act of disgust and of need. This disgust and this need are about both the body and the emotions. The bulimic finds herself in excess, too emotional, too passionate. This sense of excess is pinned to the body. The body bears the blame but *is not* the primary problem. There is a sense of hopelessness in the bulimic, a well-fuck-it-all-then, I might as well binge. This is a dangerous statement, but the bulimic impulse is more realistic than the anorexic because, for all its horrible nihilism, it understands that the body *is inescapable.*

The anoretic operates under the astounding illusion that she can escape the flesh, and, by association, the realm of emotions. The summer before I left for boarding school was the last time I would ever fully understand that I was a human being, and occasionally care about myself as such. I was about to become an anoretic. That is to say, I, the girl I knew as myself, was about to disappear. She was about to become no more than the blank spaces in the mirror where my body had once been. She was about to become no more than a very small voice.

However people know things about themselves, through premonitions or suspicions or specific plans, I knew this. And I was afraid. Yet I wanted it more than anything.

At some point, the intensity of my passion for life, the erotics of childhood, the natural hungers, and the instinctive childhood response to sate those hungers, became my greatest fear. My mind, my body, began to terrify me. I was an uncontrollable child. I could not, no matter how I tried, control my mind, its forays into distant realms, its dark curiosity. The depth and breadth of my imagination became a threat unto itself. Passion is strange. Mine is fierce, all-encompassing, a fiery desire for life. When I was a child, I knew it was there, and I lived it, a tendency toward explosion, flames, noise. This side of passion was my first perversion. The tendency toward excess veered out of control into bulimia, that state of fear and desire, that violent crashing back and forth between hunger and the abortion of hunger, between taking in and throwing back what is most needed and instinctively desired: food. The bread of life.

There is also the other side of passion. The side of me that feared fire and longed for ice, that cringed at noise and hungered for silence, that shied from touch and desired to numb itself into nothing. To implode. That side was the second to go wrong in me, perhaps in reaction to the first side. Fearing the velocity and force of life and self, I turned toward death. Fearing the constant thunder in the mind that bulimia brings, I turned toward the silence of anorexia. Afraid of the explicit passions of bulimia, I sought out what I mistook for the passionless state of starvation.

I did not know that passion will assert itself under any guise. I did not know that hunger for food, and the life-giving powers it has, could become its own opposite when thwarted, and become a different kind of hunger: a hunger for the hunger itself, a hunger for the life-taking powers that hunger has.

For a long time, I believed the opposite of passion was death. I was wrong. Passion and death are implicit, one in the other. Past the border of a fiery life lies the netherworld. I can trace this road, which took me through places so hot the very air burned the lungs. I did not turn back. I pressed on, and eventually passed over the border, beyond which lies a place that is wordless and cold, so cold that it, like mercury, burns a freezing blue flame.

Some say the world will end in fire,
Some say in ice.
From what I've tasted of desire,
I hold with those who favor fire.
But if it had to perish twice,
I think I know enough of hate
To say that for destruction ice
Is also great
And would suffice.

—ROBERT FROST, "FIRE AND ICE," 1922

In the flickering blue light of my parents' basement, June 1989, the Beijing government massacred the students of its own country. I leaned over the garbage can and was violently, involuntarily sick. Two weeks later, I boarded a plane with my choir for a tour of the Far East. In Hawaii, our first stop, we went to the beach. In my head, I looked terribly fat, at least compared to the other girls. Pictures of us show toothy grins and skin gleaming with sweat, arms flung around one another's shoulders. I look tired, pale, and plenty thin. I had the bright idea to lie on the beach in my bikini for twelve hours without sunscreen. I am extremely white. I slept, that night, under an enormous aloe leaf, my skin blistered with second-degree burns from face to foot.

We flew to Japan, my face mottled with blisters and peeling skin. My memory of the ancient cities of the East is skewed by the way my bra bit my raw skin, the way the airplane seats peeled parts of my skin off. My memory is skewed, too, by the uneasy guilt in my belly. Not to eat would be an insult to my host families, but if I ate, where would I throw up? I remember every single goddamn meal: what was served, what I ate, what I threw up. This frightens me. It was nearly eight years ago and I remember the Kentucky Fried Chicken I puked in a subway station, the fish cakes I hid in my napkin and dropped out the window at night while my roommate slept. I clearly recall the whole trout, cold, that was served on a platter for breakfast, the table of girls who sat looking at it, chopsticks poised, trying to figure out how to cut off its head.

I agonized over this lack of puking opportunity with my friend, also bulimic, as we sat on a guest room bed in our underwear in Hawaii, wincing as we rubbed aloe on each other's backs. In Osaka, I unfortunately fell in love with her. I kept my mouth shut and turned my face away as she stood in a shared bathroom, naked in the tall tub, complaining about her thighs. I glanced at her thighs and then away. I was not in the mood to compare thighs when I was having trouble keeping my hands off hers in the first place. I begged her to stop throwing up, said she was gorgeous, turned her around naked to look at herself in the mirror while she cried about what she'd just eaten. I nearly passed out from the contact of my skin with hers. It may have been the first time in my life that I really *saw* a naked woman, saw the elemental female form, saw hers not in comparison to myself but in horrible potential *connection* to myself. In hopes of getting her to eat without throwing up, I announced one day that I wasn't going to throw up anymore and I wasn't going to let her do it either. I began throwing up in secret. I expect she may have done the same.

We were on an international exchange, spreading goodwill and brotherhood, singing "Home on the Range" in six-part harmony, singing the Japanese national anthem, which we did not understand, but we smiled anyway. It was somehow very sad. I have pictures of me with my roommate, smiling, wearing traditional costumes that our hosts wrapped about us. We look profoundly white. The Beijing crisis hovered, unspoken, among us. We were headed for Canton, then called Guanjao. I have pictures of the two of us with the woman we were staying with, a tiny woman with two children and a husband who looked away from us, each of us holding up two fingers. As the flash snapped, she said, Peace.

We went to a dance club that had an enormous pink plaster Buddha at the door, paint chipping from the plaster rolls of his flesh, a garish, pupil-less smile on his face. Inside, young men with permed hair smoked Capris and asked us to dance. I was painfully embarrassed to be an American. We danced, and the glittering disco ball hanging from the ceiling spun. We sang long concerts, warned daily to keep bending our knees so we wouldn't get dizzy and fall down the risers in a flurry of pink taffeta. I bent them and bent them, and still I wavered, clutching the big bow on the backside of the girl next to me. Huge concert halls, a blur of faces dim behind the footlights, hot as hell, not enough air. I was hardly eating anything at all. Rice, bits of fish. I perfected the art of the silent puke: no hack, no gag, just bend over and mentally will the food back up.

In Hong Kong, we stayed in a hotel. The girls fanned out over the streets, murmuring to one another that we'd better buy things fast because Hong Kong would soon be the property of China. We bought like crazy, moving down the narrow streets thronged with people, the yellow arches of a McDonald's casting a strange yellow light in the late evening. In a marketplace, on a hot sunny day, I bought plate after plate of fried squid, ate it while walking through the narrow rows of lean-to stands covered with bright cloths. I ducked into a back alley, leaned over, and heaved. I straightened up. At the end of the alley stood a very old man, watching me, expressionless. I felt I should say something. I did not. I hurried back into the heat of the day, head spinning with dehydration and beating sun and an inexplicable terror. I felt I should pray. But all I could think to say, to the ears of some deaf god, was: I'm sorry.

When the tour was over, I flew to Seattle to meet my mother. We were visiting my alcoholic grandfather and his alcoholic, anorexic wife. I hadn't seen either of them since I was ten years old. In the meantime, I had, of course, gotten older, and in so doing had lost my darling-girl factor. I was now considered a threat by my stepgrandmother. She'd bought me an outfit suitable for a ten-year-old that was too tight and made me look like a sausage. I cried and said I was fat, alone in the guest room with my mother. My mother sniffed and told me to stop it.

I saved the outfit. I wore it almost every day in the hospital a few years later when I was seventeen, and it hung from the bones of my shoulders and hips, bagging at the ankles and ass.

The tension in my grandfather's house hummed like a violin string that vacation. My mother has spent her whole life trying to please her father, and I, in turn, have spent my whole life trying to please my mother. It became very obvious to me that trying to get approval was an exhausting, fruitless exercise. I was tap-dancing for her, she was tap-dancing for him, and he was staring into the sky, drunk as a deacon on holiday. Three women—my mother, my stepgrandmother, and me—competed for the Most Perfect Woman award. My mother insulted me, I insulted her, Jeanne, the stepgrandmother, insulted everything in a skirt, and my grandfather just kept right on drinking. We picked at our food, competing for who could eat the least.

When my mother was a kid, fat people were perceived by her family as slightly lesser beings. Fat people were lower class and were thus sneered at. In their opinion, fat people couldn't control themselves, not like the perfect little Williams family with their perfect skinny genes. My mother has told me that my great-grandmother, a hefty person, was mocked. Eating was seen as an annoyance. Meals were really just an excuse to have a few drinks. You were supposed to pick at your food. It's no wonder that my mother had screwy eating habits. No wonder everyone else did, too. And it is no wonder I always had the sneaking suspicion that my mother thought I was fat. Poor woman, giving birth to a normal-size child. Could I possibly have come from her body, this little round being who did totally untoward things like yell and get messy and cry? You're just like your father, she said.

Now, at the age of fifty-six, my mother tells me the problem was not that I was like my father but that I was like her. Intense. Temperamental. Driven. Bulimic. In pain.

My mother and I went for a walk. I told her about my trip to the Far East, how much it had changed me, how I felt I had learned a thing or two about the world and about myself, how I now felt more ready than ever to go away to school. She fell silent. I asked her what was wrong. She said, You talk about yourself an awful lot, Marya.

This was true. It's common in teenagers who (1) have not seen their mother in a while, and (2) are about to leave home, and (3) have recently traveled to a politically explosive part of the world. Asked about this later, she tells me I was too hyper, too excitable, nervous, babbling, and she was worried. My mother works in mysterious ways.

We went to lunch, the four of us. After the first drink, my stepgrandmother began insulting me, doing so without interruption and without pausing to eat through the arrival of the salads, the second and third drink, the arrival of the entrées, the fourth and fifth drink. She did so while I took a sudden intense interest in the napkin in my lap. An eloquent and imaginative woman, she detailed my arrogance, my uppity behavior now that I was going to some snotty arts school, how I would get a big head, how I would think I was *something* now, how my parents were spoiling me terribly and I would turn out to be a terrible person if they let me go on thinking I was talented and smart.

It truly fascinates me, the pains my family has taken to protect me from overblowing a self-image that has always resembled a pile of shit.

When I was sure she was finished, I excused myself to the bathroom and threw up. When I returned, my mother and grandfather made small talk while my stepgrandmother drank, her head trembling in its weird constant way, watching me out of the corner of her eye.

It was the last time I would see either one of them. She died a year later of a cancer no one knew she had. My grandfather died two years ago, three months after he married his third wife. He and I spoke briefly a few times over the years. The conversation always went like: "Well, is yer head screwed on right yet?" "Ha ha. I guess it is, Grandpa." My mother and I returned to Minnesota, where I packed for school and said good-bye and got in the car with my parents and began what would become an endless series of departures and arrivals, comings and goings, the latest great search for something I would never find.

We drive across Wisconsin, into the apostrophe of Michigan's Upper Peninsula, circle south and head west to Interlochen. In the hotel, I order a chef's salad. My father complains that I'm not eating enough, that I've hardly eaten since we left Edina. My parents have developed a sudden awareness of the fact that I pick at my food. I have developed a sudden disinterest in hiding it. In the room that night, my father does his calisthenics, I do mine. We have a strange competitive exchange about nightly exercises. My father says, You don't do them every night. I say, Yes I do. How would you know? He says, Hmm, and stretches his back. The inconsistency with which my parents responded to my problem would continue. A year later, just after my release from Hospitalization No. 1, I will stand in front of the mirror while my mother sits in a chair. I will weigh about 103. Trying to get some visual perspective on myself and practicing my Affirmations, I will declare: I'm pretty thin. And my mother will respond: I wouldn't call you thin.

We arrive in the tiny town where I will stay for a year, one of the sweetest years of my life. Interlochen, Michigan, is: a gas station, two pizza parlors, a Flap Jack Shack, a laundromat, and a bar. It is miles and miles of state forest. It is Green Lake, glassy and speckled with small motionless boats, held in by a dark, thick border of pines. It is a boarding school overhung heavily with trees, miniature roads winding between dorms, chapel, concert hall, studios. Farther out in the woods, the dance building, the theater, the tech building, empty cabins in the woods where old-looking long-haired children would meet, in pairs, in secret, and make use of the empty silence on bare sagging mattresses stained with time.

We moved my boxes of clothes and books into Mozart-Beethoven, my dorm, which was next door to Brahms and across a little road from Hemingway and Picasso, the two boys' dorms. The room was miniature. Along the wall, under the window, was a long desk with bookcases at each wall and two metal folding chairs. There was a very small dresser with a mirror above it, a small bathroom, a small closet.

My roommate had already moved in, her imposing presence apparent in an enormous black steamer trunk that took up half the room. I do not remember my parents leaving. They must have, because the next thing I knew, a wiry girl with a plethora of reddish hair, whom I would later come to call Tigger, bounded into the room, terrifically edgy, and, looking wildly around the room, blurted out: I didn't pick my bed yet so you can pick, I don't care which I have.

She had these incredibly long legs. She wore an enormous sweatshirt and a pair of jeans. She strode, she loped, she bounced—I have too few words to accurately describe the way her legs worked then—to the closet, swung open the door, and started rustling madly through the clothes she'd hung up. She said, more to her clothes than to me, By the way, I'm Lora.

I replied, I'm Marya.

She turned abruptly from the closet, glanced at me and then away, saying, Yeah, I know.

It was bound to be difficult. Prior to my arrival, I had considered serious questions that anyone might have before moving into a small community, sharing an infinitesimal space with another person: How will I throw up without offending? How will I do my calisthenics at night while reading a book? I expect I was not the only girl there who had these concerns. I knew from a girl who had gone to Interlochen that bulimia was rampant in the dorms. She'd told me that she and her roommate used to order pizzas and then throw up in the empty boxes. I found out later that boarding schools, in general, are hotbeds for eating disorders. I heard tales of resident advisors ("dorm mothers") posted at the bathroom doors to physically pull girls' heads out of the toilets. Later, I'd discover that the rumors were true: College dorm bathrooms rarely worked because the pipes were perpetually clogged with vomit.

There may be some validity in the common assumption that leaving home prompts waves of fear and insecurity, that eating disorders are concurrent with separation from the mother. Personally, I think it more accurate to say that, hidden from the periscope of the childhood home, people—myself included—go for broke and don't bother to hide it anymore. Leaving home is not so traumatic as to incite an eating disorder in people whose homes were perfectly Edenic. On the contrary, leaving home comes as a great relief, a sense of freedom. It is read, by an awful lot of us, as a ticket to undisturbed, self-destructive freedom.

I had not counted on rooming with Lora. I think I expected to find myself in a room with a snobby, pretentious girl in ostentatious tinkling gauzy skirts, who might, for that matter, be prone to spending time on her knees before the porcelain god.

Lora's mother was a renowned eating disorders therapist. I didn't find this out for a while, nor did Lora find out that it was relevant for a while, not until my eating disorder got so out of control that she was going nuts. For the time being, we set to the matter of the two narrow single beds. I said I wanted to sleep by the door. She said she wanted to sleep by the window. We pushed the beds this way and that. No matter how you put them, the beds (in conjunction with the steamer trunk) took up the entire room. In the end, we shoved all three together to maximize space. This meant that I had to either crawl over her to get out of bed, which she would not allow, or crawl to the foot of the bed, because I wound up stuffing all my dirty clothes between my side of the bed and the wall, leaving them there until Lora threatened to move out. She, by contrast, did laundry constantly, folding her clothes in neat piles: jeans, sweatshirts, T-shirts, socks. She smelled like vanilla and Tide.

It was fall. I was utterly in love with fall, and Michigan, and Interlochen. Leaves hurtled down from the trees that lined the walks and pillowed on the grass. Acorns crunched beneath one's boots. The lake did a slow burn at night, with sun sinking into it, sending out red heat in waves, steam rising into the chilly air.

Anorexia started slowly. It took time to work myself into the frenzy that the disease demands. There were an incredible number of painfully thin girls at Interlochen, dancers mostly. The obsession with weight seemed nearly universal. Whispers and longing stares followed the ones who were visibly anorexic. We sat at our cafeteria tables, passionately discussing the calories of lettuce, celery, a dinner roll, rice. We moved between two worlds. When we pushed back our chairs and scattered to our departments, we transformed. I would watch girls who'd just been near tears in the dorm-room mirrors suddenly become rapt with life, fingers flying over a harp, a violin, bodies elastic with motion, voices strolling through Shakespeare's forest of words.

In the writing department, I would sit sucking on sugar-free mints, the fingers of my left hand gripping the edge of a desk, face inches away from the paper, right hand curled around my pen as tight as a baby's fist. At the end of a workshop, my entire body would feel stiff, my hand arthritic, my head whirring maniacally. I have never been able to explain what happened to me that year, in those workshops, in literature classes. They made us read, and read, and read more, and then write until I thought I would never be able to write again. Entire pages were blackened with furious erasures, notations, triumphant discoveries of the *exact word, precisely that word,* notebook after notebook, ragged with torn half-pages, stapled photocopies of whatnots, paper-clipped random passing thoughts.

In biology, geometry, and German, I sat tensed, as if about to pounce, my brow a furrow of wrinkles. I did not understand. I could not keep my mind on it. I tried to concentrate, but my pen strayed to the margins, tracing and retracing small designs, scribbling bits of poems. I had maintained a running string of subpassing grades in math, science, and languages in my Edina years. It was during those classes that I wrote the bulk of the work that had gotten me into Interlochen in the first place. I swore to my parents that I would not fail my academic classes at Interlochen. I tried in earnest not to bomb out of all classes unrelated to my major. The school had nightly tutorials in academic subjects, which I religiously attended and which barely made a dent. Lora sat on the bed with my books while I paced wildly around the room, trying to listen to her explanations of proofs and cells and the subjunctive case. (Mar, do you want help with this or what? YES. Then SIT DOWN. I CAN'T.)

Fall hung back at the doorway of winter. Mornings were darker, days shorter, nights long and sleepless and black. The first snow fell and melted. We walked the two miles of backcountry road into town, bought cigarettes, loitered in the Laundromat, smoking and talking. We sat in the coffee shop, sharing our menthols, drinking our coffee, waiting for winter to come. We walked back at sundown, the last parchment leaves on the long brittle branches of trees hanging on for dear life in the very sharp wind. Pickup truck after pickup truck trundled by. We went to the pub down the road and played pool.

Lora and I didn't spend much time together outside of the room. She'd been at Interlochen the year before and had her own crowd of friends. I hung out with a scatter-shot crowd that shifted and changed with the seasons, some dancers, some musicians, several people from theater, a writer or two. As winter began, something intensified. The cold pressed us inward, closer together, kept us walking in circles, lost in work. I became utterly manic. I was not the only one.

It's not surprising that a place like this would run wild with startlingly intense children. Intensity about our respective fields was what had drawn us there in the first place. The workload was intense. Many of us, including me, had so many classes, workshops, isolated practice times, and rehearsals that we were studying ten hours a day, six days a week. The fact that we had left home at the age we had, in favor of a world that intellectually and artistically far outstripped our emotional development, was notable in and of itself. Home and childhood was not enough. We wanted more. And more we found. Many of us were lost and turned to art for direction. What we craved, in many cases, was religion.

Had we a god, it might have been Dionysus. We, his followers, imagined ourselves maenads, half-believing in divine possession, half mocking it. Either way, it was a Dionysian sort of time. Dionysus/Bacchus, it is said, was driven mad by his education. There was more information about the world, about our opportunities, about the limits and their elasticity, than we probably knew how to process. A few too many of us fell for the old romantic story of the mad artist, the genius made idiot savant by the swells and falls of music, language, color on canvas, ceaselessly, manically, playing inside his head. We wanted to be that genius, that idiot mad with the world of his mind. A thrum of self-destruction, anger and joy all tangled up, ran through the halls, the roads, the dorms.

We were very hungry.

Early on in the year, I'd decided to lose twenty pounds. Most of us had, having heard those obnoxious warnings about the "freshman fifteen" that people say girls add when they get to college. We figured the same would apply to us. It seemed to be a rite of passage beyond our control, fifteen pounds magically landing on the butt, an event that one needed to vigilantly guard against. In my dorm hallway lived several dancers, a violinist, a voice major, a harp major, Lora and I. I'd become friends early on with the voice and harp majors, who were roommates. We were in agreement that we all wanted to lose weight and swore on the pain of death to help each other do that, while insisting that the other two didn't really need to lose weight. We talked about food and weight nonstop, about how much we wanted to lose, asked each other: Do I look like I've gained weight? Lost weight? Does my butt look big in this skirt, in these jeans, when I stand like this? Does my stomach stick out, do my thighs jiggle? The two of them had a little refrigerator in their room containing Crystal Light, small tins of tuna ("It's a great lunch," said one of them to me. "There's only sixty calories in it and you're totally full."), bags of trail mix, yogurt. We took the Saturday bus into town, to Meijer's, one of those superstores, and bought bags of food in bulk: banana chips, sugar-free candies, raisins (anything with a laxative effect). We loaded up on diet sodas and ramen and popcorn and stood in the diet aids aisle, surveying the goods. Debating the merits of Dexatrim versus Fiberall. We'd wonder aloud how long a person could go just drinking Crystal Light.

You cannot trick your body. Your body, strange as it seems to we who are saturated with a doctrine of dualism, is actually attached to your brain. There is a very simple, inevitable thing that happens to a person who is dieting: When you are not eating enough, your thinking process changes. You begin to be obsessed with food. They've done study after study on this, and still we believe that if we cut back fat, sugar, calorie intake, we'll drop weight just like that and everything will be the same, only thinner. Nothing is the same. You want to talk about food all the time. You want to discuss tastes: What does that taste like? you ask each other as you devour your bizarre meals. Salty? Sweet? Are you full? You want to taste something all the time. You chew gum, you eat roll after roll of sugar-free Certs, you crunch Tic Tacs (just one and a half calories each!). You want things to taste *intense.* All normal approach to food is lost in your frantic search for an explosion of guilt-free flavor in your mouth, an attempt to make your mouth, if not your body, feel full, to fool your mind into satiety. You pour salt or pepper on things. You eat bowls of sugar-coated cereal (no fat). You put honey and raisins on your *rice.*

Eating disorders are addictions. You become addicted to a number of their effects. The two most basic and important: the pure adrenaline that kicks in when you're starving—you're high as a kite, sleepless, full of a frenetic, unstable energy—and the heightened intensity of experience that eating disorders initially induce. At first, everything tastes and smells intense, tactile experience is intense, your own drive and energy themselves are intense and focused. Your sense of power is very, very intense. You are not aware, however, that you are quickly becoming addicted.

And there's the rub. As with drugs, the longer you do it, the more you need to achieve that original high.

It is assumed that everyone wants to lose weight, so no one notices when the old topics of dinner conversation—classes, majors, guys—switches over to food, almost exclusively. It doesn't strike anyone as particularly odd, at first. Later in the year, there will be a few girls who defect: We're all just getting way too obsessed, she'll say, nibbling her apple, I'm just sick of it. But not at first. At first there is a religious fervor, a cultist sort of behavior,[1] a pact.

I made a pact with a tall, thin girl who offered to help me lose weight. When I got to Interlochen, I was at something close to my "set point," the technical term for your natural weight—mine is about 120. But 120 seemed too high, and I decided to drop that extraneous 20, down to 100 with the dancers and starving artists, and I'd been going around blathering about how I was on a diet. This girl came into my room at night, talked to me about what to eat, encouraged me in a most patronizing tone, and told me how much better I was looking. And then, one night, I "slipped." There were sundaes in the cafeteria that night. The girls had been talking about it all day—the future virtuosos of the world, cream of the crop, la di da, had been discussing in hushed voices whether we'd break down and eat a sundae. couldn't we be strong and just eat the toppings, no ice cream? that would have less fat, wouldn't it? what if we didn't eat all day, and all the next day, then would it be okay? bless me father for i have sinned i ate an ice cream sundae. I went to the cafeteria, put together a sundae, and sat with the other girls. We laughed—for once we had enough sugar in our systems, for once we were eating regular food like any other teenage kid—until Ms. Diet Police came up from behind me, leaned over, took my sundae, walked to the trash can, and dropped it in.

The furious little kid in me got good and pissed. I shoved my chair

[1] For a more complete discussion of the commonalities between cult behavior and the Western obsession with dieting, as well as an excellent interpretation of new research on eating disorders and the commercial influence on American attitudes toward weight and body, see Sharlene Hesse-Biber, *Am I Thin Enough Yet?: The Cult of Thinness and the Commercialization of Identity.*

back and ran after my disappearing sundae. This girl turned around and I *hit* her. Whatthehell? she yelled, wide-eyed. Marya, I'm just trying to help you, you said you wanted help losing weight and here you are pigging out on ice cream! Near tears, I left, feeling like a complete fool. What is my problem? I thought, heading back to my dorm. Am I such a cow that I can't live without a fucking sundae? No self-control, none. Pig.

Sometimes you break down. The body and the soul protest deprivation. We broke down from time to time, ordered pizzas or subs, sat in the main room of the dorm in front of the television, eating. Sometimes I threw up, sometimes I didn't. There was this weird unspoken agreement: If we eat together, it's okay, we've all got permission to eat. Those were good moments, when the part of us that wanted to be normal and healthy and loved food like anyone else broke through, and we sat giggling on the floor, munching away. Those moments became, for me, few and far between. Marya, do you want to order a pizza? No thanks, I already ate. I'd disappear into my room to work. Sometimes I'd come out, sit with my friends, eat the spare crusts.

Of course I didn't know then that I had all the obvious signs of having an eating disorder: strange combinations of food, eating other people's leftovers, skipping meals. Part of the reason I didn't notice was because what I was doing was hardly unique. One day, late fall, standing in the main room after classes, a girl was eating a bag of microwave popcorn and offered me some. I took a handful without thinking and popped it in my mouth. Midchew, I asked to see the bag. I read the nutritional information and spit the popcorn into a trash can. She said, Marya, that's like *really* weird. I said, it's not weird, that popcorn is fucking *full* of fat. Another girl, sitting on the couch, concurred. I'd spit it out too, she said. The popcorn girl said, that's bulimic. I said the hell it is! I ought to know, I used to *be* bulimic, and spitting food out is *not* it. She shrugged. Looks bulimic to me, she said.

I distinctly did not want to be seen as bulimic. I wanted to be an anoretic. I was on a mission to be another sort of person, a person whose passions were ascetic rather than hedonistic, who would Make It, whose drive and ambition were focused and pure, whose body came second, always, to her mind and her "art." I had no patience for my body. I wanted it to go away so that I could be a pure mind, a walking brain, admired and acclaimed for my incredible self-control. Bulimia simply did not fit into my image of what I would become. Still, I *was* bulimic and had been for seven years. It is no easy addiction to overcome. But my focus had changed.

Up to that point, the bulimia had had a life of its own. It was purely an emotional response to the world—under pressure, binge and purge; sad and lonely, binge and purge; feeling hungry, binge and purge—and actually had little to do, believe it or not, with a desire to lose weight. I'd always wanted to be thinner, sure, but I wanted to eat as well. The year I got to boarding school, I actually began to hate my body with such incredible force that my love of food was forced underground, my masochistic side surfaced, and anorexia became my goal.

Part of this had to do with the self-perpetuating nature of eating disorders: The worries about your weight do not decrease no matter how much weight you lose. Rather, they grow. And the more you worry about your weight, the more you are willing to act on that worry. You really do have to have an excessive level of body loathing to rationally convince yourself that starvation is a reasonable means to achieve thinness. Normally, there is a self-protective mechanism in the psyche that will dissuade the brain from truly dangerous activity, regardless of how desirable the effects of that activity may be. For example, a woman may wish to lose weight but have an essential respect for her physical self and therefore refrain from unhealthy eating. I had no such self-protective mechanism, no such essential self-respect. When you have no sense of physical integrity—a sense that your own health is important, that your body, regardless of shape, is something that requires care and feeding and a basic respect for the biological organism that it is—a very simple, all-too-common, truly frightening thing happens: You cross over from a vague wish to be thinner into a no-holds-barred attack on your flesh.

You stop seeing your body as your own, as something valuable, something that totes you around and does your thinking and feeling for you and requires an input of energy for this favor. You begin seeing it instead as an undesirable appendage, a wart you need to remove. "I *have* a body, you are likely to say if you talk about embodiment at all; you don't say, I *am* a body. A body is a separate entity possessable by the 'I'; the 'I' and the body aren't, as the copula would make them, grammatically indistinguishable. . . . Bodies get treated like wayward women who have to be shown who's boss, even if it means slapping them around a little."[2]

When you believe that *you* are not worthwhile in and of yourself, in the back of your mind you also begin to believe that *life* is not worthwhile in and of itself. It is only worthwhile insofar as it relates to your crusade. It is a kamikaze mission. Life and self are far less important than your single-minded goal. "Thinness" was as good a name as any for my goal. Twenty pounds, I said. No matter what.

By winter, I was starving. Malnutrition is not a joke. Whether you're skinny or not, your body is starving. As the temperature dropped, I began to grow fur, what is technically called lanugo. Your body grows it when you're not taking in enough calories to create internal heat (it's interesting how we think of calories as the Antichrist, rather than as an energy source). I liked my fur. I felt like a small bear. I grew fur on my belly, my ribs, the small of my back, my cheeks, fine downy fur, pale white. My skin grew whiter, more so than usual, when the sun became translucent, as it does in winter far north. I began to look a bit haunted. I stood in the shower, feeling the bones in my lower back, two small points at the top of my rear. I took hold of my pelvic bones, twin toy hatchets. I took Fiberall and Dexatrim. I drank gallons of water. I was perpetually cold.

Mornings, I'd haul myself out of bed at 5 A.M., put on running clothes, walk through the purple light latticed with the black arms of trees, open the doors to the long hall of the main building, and run. This was the strangest thing. I have always hated solitary exercise. When I was younger, I played soccer, racquetball, and swam on the swim team, but I had always, always hated solo running. I was very proud of myself for forcing my body to run. And run. Malnutrition precipitates mania. So does speed. Both were at play here, in large doses. But so was masochism—the subjection of the self and/or body to pain and fear, ultimately resulting in a transitory sense of mastery over pain and fear. Every morning, I ran five miles, up and down this hall, touching the

---

[2] Nancy Mairs, "Carnal Acts," in *Minding the Body*, ed. Patricia Foster, 270.

door at each end, the mark of an obsession. I had to touch the door or else it didn't count. You make up these rules, and if you break the rules, God help you, you have to run an extra mile to make up for it. When I was done, I'd go downstairs to the workout room and weigh myself.

The workout room was packed with girls. On the scale, on the bikes, on the weights, the rowing machine. Nothing wrong with a little exercise. But in such a small community, you can't help but notice the changes. The same girls, shrinking, day after day. I saw them, later, on campus, shivering in classrooms, at readings, at concerts, wrapped in wool. I'd weigh myself and leave. There was no mutual recognition. You can talk food all day with friends, but you keep your secrets. On the surface, you're doing this companionably, you're a friggin' unstoppable dieting army and you'll all go down together. On the underside, you're all competing with one another to be the thinnest, most controlled, least weak, and you have your own private crusade on which no one can join you, lest they be as fucked up as you.

By midwinter, I would run in the morning, eat grapefruit after grapefruit for breakfast (someone told me it had only eight calories. When I found out that was wrong, I ran ten miles to make up for all that grapefruit), go to class. At lunch I would speed-walk up and down the hallway while reading a book, then go to class. At the end of the day, run again, five more miles, go to the cafeteria, eat carrot sticks with mustard. Soon I made a new rule: now I had to run *after* dinner as well. By January I was running twenty-five miles a day, on a knee that was beginning to split.

In the hospital, anoretics are always amazed that they could possibly have had the energy to run, to sit on the exercise bike for hours, pedaling madly toward the vanishing point in their heads. They talk about this in group, depending on their state of mind, with either a sad sort of pride, or shock. The latter is rare. You only hear the latter from women who have come to some understanding that they have been living in an altered state, a state that cannot be maintained. The former tend to maintain their grandiose illusion that they are superhuman.

I was beginning to harbor that delusion myself, that I was superhuman. When you coast without eating for a significant amount of time, and you are still alive, you begin to scoff at those fools who believe they must eat to live. It seems blatantly obvious to you that this is not true. You get up in the morning, you do your work, you run, you do not eat, you live.

You begin to forget what it means to live. You forget things. You forget that you used to feel all right. You forget what it means to feel all right because you feel like shit all of the time, and you can't remember what it was like before. People take the feeling of *full* for granted. They take for granted the feeling of steadiness, of hands that do not shake, heads that do not ache, throats not raw with bile and small rips from fingernails forced in haste to the gag spot. Stomachs that do not begin to dissolve with a battery-acid mixture of caffeine and pills. They do not wake up in the night, calves and thighs knotting with muscles that are beginning to eat away at themselves. They may or may not be awakened in the night by their own inexplicable sobs.

You begin to rely on the feeling of hunger, your body's raucous rebellion at the small tortures of your own hands. When you eventually begin to get well, health will feel wrong, it will make you dizzy, it will confuse you, you will get sick again because sick is what you know.

I cannot explain why I remember this year with such joy. Perhaps it is because it was just the beginning. It is the last year I remember feeling whole, although I was not whole. My private self-abuse is overshadowed by my memory of Interlochen, no doubt glorified magnificently in my head, but glorious in its way nonetheless. I remember the hum of passion palpable in the studios, the concert halls, the constant music coming through the vents of the dorms from the basement practice rooms below, the dramatic voices and flailing arms in the cafeteria at dinnertime, the laughter, the undeniable Mad Hatter wildness, the extremes.

Perhaps it is because, for the first and probably last time in my life, my extremes were hardly novel. My extremes were minor, by comparison.

That year for several reasons I dated boys who were very young, aphysical, harmless. My hatred of my body, which steadily escalated over the course of the year and was not, of course, mitigated by the fact that I was losing weight, made it literally impossible for me to be even slightly physical with anyone without feeling disgusting, exposed, dirty, fat. Nighttime, in a dorm room with the door ajar ("open room" regulation, applicable only with a visitor of the opposite sex), I'd make the perfunctory noises, I'd do what I was supposed to do, short of sex, and then leave to stand in the shower, feeling my hip bones for an hour, eyes closed.

This was, given my prior history, a little strange for me. But maybe not. Maybe I was tired of sex. Sad, but maybe true. And maybe I was afraid of the intimacy, the exposure, the vulnerability. Or it may have been what so many eating-disordered women report: a fear of having their bodies seen as excessive, having their faces show response, having their voice leap out, unbidden, uncontrolled, having their passion diverted from its chosen focus—death—into something more frightening still: life. One of the boys told his roommate, worriedly, that I was "a heavy breather." I'd been faking it, of course, but I was humiliated nonetheless and kept my responses, forged or real, to myself the next time he rubbed his skinny self against me, panting and coming in his jeans, keeping his eyes averted. I listened to the laughter and shouts of the people passing by in the hall. I gave thanks for gravity and the way it pressed my belly down toward my spine, forming a little concave hollow between my pelvic bones.

A year later, in the hospital, I will hide my face in my hands as a beautiful woman starts to cry in group while blurting out that she is afraid of her own passion, her physical passion, her desire for her lover. The rest of the group, embarrassed into silence, will stare at the floor, each of us pretending we do not know what she means, each of us insisting to ourselves that we don't understand, we've never felt that. We will joke to one another later, Isn't sex just for burning calories? and laugh. I understood what the woman meant. My face burned, as if my understanding marked me as one of them, one of those women who feels things from the inside out, one of those women whose bodies sometimes rise in wordless joy. I did not want to be one of those women. In my year at boarding school, I did all that I could to starve that part of me away. The taking in of food, like the taking in of a lover, is seen as an admission of weakness and need, an admission of desire for physical pleasure, a succumbing to the "lesser," the base sides of the self. A loose woman, that's what you are, your passions beyond your control. The etiquette of our culture says that a good woman should take sex and food with a sigh of submission, a stare at the ceiling, a nibble at the crust.

Besides, sex always made me hungry. So did smoking pot. I avoided both.

Lora and I lay in our side-by-side beds in the night. Winter light is bright and blue, and cast the room in eerie shadows. The pipes banged. She was an insomniac, more so than me. We lay there speaking intermittently, of poetry and stories and writers and words, heated, blurred flurries of words about words. As the hours grew small, our voices slowed and faded. We spoke of where we would go. What we would write. Rarely did we speak of the lives we'd left. As the clock crept toward dawn, we rambled nonsensically. She called me Max.

As winter went on, longer than long, we both freaked out. My mania grew to insane proportions. I sat in the study room at night, wildly typing out Dali-esque short stories. I sat at my desk in our room, drinking tea, flying on speed. She'd bang into the room in a fury. Or, she'd bang into the room, laughing like a maniac. Or, she'd bang into the room and sit under the desk eating Nutter-Butters. She was a sugar freak. She'd pour packets of sugar down her throat, or long Pixie-Stix. She was in constant motion. At first I wondered if she too had some food issues, subsisting mostly on sugar and peanut butter-and-jelly sandwiches on Wonder Bread, but my concern (as she pointed out) was "total transference, seriously, Max. Maybe you're just *hungry*." Some Saturdays, we'd go to town together, buy bags and bags of candies, Tootsie Rolls (we both liked vanilla best; she always smelled delicious and wore straight vanilla extract as perfume, which made me hungry), and gummy worms and face-twisting sour things and butterscotch. We'd lie on our backs on the beds, listening to The Who and Queen, bellowing, "I AM THE CHAMPION, YES I AM THE CHAMPION" through mouths full of sticky stuff, or we'd swing from the pipes over the bed and fall shrieking to the floor.

People have this idea that eating-disordered people just *don't eat*. Wrong. They have rules about what they eat, and eat "safe foods," as we'll call them in the hospital in a few months. Sugar was an obvious choice: fat free and it makes you hyper to boot and just think how much work you can get done when you're wired to the gills on cocaine, caffeine, and sugar! A steady stream of strange short stories spilled from my typewriter, weirder and weirder, more and more breathless and abstract.

Reading over them, years later, I can almost picture myself lifting up from my chair, levitating midair, staring off into space, the words that spilled out completely cerebral, not grounded in physical reality, all magical realism, all hallucinatory image, a clear, bizarre progression of stories about women who grew increasingly silent, increasingly pale, thinner and thinner, building to my pitiful literary denouement of that year. I wrote of a woman who disappears into thin air. Then of one who, while walking, finds herself crumbling into a pile of porcelain dust. *Disturbing and vivid,* scribbled the teachers, *Eerie, ungrounded.* On the last one: *Marya, come back down. You've gone too far with this one.*

Lora wrote madly with a purple pen and worked herself into incredible states, trying to get the lines of her poems EXACTLY RIGHT. I was buzzing with weird energy. Mania is easy when you're not eating because, of course, you have to keep your mind off food as much as possible. Food is such a hindrance to your progress, and you must keep yourself awake because if you fall asleep you're not burning any calories and not getting anything done. Time is of the essence when you're manic, you MUST GET THINGS DONE, anything, everything, and you must DO IT IN TIME, the White Rabbit dashing about looking at his pocket watch, I'm late! I'm late! The world won't stop for me and I have to catch it before it goes flying by and I MISS MY CHANCE to be INCREDIBLE. There is a deadline on incredibility and the clock is ticking away. My days and nights were planned in fifteen-minute slots in my notebooks. I was always checking my notebooks to see what I had to do next.

Lora and I started fighting over nothing. Well, not really over nothing.

I was taking my shirt off, my back to her.

"Max, let me see your back." Her voice was sharp. I had stopped changing in front of her. I had slipped.

"What? No." I pulled my pajama tops on and went into the bathroom, locking the door.

"Max!" She banged on the door. "What the fuck is up with your back?"

"What are you talking about?" My hands ran their panicked course over the bones of my back, my collarbones, my wrists, my knees.

"Max, you *aren't eating! Come out here!*"

I came out and stood in front of the mirror, brushing my hair. It fell to the floor in thin dark clouds.

She stood at her desk, banging things. "You know, Max, this is, like, bullshit."

I didn't say anything. I looked at myself sideways in the mirror. I was thinner, but not thin enough yet.

"I mean, like, you could talk to someone about this, or something."

I got into bed and vigorously cracked open a book.

"MAX," she screamed.

I looked up, waiting.

"Fuck you," she said. "I mean, about this. Just *fuck* you."

She slammed out of the room.

I began to chain-smoke. I stood on the back of toilets in the dorms, tight up against another girl, our faces lifted, baby-bird-like, our illicit, punishable-by-expulsion cigarette held up to the vent. I signed out to leave campus, walked, sometimes alone and sometimes not, down the worn road, into the woods. This was the first time in my life when I began to like being alone. I had always had a sharp fear of solitude, but now, the walks were necessary. I wanted the exercise. The girls and I had discussed the length of the walk from campus to the strip of shops at the edge of Interlochen. We estimated about two miles, and we debated at length whether you estimated how many calories you burn by the length of the walk or the time that it took. I figured by length because it would mean more calories.

I wanted the solitude. I walked, my steps matching the rhythms of words in my head. Words, a sudden unfailing companion: Turn left at the gate of the school, breathe, walk a while, and then the words would come, swinging like a metronome in my head. I'd walk and with each line breathe in, and with each line breathe out, and step, and step.

On weekends, we were 350 children dressed up to attend evening performances, the like of which I've not seen since. Still as snow, we sat in the audience, holding our collective breath, hearing the music in the dark. Our fingers clutched the programs in our laps, our muscles followed, involuntarily, longing, the figures in their dance. On Tuesday nights, we shook our heads in time with the barefoot and goateed jazz combo, their calloused hands seducing sax and string bass into some song that moved, belly deep, through the swaying, sweating room.

Winter inched into the small world where we lived, drifting through small fissures in our walls, wind leaning its shoulder into the buildings, making them groan and sigh, the ground high and white, roads crunching under our feet. The snow fell in soft convulsions, quilts of white drifting over our heads. In wool and scarves we blew from class to class, breath coming in small white explosions from our mouths. Inside, short of breath, fat flakes clung to our hair, their perfect geometries melting into patterns of crystalline drops.

In the cafeteria I'd pour myself coffee and dribble one-third of a teaspoon of cream on the top. A small plate: carrot sticks, celery, mustard. As the year went on, I began to fill a bowl with a ridiculous amount of mustard, eat mustard straight, using a carrot stick more as a spoon than as an edible. It didn't actually seem that strange to me at the time, no matter how often people told me it was weird or made jokes about it. I was first and foremost concerned with the loss of weight, and hell, if mustard and carrots had no fat, no calories, and filled me up, then what the hell did I care? No one else was eating normally either, so who were they to talk? Most of the time, a big group of girls, including me, would jabber on about our diets, how much we'd lost. Other times it would look like someone was pulling ahead of the pack: so-and-so is throwing up, one girl says, and we'd all freak out. Oh no! we'd cry, as if we weren't all doing it. That's awful! Or the famous anoretic on campus, a dancer who (we whispered) had been in the hospital once (gasp) and had (we leaned closer) only *four percent body fat!* We said, No WAY. Are you SERIOUS? (The healthy range of body fat for most women is between 18 and 25 percent. Did it occur to us that four percent was potentially fatal? No. We were jealous.) Of course, there was body fat testing day for the dancers, and they all came back crying. Or if there was someone who usually ate more food than the rest of us, but who ate only celery for dinner one night, we'd be all over her like a pack of dogs, yapping and snarling that That's like REALLY dangerous, you won't have any energy, STOP THAT RIGHT NOW! She'd burst into tears and say that her boyfriend wanted her to lose weight. Fuck him! Who needs it? we cried, and gave her hugs.

If I was terrifically hungry, I'd eat a few pretzels, a bit of corn, or some rice with lots of salt. Like, a really disgusting amount of salt. Dehydration, induced by both incessant vomiting and a lack of nutrients, makes you crave salt in the worst way. It makes mustard delicious. It makes you want a salt lick. People stare, then try not to as you shake and shake and shake on the salt. You glance up, say, "What?" When you get to the hospital, you will scream at the nurse, the nutritionist, the doctor, the laundry boy, because you only get one of those little teeny packets of salt with your meal. You want handfuls and handfuls of salt.

Sundays, we'd binge. Several of us, unspoken. On Sundays there was a dress-up brunch in the cafeteria, buffets of sugary institution rolls, muffins, Danish, coffee cake, huge stainless steel trays of crusting mashed potatoes, eggs, sausage, hash browns. We'd eat and eat and eat. But we ate strange things: seven blueberry muffins, an entire plate of salty mashed potatoes, fourteen chocolate chip cookies. Sunday afternoons, you'd see us, faces pinched, hopping aerobically up and down, pedaling wildly on ancient stationary bikes. One Sunday, standing in the cafeteria with Lora, eating frozen yogurt, a friend of hers said to me: God, do you do anything other than run and eat?

I said, defensively: I don't eat that much.

The bragging was the worst. I hear this in schools all over the country, in cafés and restaurants, in bars, on the Internet, for Pete's sake, on buses, on sidewalks: Women yammering about how little they eat. Oh, I'm starving, I haven't eaten all day, I think I'll have a great big piece of lettuce, I'm not hungry, I don't like to eat in the morning (in the afternoon, in the evening, on Tuesdays, when my nails aren't painted, when my shin hurts, when it's raining, when it's sunny, on national holidays, after or before 2 A.M.). I heard it in the hospital, that terrible ironic whine from the chapped lips of women starving to death, But I'm not *hun*-greeee. To hear women tell it, we're never hungry. We live on little Ms. Pac-Man power pellets. Food makes us queasy, food makes us itchy, food is too messy, all I really like to eat is celery. To hear women tell it, we're ethereal beings who eat with the greatest distaste, scraping scraps of food between our teeth with our upper lips curled.

For your edification, it's bullshit.

Starving is the feminine thing to do these days, the way swooning was in Victorian times. In the 1920s, women smoked with long cigarette holders and flashed their toothpick legs. In the 1950s, women blushed and said tee-hee. In the 1960s, women swayed, eyes closed, with a silly smile on their faces. My generation and the last one feign disinterest in food. We are "too busy" to eat, "too stressed" to eat. Not eating, in some ways, signifies that you have a life so full, that your busy-ness is so important, that food would be an imposition on your precious time. We claim a loss of appetite, a most-sacred aphysicality, superwomen who have conquered the feminine realm of the material and finally gained access to the masculine realm of the mind. And yet, this maxim is hardly new. A lady will eat like a bird. A lady will look like a bird, fragile boned and powerful when in flight, lifting weightless into the air.

We feign disinterest and laugh, and creep into the kitchen some nights, a triangle of light spilled on the floor from the fridge, shoveling cold casseroles, ice cream, jelly, cheese, into our mouths, swallowing without chewing as we listen to the steady, echoing *tisk-tisk-tisk* of the clock. I have done this. Millions of people have done this. There is an empty space in many of us that gnaws at our ribs and cannot be filled by any amount of food. There is a hunger for something, and we never know quite what it is, only that it is a hunger, so we eat. One cannot deny the bodily response to starvation, and that is part of the reason, some nights, I sat in the basement of the dorms, locked in a bathroom, watching myself in the mirror as I stuffed candy bars, chips, vending machine anything into my mouth, and then threw up. There is also a larger, more ominous hunger, and I was and am not alone in sensing it. It squirms under the sternum, clawing at the throat.

At school we were hungry and lost and scared and young and we needed religion, salvation, something to fill the anxious hollow in our chests. Many of us sought it in food and in thinness. We were very young at a time in our lives when the search for identity, present and future, was growing intense, the hunger for knowledge and certainty extreme. Many of us came from less-than-grounded families. We were living inside a pressure cooker, competition tough, stakes very high, the certainty of our futures nonexistent, the knowledge that one is choosing a difficult life clear and the awareness that one's chances of "making it" were slim. This created, quite simply, a hunger for certainty.

We lived in a larger world where there is also a sense of hunger and a sense of lack. We can call it loss of religion, loss of the nuclear family, loss of community, but whatever it is, it has created a deep and insatiable hunger in our collective unconscious. Our perpetual search for something that will be big enough to fill us has led us to a strange idolatry of at once consumption and starvation. We execute "complicated vacillations . . . between self-worship and self-degradation,"[3] the pendulum swinging back and forth, missing the point of balance every time. We know we need, and so we acquire and acquire and eat and eat, past the point of bodily fullness, trying to sate a greater need. Ashamed of this, we turn skeletons into goddesses and look to them as if they might teach us how to not-need.

Not everyone at school was obsessed with food. There were the others. Oddly enough, my closest friends there were marginally healthy about diet (of course, several of them were male), and simply by virtue of being young, very few of my friends knew anything about eating disorders beyond their conceptual existence. This problem, rampant as it was, did not share the same very public sphere at Interlochen that drugs and drinking did. As the dead of winter set in, my friends began to worry. I ate strangely. At meals, they'd say, too casually, Mar, don't you want some? They'd push food at me. You need protein, Anna would say. Have some cottage cheese, have some beans, eat something, you must be hungry. By December, I had decided to ingest one hundred calories a day. It seemed a good number, a tidy number, a "diet" rather than a disorder, a Plan. Carrots, mustard, two pretzels, the milk in my coffee. My friends would sit down at breakfast, loudly saying: Oh, yum, I love oatmeal. Mar, go get some oatmeal. It's really good today, Mar. Oatmeal is

---

[3] Ibid., 270.

low fat, they'd say in a singsong voice, waving bowls of oatmeal under my face as I scowled, pulling back from it like a baby having a good pout. Mar, you'll be hungry, they'd say. I'd change the subject.

Christmas break came. I flew home. In the Traverse City airport we sat, nervous and sad, distracted, laughing too sharply. Few of us wanted to go back to where we came from. I got drunk in the Detroit airport, and even drunker on the plane. Calorie counting was pushed aside in favor of oblivion. My mother picked me up. Her face was tight, her mouth pressed together in a thin line. I looked about thirty. My skin was ghastly pale, my red lipstick garish, black clothes too loose and too old. She gave me a stiff hug. We walked to the luggage carousel, barely speaking. Surely she was worried, that's all it was. But I was only fifteen, and my mother is a difficult woman to read. Her face clenched with—distaste? irritation? what had I done now? I said, sarcastically: Well, *you're* glad to see me. She made that *tssk* noise and said, Oh Marya. I said, What? She *tssked* and turned her head, moved quickly, professionally, efficiently. We swooped through the airport like witches on twin brooms.

January was cold, February colder. During my vacation I had achieved the acclaim I'd wanted in the form of compliments for having lost weight, giving me an oddly flat, fleeting sense of accomplishment. I couldn't figure out how to say "no Christmas dinner for me, thanks" without causing a ruckus, and upon my return to school I decided to eat once a week, in penance for the minimal eating I'd done at home. I ate on Sundays. Rice.

I did this until I began bingeing and purging almost autonomously. This sounds very odd to people who haven't been malnourished, maybe even to those who have, but scientifically speaking, your body will actually override your brain and *make* you eat. You suddenly find yourself hanging up the phone after having ordered a pizza, with no way to hide either pizza or the hunger it implies. You lock yourself in your bedroom and eat it and puke. Or, you find yourself alone in the cafeteria, filling plate after plate, and you're so bloody hungry that the smell of the food, the existence of all-you-can-eat buffets, the garish light and the laughter and hundreds of mouths opening wide and taking in food, take over and you eat and eat and eat and run to the bathroom and puke. Or, one day you find yourself walking along, and you impulsively stop in a restaurant, order an enormous dinner, and puke in the woods.

Maybe the issue is that your body remembers a time when you did eat normally. When you were hungry, you stopped at a restaurant and ate. There is a kind of buzzing that goes on in your brain, and you miraculously forget, at least long enough to eat, that you are studiously trying to be a good anoretic. Midway through the food you remember, but then it's too late and you're still fucking hungry and you're hungry even after the food's all gone, but then you feel so unbelievably guilty and hideous that you have to, you *have to throw up*, and so you do and everything feels better.

That's really the worst of it. That's what mortifies me now when I listen to women in the thick of it telling me how much better they feel when they barf, when they talk about the release, the comfort, the power, however illusory and short-lived, of being able to conquer nature. Of being able to spit in the face, or rather puke on the shoes, of this material realm. I remember that relief, that power. I miss it. It hurts like a sonofabitch. It's disgusting, but it was my safeguard, my sure thing, my security, my life for all those years. It was something I knew for sure, no question, that I was good at. I knew it would be there for me when I needed it. That's the thing: It's still there. It wheedles at me, after dinner: Come on, you're stressed, wouldn't it feel better? You wouldn't be so full. Come on, just this once? It's always there, every day. The bathroom is right down the hall, precisely ten steps away from where I sit at my desk—and I have counted those steps, pacing back and forth some afternoons, ten steps, ten tiny little steps. If the need was great enough, I could make it in three long strides.

Right down the hall from me lies certainty, comfort, but it's a comfort that I cannot have anymore. Every goddamn day, I have to remind myself that right down the hall, right after the certain comfort, comes a grotesque death. I picture my husband finding me that way—on the floor in a pool of blood and vomit, dead of gastric rupture or a heart attack or both—and I plunk back down at my desk.

That is control for me, sad as it sounds. But the fact of the matter is, a few years ago, I would not have been able to make this daily choice. I would have believed that the throwing up, perhaps even the death itself, was control. I would have been very wrong.

February was claustrophobic, and things got stranger still. There was a sudden rage that swept over campus of desperate sex and cocaine and booze, a sudden spate of people kicked out of school when caught. A single cellist playing a sonata in the snow. People shuffling into class in their pajamas, a wild matted look to eyes and hair. There was my own mania one night—all I can say is that I wanted to make everything in my head stop moving around and jabbering at me, and that I may have done just a touch too much speed—that led me to the bathroom cabinet and had me swallowing all the pills we had, Fiberall, vitamin C, codeine, Motrin, aspirin. I remember the curious way the floor flew up at me. There was my early morning walk-crawl in the dark to the infirmary, asking to be excused from class, I just wasn't feeling well. They said no. The following week was a haze of classes that swerved in and out of focus, close-up and distant shots alternating madly through my eyes.

I began stashing uneaten food in my room. I had a little pencil box where I kept crackers, hard candies, stale pretzels, the occasional rubbery carrot stick. Lora brought me food from meals, which I rarely went to anymore. She'd toss packets of crackers on the book over which I was bent. I stashed them in my box. I kept them, in case.

This is a common habit of anoretics. There seems to be a biological basis for it. When a study was done on a group of young, healthy *men* whose daily caloric intake was cut to just under a thousand calories, they began to: stash food surreptitiously, talk about food constantly, chew gum and mints perpetually, read recipes for dishes they couldn't make. As the study went on, they were frequently caught digging through garbage cans, sneaking into the hospital kitchen to binge. They began to purge, and—interestingly enough—they became incredibly worried about their weight, the shape of their bodies, and began to *diet*. They worried about getting dirty, got disgusted with their own biological functions, and didn't want to touch food anymore.

Hmm.

I don't know where the body begins and the mind ends. Perhaps one of the fallacies endemic to both eating-disorders specialists and our culture in general is that there is *either* a biological cause *or* an emotional cause for eating disorders. But the two become entangled. You yourself get terribly tangled up in both, and you don't know how to get out.

Whether the cause was malnutrition, neurosis, or an ineffable combination of the two, what changed very suddenly in that year was the way my mind worked. For as long as I had been bulimic—seven years, by that point—I had never before reached the state of complete and constant obsession that began that year at school and would characterize the years to come. A friend of mine who I'd meet later in life, one who never had an eating disorder, told me that she'd bent over the toilet once and began to throw up. But then she was suddenly gripped, she said, by a sudden sense that what she was doing was *wrong.* Not wrong in the sense of sinful, but wrong in a human sense—a crime against nature, the body, the soul, the self. She stopped. I think that prior to my sixteenth year, I had always understood in the back of my brain that this was true. I had a clear, haunting knowledge that my eating disorder was cruelty. We forget this. We think of bulimia and anorexia as either a bizarre psychosis, or as a quirky little habit, a phase, or as a thing that women just *do.* We forget that it is a violent act, that it bespeaks a profound level of anger toward and fear of the self. That year, the questioning, whispering voice in my head fell silent.

With that voice gone, my eyes changed, and subsequently my world changed as well. Through the looking glass I went, and things turned upside down, inside out. Words turned themselves around, and I heard things in reverse. Inside the looking glass, you become the center of the universe. All things are reduced to their relationship to you. You bang on the glass—people turn and see you, smile, and wave. Your mouth moves in soundless shapes. You lose a dimension, turn into a paper doll figure with painted eyes.

You become fearless in a very twisted way. Reckless, careless, a cartoon character spinning its legs in glee as it falls from a cliff, splats flat, bounces back up. You sneeze, and your nose, cocaine torn, spatters blood. This pleases you, just as the small knives of pain please you when you run, the stabbing pain of each step, just as the worried, muted words of friends please you, just as your own voice pleases you when you say to them, I just can't stop. You've made a decision: You *will not* stop. The pain is necessary, especially the pain of hunger. It reassures you that you are strong, can withstand anything, that you are not a slave to your body, you don't have to give in to its whining.

In truth, you like the pain. You like it because you believe you deserve it, and the fact that you're putting yourself through pain means you are doing what you, by all rights, ought to do. You're doing something right. It's hard to describe how these two things can take place in the same mind: the arrogant, self-absorbed pride in yourself for your incredible feat, and the belief that you are so evil as to deserve starvation and any other form of self-mutilation. They coexist because you've split yourself in two. One part is the part you're trying to kill—the weak self, the body. One part is the part you're trying to become—the powerful self, the mind. This is not psychosis, this splitting. It is the history of Western culture made manifest. Your ability to withstand pain is your claim to fame. It is ascetic, holy. It is self-control. It is masochism, and masochism is pleasurable to many, but we don't like to think about that. We don't like to think that a person could have a twisted autoerotic life going on, be both a top and a bottom, and experience both at once: the pleasure of beating the hell out of a body shackled at the wrists, and the pleasure of being the body and knowing we deserve each blow.

The year became psychedelic. Winter began to break in March, the sun changing from white to pale yellow, daylight creeping in earlier, the packed snow on the paths beginning to melt. I was severely malnourished and moving faster and faster, with the bravery particular to fools, toward sickness, seeking out sickness with a passion. It was not that I *thought* that I wanted to be sick. It was simply that I was actively doing all I could do to be sick. On one level, I wanted very much to get caught. I did not want to get caught to be saved. I wanted to get caught to be seen as something, to have a claim to greatness, to have the sick admiration that comes to those of us who destroy ourselves particularly well. My god! people say. You have so much *self-control!*

And later: My god. You are so, so sick. When people say this, when they turn their heads, you've won your little game. You have proven your thesis that no-body-loves-me-every-body-hates-me, guess-I'll-just-eat-worms. You get to sink back into your hospital bed, shrieking with righteous indignation. See? you get to say. I *knew* you'd give up on me. I knew you'd leave.

But then what do you do? What are you worth if no one's looking? How do you know you're even *there?* Back to the mirror you go, then, looking for something other than bones, other than the shadow of death at your back. It takes a long time to learn to see.

Death is a fascinating thing. The human mind continually returns and returns to death, to mortality, immortality, damnation, salvation. Some fear death, some seek it, but it is in our nature to wonder at the limits of human life, at least. When you are sick like this you begin to wonder too much. Death is at your shoulder, death is your shadow, your scent, your waking and dreaming companion. You cannot help, when sleep begins to touch your eyes, but think: What if? What if? And in that question, there is a longing, too much like the longing of a young girl in love. The sickness occupies your every thought, breathes like a lover at your ear; the sickness stands at your shoulder in the mirror, absorbed with your body, each inch of skin and flesh, and you let it work you over, touch you with rough hands that thrill.

Nothing will ever be so close to you again. You will never find a lover so careful, so attentive, so unconditionally present and concerned only with you.

Some of us use the body to convey the things for which we cannot find words. Some of us decide to take a shortcut, decide the world is too much or too little, death is so easy, so smiling, so simple; and death is dramatic, a final fuck-you to the world.

> *Dear Father, I have no intention of making a peace pact between my body and my soul, and neither do I intend to hold back. Therefore, allow me to tame my body by not altering my diet; I will not stop for the rest of my life, until there is no more life left. You should not think that my body is so mortified and weak as it seems; it acts this way so that I should not demand the debt it contracted in the world, when it*

liked pleasure. . . . Oh my body, why do you not help me to serve my creator and redeemer? Why are you not as quick to obey as you were to disobey His commands? Do not lament, do not cry; do not pretend to be half dead. You will bear the weight that I place on your shoulders, all of it. . . . I not only wish to abstain from bodily food but I wish to die a thousand times a day, were it possible, in this mortal life of mine.

—SAINT MARGARET OF CORTONA, IN A LETTER TO HER CONFESSOR ORDERING HER TO EAT. D. FEBRUARY 22, 1297, OF STARVATION.

March. Two friends and I lay on the bed in a dorm room. We talked about sex, one-upping each other with what we'd done. Flopped on our backs, we brag of the careless use of our bodies, our common disdain for the boys or men. I didn't feel a thing, we'd say with pride. We talked about food and weight, we talked about diet and loss.

The air warmed and the trees began to bloom small green buds. It was breezy, sunny spring. I walked roads in late afternoons, out to an empty school yard, through the woods to a creek, with two other girls or alone, took off my shoes and rolled up my pants, dipped my feet into the brook, the ice water of melted snow. Sun played on the ripples and wet rocks, shone through the clear water to the pebbled brook floor. On brave days, we took off our clothes and swam, breathless and laughing with the shock of cold, the shock of water's motion after months of the ice's stillness.

My friend Jeremy remembers this time, the rush of spring and pollen, the way people move more quickly, bodies thawing, blood coursing through the veins like cold streams. He remembers knocking on my window one night. Lora told him that I was at the top of Kresge Auditorium, an enormous coliseum of an auditorium with stone floors and steel supports, a web of metal and wire that held up the arched roof. The top? he said. She said, Yeah. She climbs up into the rafters to smoke.

I picture myself up there—I was certainly not the first to go—a small girl, a pile of sweatshirts, perched on a metal beam by the ceiling, smoke coiling about my head. I remember looking down, the dizzy, heady feeling of the head's weight pulling forward, pulling toward the stone floor some hundred feet down.

A rustle of wind off the lake swept through the campus, tousled hair, and the craziness shifted again. Talk of contests and auditions and graduations was constant. There were late nights and endless workshops. Lora and I both won national writing awards that spring. We grew increasingly distant, as I spent more and more time in the company of other dieting girls who didn't ask, or alone. Lora saw too much and was too angry, and I was too bent on not-eating. It was impossible for her to ignore it, and it pissed her off. Fights grew more frequent. She knew what was going on. She occasionally hauled me bodily to the cafeteria and then sat there glaring at me while I ate Jell-O. She told the resident advisor, who spoke to me briefly about it. At breakfast, a girl said to me, admiringly: Oh my god, you've lost so much weight! You look great! I'm so jealous. Lora furiously said, Jesus Christ, don't encourage her. She pushed her chair back and started slamming her things together. The girl put her hand around my arm, forefinger touching thumb. Wow, she sighed. Lora shoved her chair in and said, Don't expect me to be at your funeral, and walked off. Someone said, What's up her butt? I shook my head. Nothing, I said.

There was some part of me that could not understand, at that time, why she was so angry with me. There was a part of me that believed it was none of her business, not her problem. It was strange, because other people's concern, their hugs and advice, just fed into it. I just wanted to get more sick. Lora's anger scared me. I think it reminded me that I had no right. And as I would do for years to come, I got angry at the people who loved me the most and therefore pulled no punches. I wanted to be coddled. I wanted someone to say, Oh, poor baby, everything will be okay, we'll make it better. I did not want someone to say, This is bullshit. No one wants to hear the truth about themselves. Lora was telling the truth, and I moved out.

It happened after spring break.

It happened in late morning, a few weeks after we got back. I went to breakfast, my zest for starvation renewed by weeks of bulimia. I was wearing pink sweatpants and a white sweatshirt. I remember it was cool but bright, incredibly bright. The light hurt my eyes, the scattered sudden white light between leaves that moved in the breeze was sharp. I must have been looking up because I remember the trees, and the light, and the pain in my forehead, my squint. I remember the three glasses of water I drank at breakfast, the pain in my chest, the nauseating fullness I always felt after the water. To this day I hate water. The taste of water feels empty, hungry, sick. I drank coffee, two cups. I had stopped using cream. I drank it black. When we finished breakfast, I stopped at the buffet line and picked up twelve chocolate chip cookies, putting them in the inside pocket of my bag. I remember the chocolate chip cookies: bendy, chewy. I hadn't eaten them in months, but I liked to have them around. I went out the front door of the cafeteria, turned right, crossed the main square of the campus. I went in the door of the classrooms building, walked down the hall, went into the English department, turned left, walked into fiction workshop, said hello, and passed out.

It was not the first time I'd fallen. It wasn't even the first time I'd faded, slipped, and fallen, not the first time I felt my vision blur and dim. But before there had always been a few things to warn me: the knees buckle, the center of gravity dissolves and the arms feel like they've begun to float, the ears ring, the eyelids flutter. It's just like the movies. I could always see myself falling, I'd always known. This time it just went black.

I don't know what happened next. My next memory is of someone helping me up the stairs to the dorm. A friend of mine happened to be standing at the desk and saw me held up by the shoulders, unable to focus. She caught me and yelled for someone to help. Someone came running, and got me from there to the infirmary. I remember trying to walk and being unable to. I remember the feeling of gravity pushing us backward. I apologized for being so heavy. I was laid down on a bed. Someone took my temperature, another pulled me upright to a sitting position and veered dangerously close to my face with orange juice in one of those little paper Dixie cups they keep in infirmary bathrooms. Someone had one hand on the back of my head and one on the cup, was forcing my mouth open, tipping my head back, pouring the juice down my throat. This I remember: As they stood there, still holding my head, I threw the juice up, on purpose, back into the cup. I fell back onto the bed and said: I have the flu.

Eating disorders have the centripetal force of black holes. I remember, that day, pulling into myself and not caring about who I was sucking in after me—the friends at the bedside, the nurses. I remember curling up under the thin white blanket, fading in and out of sleep, panicked by the faint taste of orange juice on my tongue, lulled by the memory that I had thrown it up, it was okay, it hadn't gotten in. That, I remember: the sorry little mantra I sang in my head, the lying lullaby, It's-okay, it's-okay, it's-okay. I remember the sunny day outside the window, the tops of the trees that tapped on the panes.

And I remember being utterly, utterly pleased with myself.

Why?

Because I was disappearing. A disappearing act, the act of becoming invisible, is, in fact, a visible act, and rarely goes unnoticed. There is a strange sort of logic to this: We expect, in this world, that human beings will bear a human weight and force—there is a fascination with all human rebellions against material limits, with that small step into the supernatural, or what we imagine to be supernatural. I am not saying that the act of erasing the body *is* magic, but it *feels* magical. Houdini, barefoot, walks across the coals, and the gathered crowd sucks in its breath. Houdini disappears into thin air; the gathered crowd murmurs and looks around wildly.

There is an even more urgent appeal to the anorexic body. We know, we've learned through the indoctrination of cultural babble, that we too can strip away the flesh, we too can "magically" drop pounds, "melt away" pounds, watch the pounds "disappear." The skeletal body can be ours for a nominal fee. As the average American steadily grows heavier, the passionate fascination with and fetishization of the anorexic body also grows. Women fling themselves headlong down the rabbit hole, everyone else is going, it can't be so dangerous. There are people reading this who may think to themselves: What if I just tried it? What if I just lost a few more pounds? After all, *she's* still alive.

Not quite.

I spent a few days in the infirmary. My friends and the boy I was seeing came to visit me. We found an ancient box of Girl Scout Trefoils (shortbread) in a drawer. I ate them all and threw them up. It baffled me, even then, that the nurses didn't go into a frenzy. They periodically took my blood pressure and my temperature, and congratulated me on my (dangerously low, I will soon find out) blood pressure—I didn't know, at the time, that my blood pressure bore a relation to my health—and put me back to bed. I didn't know, then, that the only medical professionals acquainted with the signs of an eating disorder were specialists.

Friends would visit me in my little infirmary nest in the late evenings, when the yellow light from a cheap lamp would spill over the bed where we all curled up. I was full of good cheer, the picture of contrition, avowing my commitment to health. I did a funny thing. I agreed with a friend of mine that I needed to go into AA. In truth, I did have a problem with chemicals: I was using them as a substitute for food and had been for years. In truth, what I wanted was a group of people who wouldn't judge me, wouldn't lurch up in their seats with alarm when I said: I'm sick. There was a little AA clique of underage recovering alcoholics and addicts at school. They had special permission to take the bus into town on Sunday mornings and sit in the room where AA met, smoking to their hearts' content. I called my parents that day and told them I was going into AA. My father said only this: Why?

Sunday mornings, we left campus, and the sky seemed suddenly wider. The laughter on the bus was, I would later note, a great deal like the laughter of the girls on the hospital unit when we got to take a three-block walk, when the miniloonies from the bin took a little field trip to the pool. It was a reckless sort of laughter, as if a sudden rush of oxygen had hit the brain. We sat in the room, smoke so thick you couldn't see. After a few meetings, I sat up and announced: Hi, my name is Marya. (Hi, Marya.) I'm cross-addicted. I paused. I said: And I think I'm bulimic.

As the words came out of my mouth, they felt like a lie. I felt, God help me, like I was *bragging.*

I loved the group. I loved feeling that things would be okay, that if I just went to meetings, and Stuck to the Program, all would be fine. I especially loved the step that said: I am powerless over this disease.

I think this assumption of powerlessness is the most dangerous thing an anoretic can hear. It grants license, exoneration. I liked sitting back in my chair, chain-smoking, sighing with relief and thinking: This is beyond my control. The mind lifts its hands from the wheel and says: I hand this over to a higher power. God, don't let me crash.

People who've Been to Hell and Back develop a certain sort of self-righteousness. There is a tendency to say: I have an addictive personality, I am terribly sensitive, I'm touched with fire, I have Scars. There is a self-perpetuating belief that one simply cannot help it, and this is very dangerous. It becomes an identity in and of itself. It becomes its own religion, and you wait for salvation, and you wait, and wait, and wait, and do not save yourself. If you saved yourself and did not wait for salvation, you'd be self-sufficient. How dull.

At Interlochen, there is no prom, but rather Morp, *prom* spelled backward. I had convinced the several dorm parents that I was well enough to go. I had to promise that I was telling the truth and knew that if anything went wrong, I was in deep shit. I remember one woman, a small, tough woman, who looked me in the face and said: If you're lying, you're out of here. It was a threat that hung, with good reason, over the heads of most of the students. Expulsion lurked in the background waiting to catch you in the act of sex, smoking, drinking, drugs, and now, illness. I wheedled, I cried. I was getting rather good at both. I went.

The costumes were fantastic. A bunch of us got dressed in our room. There had been a debate over shaving our armpits, and we eventually did, and were subsequently bereft. We took a bus to a restaurant on the bay and had dinner. I ate a potato, excused myself, quietly threw up while my friends redid their lipstick. My date and I walked on the beach, high on the smell of salt and the sunset. I took off my shoes (teenage love is terribly dramatic). My head began to spin, just slightly. We took the bus to the club. The dance floor throbbed, skin flashing wet and red under colored lights, eyes glassy. My friends and I moved through the club, from pool tables to dance floor and back again. I leaned against a wall, trying to breathe. Smiling very bright. My black satin dress began to cling, cold and damp, to my skin.

While dancing, I stumbled. I made my way through the bodies to the bathroom, sat down in a stall, leaned my face against the cool metal of the wall. I steadied. I stood. Back on the floor, strobe lights were flashing, and I couldn't balance. There was too much spinning, too much flashing, faces suddenly garish, absent-eyed smiles flickering on and off, limbs moving too quickly, too close. I began to flinch, holding my hands up to my face, trying to focus, and stumbled off the floor to return to the bathroom, my friends at my heels. I bent over at the waist and began to cough, blood spattering on the white porcelain tile, rasping out the words: I'm fine, I'm fine while my friends screamed. With my back to the wall, I slid to the floor: A distinct drop in altitude, a feeling rather like slipping under water, temperature falling, gravity losing its hold.

A friend furiously slammed out of the bathroom and got one of the chaperons. She stood above me, listening to the chaotic noise of my friends telling her in shrill voices what had happened, me insisting that I was all right. She finally cut in with: All of you, shut up. Marya, you're full of shit. We're leaving. She pulled me up by one arm and hauled me out while I yelled and tried to pull away. I had a very hard time not laughing. It all seemed like a great joke.

In the car, I passed out. Back to the infirmary. My parents were called. They were told that while this was obviously not a good thing, I was in no way too thin and had probably just been taking diet pills that hadn't agreed with me. It was May. The year was almost over, and I think it must have been decided that I could finish the year. In all likelihood, I probably convinced my parents that this was much ado about nothing. Nonetheless, I was sent to a psychologist off campus.

I do not think eating disorders were my therapist's specialty. I was *profoundly* pissy. I remember taking a cab there. She asked me, I think, if I had an eating disorder. I said no. Then what's going on? I shrugged. I don't remember anything else about it.

The year sped up. Spring turned to early summer, preparations for graduation week began, people worked like mad getting ready for performances and readings and exhibits. We laughed easily. The sky was bluer than blue, the air warm and very sweet. Now that the cat was out of the bag, I had to change my tune a bit. I convinced my friends that the "real" issue was my bulimia, and since I wasn't throwing up, everything was really fine. Besides, my stomach is all messed up and food makes me feel sick, so I can't eat very much, so I can't eat at all, today. I'm trying, I swear to god I'm really trying. With that, I'd take a bite of toast, start to cry, and set it back down on the plate. I just can't do it, I said, and they cried and I cried and they told me what a good job I was doing, not throwing up and all. I nodded and wiped away my crocodile tears and I still did not eat. I fell again, while returning from smoking in the auditorium with a friend. It was early morning, still cool. We came up the hill, toward the cafeteria. I swayed and fell.

For the first time, I was scared. But only for a minute. I said: I'm just tired. Maybe I had a bad cigarette. She said, Come eat something, and I said, Oh no, that would make me throw up, I don't feel good, and she helped me walk into the cafeteria. I drank my coffee and held my head.

The last weeks are a blur. Friends were crying in administrators' offices, trying to get them to *do something!* They would respond, quite understandably, What do you want me to do? I would sit slouched in my chair, arms crossed, telling them and almost believing that things weren't as bad as they looked. In truth, I didn't think they could possibly be that bad. I wasn't that thin. There were people far thinner than me, and that was all there was to it. I mean, we all know the dangers of starving, but bulimia? That can't be that bad. It's only bad when you get really thin. Who worries about bulimics? They're just gross.

We packed up our rooms, soared through finals, notched our belts with awards. Lora and I had little to say to each other, so we did not speak. Murmurs of destinations hummed through the dorms: Julliard, NYU, Oxford, Harvard, Oberlin, RISD, Yale, L.A. Chatters of who would be back, who could take it, who was going into treatment, who was touring Europe, who'd been signed, who'd made it, who hadn't. I was planning to come back, planning to sweep the writing awards the next year.

Part of me, the part that was still attached to the ground, walked into a teacher's office, knocked, closed the door behind me, and told him I was going into treatment. The strange thing was, I didn't know that at the time. My fiction teacher, who had worked closely with me all year, pushing me so hard I at times thought I would die, who believed in my writing, sat back in his chair, baseball cap perched on his head, and rubbed his beard. He said: I'm sorry this is happening. He said, leaning forward: I want you back here next year. Got that? I nodded, looking away, trying not to cry. He said: Okay, punk. Don't you stop writing. I shook my head and said: See ya.

It was not so much that I knew I wasn't coming back to Interlochen. It was that I had a funny feeling I wasn't coming back anywhere.

My brain had split into two poles. At one pole was the basic survival instinct, the desire common to animals, beyond language and reason, to live. This side, the innate biological need to survive, is the one with which anoretics are at war. The survival instinct is what maddens anoretics and bulimics more than I can even articulate. Whereas most people, when hungry, eat, and when sick, go to bed, I was cowed and infuriated by the blind binge, the sudden fall to the floor, each implying my body's needs, weakness, and ultimate mastery over *me.* Refusing to starve, my body ate; refusing to stand any longer, my body buckled and fell. The awful paradox is that, to me, it seemed that my emotional survival, my basic personal integrity, was dependent upon my mastery, if not total erasure, of my physical self.

At the opposite pole of my brain there was a desire to throw in the towel at an early age. Turn over the survival instinct and you will find its wet white belly, the instinct that tends toward death. I felt no anger toward this instinct and, curiously, had little fear of it—not yet—and I turned to it as an ally in my little war.

Eating-disordered people are aware, to a limited extent, that their behavior is dangerous. We may be deluded in a number of ways, but we are not so far gone that we cannot see the way our crusade—emotional survival, physical death—cancels itself out altogether. The body, many of us find to our great dismay, will always win. Either it will survive despite our best efforts, dealing a blow to our egotistical notion that we can control it, or it will die, making emotional survival utterly moot. People who have eating disorders are all very different. I am certain that there are people who just get eating disorders and are not necessarily trying to starve themselves to death. I was not one of those people. I was trying to die, in a curious, casual sort of way. Some women I've talked to say they were just testing the limits of the human body—eating-disordered athletes in particular seem to have this idea—but they speak in a bizarre, almost proactive tone, as if they had always intended to stop. The eating disorder just got out of hand.

I did not intend to stop. I was not testing the limits of the human body—which implies a certain respect for those limits—so much as I was wondering what it would take to break through them. I wanted to see what was on the other side.

In retrospect, I can see that my manic run toward success may have been based on the belief? knowledge? that I had only a small window of opportunity in which to succeed. One night, earlier in the school year, Lora had asked me how long I thought I would live. I lay there in bed and considered the question for a minute. I said, "Maybe twenty."

I figured it would take me about that long to starve to death. I came very close. Three years later, two months shy of my nineteenth birthday, the doctors gave me a week to live.

I didn't particularly want to live much longer than that. Life seemed rather daunting. It seems so to me even now. Life seemed like too long a time to have to stick around, a huge span of years through which one would be required to tap-dance and smile and be Great! and be Happy! and be Amazing! and be Precocious! I was tired of life by the time I was sixteen. I was tired of being too much, too intense, too manic. I was tired of people, and I was incredibly tired of myself. I wanted to do whatever Amazing Thing I was expected to do—it might be pointed out that these were my expectations, mine alone—and be done with it. Go to sleep. Go to a heaven where there was nothing but bathtubs and books.

The usual line on eating disorders is that they are an attempt to become a child again, a regression. Rather than looking at eating disorders as an infantile desire to return to an *ex utero* symbiosis with the mother, I think it's important to note that they might be a cultural and generational phenomenon of plain old-fashioned burnout. My generation was weaned on subliminal advertising, stupid television, slasher movies, insipid grocery-store literature, MTV, VCRs, fast food, infomercials, glossy ads, diet aids, plastic surgery, a pop culture wherein the hyper-cool, blank-eyed supermodel was a hero. This is the intellectual and emotional equivalent of eating nothing but candy bars—you get malnourished and tired. We grew up in a world in which the surface of the thing is infinitely more important than its substance—and where the surface of the thing had to be "perfect," urbane, sophisticated, blasé, *adult*. I would suggest that if you grow up trying constantly to be an adult, a *successful* adult, you will be sick of being grown up by the time you're old enough to drink.

I got tired of trying to be that kind of adult. I don't think I was the only one. I couldn't imagine what the hell I was going to do with myself once I attained "success," but I couldn't give up the panicky need to achieve it either. My idea of success was about to take a rather perverted twist.

Bear in mind, people with eating disorders tend to be both competitive and intelligent. We are incredibly perfectionistic. We often excel in school, athletics, artistic pursuits. We also tend to quit without warning. Refuse to go to school, drop out, quit jobs, leave lovers, move, lose all our money. We get sick of being impressive. Rather, we tire of having to *seem* impressive. As a rule, most of us never really believed we were any good in the first place. I got tired of the feeling that I was constantly onstage, wearing someone else's clothes, saying someone else's lines. I quit the charade of excellence and sought out something that seemed like an easy route to the respect I wanted, a *real* respect: an eating disorder.

I didn't realize that I would apply the same unrealistic expectations to my illness. I didn't know in advance that I would never feel like I was good enough, like I was a "successful" eating disordered person until I was at death's door. Actually, not even then.

My mother arrived in the last week of school, her mother in tow. I was wearing some sort of gauzy white thing. She hugged me. As we walked, smiling, passing through the throng of students and parents, she said, You look like hell. What? I said, waving to friends. She said, Your face is covered with fur. My hand flew up to my face, felt the fine silky down on my cheeks. I said, Look how much weight I've lost. She said, sarcastically, Yes, dear. I can see how much weight you've lost. I asked proudly,

Don't I look good? She replied, You look like a ghost. You're gray.

We went to see Beckett's *Waiting for Godot*, a concert, a reading. I introduced her to everyone. She was looking at me funny. She was being unusually sweet—not that my mother isn't a nice person, just that *sweet* is not the first word that comes to mind to describe her. She didn't know what was going on, but she was clearly going nuts with worry, though I think she was trying not to upset me. At graduation ceremonies, I sang with the choir, *I took the road less traveled by, and that has made all the difference, all the difference.*

That afternoon, everyone hugging and waving and bawling, I climbed into the car and we drove to Chicago. I don't remember the first day except for the memory of badgering my mother to let me drive. High on speed and starvation, I'd done my driver's training that winter, learning to drive on icy, snowy Michigan roads. Maybe drug and blood-sugar testing ought to be mandatory for fifteen-year-olds in driver's ed. We pulled into Chicago late in the evening, my grandmother bitching, my mother white-lipped and terse, me dizzy and cranky. There was an enormous convention or festival going on, and the streets were gridlocked, the hotels full. We wound up at the Hilton or the Hyatt in a ridiculous suite with a separate room for the bathtub, which I promptly sank into, watching myself from all angles in the mirror-covered walls.

I decided, quite randomly, that I was hungry and proceeded downstairs to the five-star restaurant. I ate *quail*. To this day I have no idea what possessed me, but I remember that meal as if it was my last request before execution, the elaborately arranged corn thingamajig appetizer, the cold soup, the quail, the thick black coffee at the end, the mint. As I ate, I read. I signed the bill, went upstairs to the room, bent over the toilet, and began to throw up, when I decided the meal was too expensive to just flush. I stopped puking. The whole affair was completely out of character. I lay down in bed and read for a while, pulled the little dangling cord of the bedside lamp and fell asleep, full at last.

The next morning, feeling guilty and rotund, I did not eat. We sat in a café on Oak Street, my grandmother picking at her food as she always did, admonishing me to drink my smoothie, my mother glaring at me. A bizarre dust storm upturned semis on I-94W and rain began to pour. I remember the windshield, a sheet of running water, the murky green sky that comes before midwestern tornadoes. I bitched and whined the entire time, insisting that my mother ought to let me *drive*. It didn't seem to me that it would be so hard to drive in a tornado. I picked a fight with my mother, who was damn close to smacking me. I took that opportunity to tell her how she never let me do anything, that she thought I was just a little kid and never took me seriously. She sat silently, bent forward over the wheel. I jabbered on and on, reminding her of the last time we'd been stuck in the car together during a storm in the summer of 1987. I said: You HIT me! She said: I didn't hit you. I said: YOU DID! We were driving along and you were pissed because you didn't get that job you wanted and you were just in a bad mood and you SMACKED me! You did! (Can you blame her?) Finally she hissed: *Marya shut up! I cannot deal with you right now!*

By the time we got to Edina, I had probably convinced her that I'd lost my mind. I, however, was planning my summer job, my summer books. We pulled up to the house, and my father ran out to give me a hug. In the refrigerator sat a big bowl of grapes with a sign that read: WELCOME HOME GRAPE HOG! When I'd lived at home I'd always eaten all the grapes before anyone else got to them. Grapes have–hmm–a laxative effect. I had the good grace to force a laugh and thank my father. He moved around the kitchen, hyperkinetic, worried, hugging me often, patting my back. I would later realize that their constant, unprecedented touching was a test. I would learn the difference between a hug and a bone count, hands roving down the spine with a bump-bump-bump, palm tripping on a shoulder blade.

Over dinner, they told me I had an appointment on Tuesday. We just want to make sure you're okay, they said. I was game. I didn't figure anyone *real* would be worried. We drove into the heart of Minneapolis, sat down in the waiting room of the Teen-Age Medical Services (TAMS) clinic. Both of my parents were there, which felt funny. My dad had always been the one to take me to the doctors before I left home. We had always gone to McDonald's afterward. It was something of an event. I remembered that I couldn't go to McDonald's anymore. I paged through magazines. I looked at the pamphlets on the wall: birth control,

STDs, Do You Smoke?, Getting Along with Parents, little sketches of smiling boys-n-girls. My father put his arm around me and felt my shoulder bones. He punched my arm lightly and then looked away, who—me? It was our old joke. I punched him back.

A voice from behind me: "Marya?"

Something was wrong. She pronounced my name right. Someone had been talking to her.

She was short, dark-haired, pretty, had a beautiful but worried smile. I put down my magazine, stood up, folded my arms across my chest, listened suspiciously as she greeted my parents, "Hi, Jay. Judy."

Jay and Judy? What were they doing on a first-name basis?

She put her hand on my shoulder. I jumped. She dropped her hand and said, Come on back. By the way, I'm Kathi.

Mmm-hm.

We walked down the hall. She asked, Okay, do you know what's going on here?

I answered loudly: NO. I watched her pull out a thick file with my name on it. I'd never been there before. What the hell was in the file?

She said: We're doing an eating-disorders evaluation. You—

I interrupted: I don't have an eating disorder.

Okay, she said. Then this will be quick. In the meantime, you're going to see the doctor first, and then come up and talk to me. Sound good?

No.

She laughed. You're right, she said. I'll cut the Pollyanna act.

I smiled.

In the examining room, my feet were cold. My hands were cold. I am convinced they keep doctors' offices at forty degrees. Even my knees got cold. The doctor came in. He was young, pleasant-looking, brisk. He put his hands at my throat, felt the swelling below my jaw.

How long since you've thrown up? he asked.

You're assuming I throw up, I said.

Yep.

Yesterday.

How many times yesterday?

Once.

How many times yesterday?

Once.

From the swelling here, I'd guess three, minimum.

I almost fell off the table. He was right. He moved in front of my face, shined a little light in my eyes.

Did you know your eyes don't focus?

Um, no.

They don't.

He wrote on my charts. He wrapped a cuff around my arm. It was too big. He pulled out a cuff that said, in big delightful letters, CHILD'S CUFF.

That pleases you?

What?

That an adult cuff is too big?

No.

You look pleased. Stand up.

He took my pressure. I began to get the idea that blood pressure had something to do with eating disorders.

I asked: Is it normal?

He said: I don't know yet. Lie down.

He took it again.

Nope, he said. It's not. All right, walk heel-to-toe from the door to me.

I went to the door. I started walking.

Don't look at the floor, he said. I looked up, took a step, stumbled, caught myself on the table, laughed nervously. I asked, How many tries do I get?

He didn't laugh. He said: Shut your eyes, put your arms out to either side of you, and touch your nose with your index fingers.

I said: You've got to be kidding.

He shook his head.

I couldn't do it.

He sat me on the table, tested my reflexes with his mallet. No response whatsoever. My legs hung down, limp. He tested again. Nothing. He took one of my hands, peered down at the nails, chipped the polish off one finger. The nails were blue. He wrote it down.

He lay me down on the table, pressed at my stomach for a while.

You've got a good coat of fur here.

Thanks.

He weighed me, took blood, took a urine sample. As he scribbled his last notes on my chart, I asked cheerily, So, did I fail?

He glanced up at me and said: Pretty much.

Upstairs in Kathi's office, I curled into the corner of the couch and took test after test: Eating Disorders Index, Body Perception, this and that. I was relatively honest. *Do you think you need to lose weight?* Yes. *What is your ideal weight?* Eighty-four. *Would you say that you'd give anything to be thin?* Yes.

Ask a woman in your life how she'd answer these questions and see what kind of answers you get. None of these things are so shocking. Statistically speaking, this is not so far from the norm. I didn't figure I had anything to worry about.

When I was done I chatted with Kathi, whom I rather liked. She was funny and sharp. We talked for an hour or so after she'd reviewed my tests and the lab results. We talked about life, food, weight, stuff.

She said, So, you don't have an eating disorder.

Nope.

That's not what your body says.

Excuse me?

Your blood is anemic. You have ketones[4] in your urine, your blood pressure is completely unstable. Your heart rate is pitiful.

But I'm not skinny.

Not as skinny as some, no.

So it's not that big a deal.

It's a very big deal.

I started laughing. She smiled at me.

I'm checking you into Methodist Hospital.

WHAT?

Sorry. You need to be in the hospital.

---

[4] Ketones are a class of acid compounds. A ketone body is "a ketone-containing substance . . . that is an intermediate product of fatty acid metabolism. Ketone bodies tend to accumulate in the blood and are excreted in the urine of individuals affected by starvation or uncontrolled diabetes mellitus" (*American Heritage Dictionary*).

I lost it. I started screaming. She sat there.

And then I was in the car with my father. I said, I suppose all I'll need to take is a nightgown, now that I'm going to lie around for a month. He laughed. He tried to make a joke: What does the dyslexic insomniac think about all night? (The existence of Dog), but it came out: What does the insomniac anorexic—wait—oh, shit—and we laughed and laughed.

That was on a Tuesday. The following Monday, I went into the Methodist Hospital outpatient clinic for a final evaluation. I sat on the table, freezing cold in my little paper gown, rubbing my feet together with a noisy *scritch-scritch.* There was a blanket in there—they were used to us—and I pulled it over myself. I put on my jacket. I lay down. The doctor came in. He said simply, "Cold or tired or both?" I sat up. He put me on the scale. He was gruff, didn't meet my eyes, ran through the battery of tests. My vital signs had fallen significantly since I'd been seen the previous Tuesday. He mentioned this to me. He checked me in. I watched my father sign the forms.

MARYA JUSTINE HORNBACHER. F. DOB 04-04-74.

I. AXIS I:

A. Bulimia nervosa, 307.51 (w/anoretic features)
B. Substance abuse, 305.00
C. Major Depression, 296.22

Interlude

September 22, 1996

I suppose you'd call it amnesia. I read the charts. I sit in a back office in TAMS, reading my charts. Medical and therapeutic. Charts (blue) regarding a person (sixteen, female, white) named Marya (chronic, total denial) who is clearly very sick. These do not look like my charts. I do not have charts. I am a regular person. Why would I have charts? This never happened to me. These look like my research. I am taking notes as I always do, flipping pages, footnoting, regarding the case at hand. I sit in my chair, suit and red lipstick, professional, smiling brightly as the doctor—my old doctor, the one who watched me get sick and get well and get sick and so on for years—comes in and asks, How are you? Wonderful, thank you. He sees me reading the charts. He says, It must be hard. I say, A little strange, yes.

Rain flings itself down at the pavement. Outside the window, a siren goes screaming by. The doctor smiles at me. I am a grown woman. I am married. I am employed, I am Recovered. I sit here in my suit, hunched over the desk, smiling redly. They are proud of me. It was a Long Haul, but I Made It.

And I read the charts. They make me sad. For the girl and for her family. A family trying very hard to understand, a girl trying very hard to die. The charts make me shake my head in disbelief that the family could be so obtuse, that the girl could be so insensitive, so wrapped up in her own little world, that she could be so blind to the ramifications of her own behavior. "The most striking characteristic of Marya [is] her complete disdain for any risks or dangers involved in her eating disordered . . . behavior. States that they might be dangerous for other people, but not for her."

I am that girl, still. The ramifications occupy space in every cell of my body, every damaged organ and nerve, every memory tainted and skewed by the obsession that was and is my life, every plan for the future that is highly speculative, qualified: Will there be a future? How long? I turn the pages, watch the weight rise and fall, listen through a din of years to the pleading, wheedling, delusional, lying voice of this girl.

Because, in these charts, even I can see that the girl is lying. And that she will fall again.

And again.

4 Methodist Hospital, Take 1

Summer 1990

So, so, Herr Doktor,
So, Herr Enemy.
I am your opus,
I am your valuable,
The pure gold baby
That melts to a shriek.
I turn and burn.
Do not think I underestimate your great concern.
Ash, ash—
You poke and stir.
Flesh, bone, there is nothing there.

—Sylvia Plath, "Lady Lazarus," 1966

The hospitalizations at Methodist have a tendency to blur, one into another, since I was there three times in less than a year. Hospitalizations in general are blurry. The days are the same, precisely the same. Nothing changes. Life melts down to a simple progression of meals. They become a way of life fairly quickly. You used to be a normal girl with a normal life. Now you are a patient, a case, a file full of forms. You may welcome this transition. It may seem inevitable to you. You have been removed from the world. You have been found flawed and wanting. You could have told them this years ago. It is all right, in a way, because there is nothing so sure, so safe, as routine. There is nothing so welcome to the anoretic or bulimic, much as she protests and howls, as a world wherein everything, everything, revolves around food.

And there is nothing so wonderfully conducive to eating disorders as treatment.

There are the certainties. You will be given slippers—little socks with rubber treads on the soles—and a paper gown. From the doorway to your room, the room will have a bathroom on the left. You will turn the doorknob, but it will be locked. To your right, built into the wall, a small closet. Three drawers beneath a mirror hung too high to see your butt or even your waist. You will be forced to focus instead on your arms, your shoulder bones, the flesh of your cheeks or throat.

Ahead of you, on the left side of the room, two beds, a curtain shoved back to the wall in between. Apparently you will be sharing the room with another patient. Perhaps the two of you will conspire. On the right side of the room, against the wall, sit two hospital chairs, vinyl-covered, gray metal frames. One of these beds is for you. It will be a hard bed, but you are exhausted. In the hospital you will sleep deeper than you ever have, or ever will again. There will be a little table by your bed with buttons on it. You can turn on the radio, call a nurse, flip the light. None of you ever use the nurse call button, even if you are having a heart attack, because you aren't really sick. To call a nurse would be ostentatious, as if you thought you really warranted worry, as if you were so weak as to want to get well. There will be a window in your room that will look out over rooftops and winding streets. Depending on what time of year you are there, the trees will either be full or bare.

There will be a main room, which will have a television and a long bank of windows looking out over the city on one wall. The rest of the walls will have Plexiglas windows through which you will be watched. The room will have one or two couches, end tables, institutional carpeting covering the concrete floor. You will carry your pillow with you everywhere, in its rough white case. You will sit on it, because the floor will hurt the bones poking out through your ass. Or you will lie on the floor on your belly and move the pillow frequently, from under your rib cage to under your elbows to under your pelvic bones. There will be decks and decks of old cards, board games, news magazines. There will be no fashion magazines, and your friends and family will be warned not to bring them to you, because they are bad for you. They may not bring food or drink. If you are lucky, you will be in a hospital where they are allowed to bring decaffeinated coffee. The coffee is never caffeinated—you might be using caffeine to artificially boost your metabolism, or if you are experienced, your heart rate. In Methodist, not even decaffeinated coffee will be allowed, because you might be using it to boost your weight, knowing as you do that you are retaining fluids.

There will be nurses, several of them, on rotating shifts. They will be nice, or they will not. There will be bathroom times, usually every two hours on the hour. At those times, a few nurses with heavy, jangling key rings will open the door for you and lean back against the closet door. Everything rests on the nurse: The very nicest of them will let you leave the door open just a crack, a token, and she will talk to you while you pee to keep your mouth too busy to lean down and puke between your legs. Most of them will stand there, door wide, but will avert their eyes and talk to you. They always cross their arms. They act nonchalant. Some of them are not that much older than you. You hope they feel horrible. Some nurses will let you turn on the water while you go, so that the noise of your piddling into the little plastic container—called a "hat"—which measures your fluid output is not quite so thunderous. There are also the awful nurses, who swing the door wide and *watch*. These are the ones who diet. You hear them talking on the nurses' station when they think you aren't listening—idiots, you're *always* listening—about their fat thighs. These are the ones who do terrible, cruel things to their hair, perming it into thin strands of curled straw and dyeing it colors not found in nature. And they stare at you, your pants around your knees, your arm folded over your belly to hide what you can, and when you ask them, "Can I please turn on the water?" they will say not simply no but "Why?" And you will say, "Because this is a little embarrassing." And they will say, "Why?" And you will drop it, sitting there, attempting to will your body into silence.

Taking a dump will become an obsession. Taking a dump will be a topic of conversation, often a topic of terrific bawdy glee among the patients, sitting curled up on the couches, or beached, after meals, laid out on the floor, hands on the belly, groaning, distended, in no small measure of pain. The nurses will eventually get embarrassed and silence you: Let's move on to another subject, they'll say, and silence will seep over the room again. The fact of the matter is that you cannot take a dump. None of you can take a dump. You will beg for laxatives, but they cannot give you laxatives because more than half of you are addicted to them already, and they could kill you. You personally are not addicted to laxatives at that point, and the whole idea of using them for weight loss will seem utterly stupid to you, because it's not *real* weight you lose by shitting all day long. It's just *water* weight, which isn't as *good*. Of course you do not know then that in less than six months, you and your disdainful ass will move into the bathroom for days at a time because yes, you too! will be eating whole boxes of chocolate Ex-Lax three times a day. Your bodies are in shock. Your intestines, not used to having food in them, or keeping it, will grip the six meals a day like a vise, tighten on the food, refuse to digest. You will lie in bed at night, picturing each item you've eaten, stuck somewhere, arranged in order of consumption: In your large intestine, Tuesday's meals, compacted but still whole; in your small intestine, Wednesday's and Thursday's, part of Friday's; in your stomach, Saturday's and Sunday's; Monday's meals are stuck in your esophagus and lunging toward the back of your throat. If you go too long without taking a dump—say, six to ten days—they will take you away to another part of the hospital and give you a barium enema. This is a nightmare. Barium is an explosive.

Your day will go like this: You will wake up in the wee hours of the morning with dreams of a boa constrictor wrapping around your arm. It will be a blood pressure cuff. You will, in hazy tones, ask the nurse how your pressure and pulse read. She may or may not tell you, depending on whether she's a regular nurse on the unit (won't tell) or a sub (will). You will sink back into sleep. In the morning, if you are me, you will wake up very early. This will get you in trouble because they will think you are waking up early to have unmonitored time to yourself, to exercise. You are simply used to waking up early, but you take their suggestion nonetheless and spend these early hours listening to the sheets hiss as your legs move up and down.

When the light turns from dark blue to pale gray, a nurse will come to the door to wake you up. Good morning, she'll say. You'll mumble, Morning. You will stand up too fast because you never, never get it through your thick head that your body is fucked up. You will sway and sometimes fall over, which will put you on watch for the rest of the damn day. You will put on your paper gown, shivering, and get back under the covers to wait until it's your turn.

When it's your turn, a nurse will come to the door and usually hold your elbow as you go down the hall. You will stand on the high-tech scale that was probably constructed for eating-disorder units because the numbers face away from you. When you peer over to look at them, you find your weight reads in kilos. You don't know metric. You are furious. You are in a state of total disarray, as is everyone else on the unit. Most of you have known your weight minute by minute for some time. It has become the center of your life, and this not-knowing simply will not do. You beg to know your weight, because you're new. When you've been there a little longer, you will listen to other new women beg with the same desperation, and you will exchange little knowing glances with the others in the hall. They never tell you. Your life comes apart at the seams.

You live, all of you, in a state of constant, crazed anxiety. You know you're going to gain weight. There's really no way to get around it. You can play all sorts of little games, and you will still gain weight. There is no way to describe the tiny, constant implosions of your chest when this thought hits you, as it does, often, day in, day out.

You take a shower in a stall with no curtain. You have to sit down on the little stool in the shower. You argue with the nurse about this. "Why?" you ask. Most of the nurses will turn away in the chair where they keep watch, but not all. You will learn quickly which nurses you hate, which ones you do not hate. The ones you hate will watch. Because you are a little bitch, you will ask the one you hate most, "What, are you jealous?" She will attempt to shake her head in scorn.

But she is jealous. Most of them are not. Most of them think you're pitiful. But a very few have, shall we say, eating issues of their own.[1] You have a trump card.

Your forbidden things will be kept in a little plastic cubby in the nurses' station: Razors, matches, cigarettes. You will be allowed, upon request, to shave your legs. Most of you will shave your legs every day. You will also agonize daily about what you will wear, and you'll apply your makeup perfectly, and curl and tease your hair, as if you had somewhere to go, as if you will not spend your day and the next and the next

[1] Judging by the number of women I've talked to who have gone through hospital-setting treatment, it is fairly common to have nurses who have eating issues of their own. They are certainly a source of serious irritation to their patients, who often find it difficult to listen to advice from women talking out of both sides of their mouths. It seems reasonable that hospitals should carefully screen nurses slated for rounds on an eating-disorder unit.

on the eighth floor of a hospital, with no one to see you but the nurses and the other fuck-ups in the cage. Almost all of you have been spending at least an hour daily refining your appearance since puberty. It is part of your routine, and your routine must be maintained, if only in name.

You will sit in the main room playing solitaire on the floor. You like mornings, because you feel peaceful then. You look forward to your day. Every day, the routine is as such: Breakfast, morning check-in, physical therapy, snack, morning class, lunch, occupational therapy, snack, free time, dinner, visiting hours, snack, evening check-in, bed.

It's like being at camp.

You will not realize until you get to treatment just how deep and abiding your obsessive love of food really is. It's not the way most people like food—the feeling of fullness, of communion with friends and family. Food *qua* lover. I remember the day I met Jane as she sat on a couch, doing something to an apple with her mouth that was positively erotic. She was still pretty sick. I asked: What are you doing to that apple? She looked up at me, startled, her tongue on the wet, white flesh. She laughed and said, "I'm making love to it." It was funny, but true. With both anorexia and bulimia, food becomes the object of your desire. You either prefer the desperate hunger of unfed passion, or the battering cycle of food moving in and out and in and out of your body in a rhythm that you never want to end.

Treatment, that first time, turned out to be divine. I had it easy. I was classified as bulimic, so I did not have to gain too much weight. I got to avoid the weird agony some of the other women were going through, though I would later experience the frenzied panic at weight gain upon my frequent returns. Treatment, that time, turned out to be a grand buffet. They feed you normal food, and lots of it. In earlier years, eating-disorder facilities were big on force-feeding and providing massive quantities of high-calorie food, but they soon figured out that this treatment gave way to almost immediate relapse. Now they give you a nutritionist who attempts to convince you that food is simply a necessary thing, neither Christ nor Antichrist. After the first week, when I flat-out refused to eat anything—it was more a statement than an actual fear of food—I went through the motions that we all went through, bitching and moaning about how awful it was to have to eat, balking at the slightest drop of grease on our poached fish, taking as long as we possibly could to finish our food. The fact was, I was in seventh heaven. My life revolved around meals. Never believe an eating-disordered person who says she hates food. It's a lie. Denied food, your body and brain will begin to obsess about it. It's the survival instinct, a constant reminder to eat, one that you try harder and harder to ignore, though you never can. Instead of eating, you simply *think* about food all the time. You dream about it, you stare at it, but you do not eat it. When you get to the hospital, you have to eat, and as truly terrifying as it is, it is also welcome. Food is the sun and the moon and the stars, the center of gravity, the love of your life. Being forced to eat is the most welcome punishment there is.

In the little eating room, a nauseating late-1980s aesthetic will prevail. Heavy on the mauve. There will be a schoolroom clock on the wall, round glass face glinting with the ugly light of those long, humming fluorescent bulbs. You will stand in the doorway for a minute, looking for your tray. It will have your menu beside it. You will spot it, like spotting the face of a lover in a crowd, move toward it, feign disgust, pull your chair back, sit down. At first, you will honest-to-god be mortified, and really not hungry. Your stomach is shrunken, you are very simply afraid of food, and you will cry in despair. But as the body begins to come alive again, you begin to feel hunger, a racking sort of hunger, and you will damn near cry for joy.

Your menu: you have been given a chart, which tells you how many calories you have to eat per day. It breaks that number down into categories: Proteins, breads, milks, vegetables, fruits, desserts, "satieties" (fats). These numbers dance like sugarplums in your head. The obsessive-compulsivity[2] that you used to channel into hyperactive management of time and work is rerouted to a place where it can do some *real* good, and it twitches in your face like a tic when you sit down, each day, with your

[2] The obsessive-compulsive behaviors that creep up concurrent with eating-disorder symptoms are not necessarily the same as obsessive-compulsive disorder (OCD). The eating disorder, and the biochemical malfunctions that it causes, also cause obsessive thoughts and behavior, which often decrease or disappear when the eating disorder is under control. OCD is a separate disorder, and while it is relatively common in eating-disorder patients, the two do not necessarily go hand in hand. I myself do not have OCD, but when anoretic I sure as hell seem to.

chart and your menu. You spend hours poring over it, trying out every possible combination of items that might fulfill your quotas. You love the neat *X* in the box, the tidy circle around optional items, butter and jam, French or ranch. You will look forward to every meal, every snack, with a completely ridiculous level of excitement. All of you will pretend to dread them. All of you are full of shit.

This time around, it will be summer. At meals and snacks, someone will turn on the radio, which sits on the counter running along one wall, under the cupboards where they keep the Ensure. You will remember the Ensure, a nutritional liquid that you will get when you do not finish your food within the allotted time: half an hour for meals, fifteen minutes for snacks. As soon as you walk into the room, a nurse will look up at the clock and write down a time on the white dry-erase board on the wall. A nurse will sit down at the head of the table to watch you. She will not eat. She will not read a magazine. She will simply watch you. If she is young, she will join in the conversation, if there is one. Usually there won't be because you are all peering suspiciously at your food. If she is old, she will not talk. When the conversation inevitably turns to food, weight, exercise, she will speak. That's a nonissue, she'll say. You will find this incredibly ironic.

She will scrutinize your eating habits. If you are scraping the tines of your fork against your teeth, even silently, if you curl your lip back from the food in an involuntary sneer, if you are pushing your food around on your plate, or eating things in a particular order, day after day, as I did—liquids first, followed by vegetables, starch, fruit, entrée, and dessert—if you do any of these things, the nurse will pipe up: Marya, that's a behavior. When you are new, you'll ask, A *behavior?* You will sit there, trying to keep your lip as far from the food as possible without being obvious, thinking of all the connotations of a *behavior.*

Or if you commit a cardinal sin—spitting food daintily into your napkin, folding it expertly under the table, casually slipping the pats of mandatory butter into your pocket, hiding the last bites of food under your tongue (hiding it in your cheek never works, your cheeks are sunken and stretched)—you will find yourself in serious shit. If you do not finish your meal on time, you will be kept after. You will sit, with one or two other girls, while the nurse calculates the number of calories left on your plate. How are you figuring this? you cry. How do you know how much Ensure to give me? That's too much! That's bullshit! Watch your language, Marya, she warns as she pours the white liquid into a little plastic cup with measuring marks along the side. You will be given ten minutes to finish the Ensure. I'd speed it up, she'll advise, watching you sip as slowly as you can. You're making a choice, she'll say. This is supposed to be empowering. If you do not finish, you will be tube-fed.

You will remember the silence, the ding of tin fork to plate. You will remember the radio, KDWB bouncing along. Everyone will come to know every song on the playlist backward and forward. You will remember a table of women, intently staring at their food, glancing at one another's plates, unconsciously mouthing the words to the songs between slow bites.

When I got to treatment the first time, I was not one of the emaciated ones. I was definitely slim, far thinner than is normal or attractive, but because I was not *visibly* sick, the very *picture* of sick, because I did not warrant the coveted title of Anoretic, I was embarrassed. Ignore the fact that my diastolic pressure had a habit of falling through the floor every time I stood up, putting me on watch for sudden cardiac arrest, or the fact that my heart puttered along, slow and uneven as an old man taking a solitary walk through the park. Ignore the fact that I had a perforated esophagus and a nasty little habit of coughing blood all over my shirt. In treatment, as in the rest of the world, bulimia is seen as a step down from anorexia, both in terms of medical seriousness and in terms of admirability. Bulimia, of course, gives in to the temptations of the flesh, while anorexia is anointed, is a complete removal of the bearer from the material realm. Bulimia hearkens back to the hedonistic Roman days of pleasure and feast, anorexia to the medieval age of bodily mortification and voluntary famine. In truth, bulimics do not usually bear the hallowed stigmata of a skeletal body. Their self-torture is private, far more secret and guilty than is the visible statement of anoretics, whose whittled bodies are admired as the epitome of feminine beauty. There is nothing feminine, delicate, acclaimed, about sticking your fingers down your throat and spewing puke. Denial of the flesh, however, is not only the obvious culmination of centuries of bizarre ideas about the dainty nature of women but also an active realization of religious and cultural ideals.

And yet this is a culture where we seesaw madly, hair flying and eyes alight, between crazed and constant consumption, where the insatiable hunger is near universal, as is the fanatical belief in the moral superiority of self-denial and self-control. Culturally, we would be diagnosed as bulimic, not anorexic, daily veering back and forth between two extreme points, bingeing and purging. The frenzied adoration of the anorexic body, and the violent hatred of fat, on ourselves and on others, reveals not that anorexia is beautiful, nor that fat is particularly despicable, but that we ourselves are intolerably torn, and we have to choose sides.

You, Doctor Martin, walk
from breakfast to madness. Late August,
I speed through the antiseptic tunnel
where the moving dead still talk
of pushing their bones against the thrust
of cure. And I am queen of this summer hotel
or the laughing bee on a stalk
of death.

—ANNE SEXTON, "YOU, DOCTOR MARTIN," 1960

The doctor, one Dr. J., had been an army physician prior to his advent in EDI (Eating Disorders Institute) as resident paterfamilias to a family of shrunken pygmy girls. We wondered aloud at what had moved him to make this odd career change, to stride, white coated and unsmiling, into our midst with his clipboard of questions and bottles of pills.

My parents remember him differently than I do. It is worth noting that I lived on the unit, they did not. My parents were (briefly) under the impression, as most people are, that treatment would fix me. Dr. J. was seen, however unconsciously, as my potential savior. Dr. J. has since gone into the medical insurance business, and I am sure that he is very good at it. He, as might have been predicted, was not very good as Christ.

To the best of anyone's knowledge, we were the most annoying creatures Dr. J. had ever come across. He did not laugh or smile, did not noticeably give a damn. To his credit, he did tell my parents that the only person who was going to save me was me. They did not, at that time, believe him. Dr. J. did not care for me much. I was difficult, mouthy, disruptive, "not receptive to treatment," unpleasant, rude. I did not much care for him, either. We saw him on his rounds once a day. He asked how you were feeling and granted or denied you a pass to leave for an hour or a day. He asked if you wanted prunes and bran with breakfast, and if you wanted happy pills. He determined whether you would be allowed to take a stroll with the nurses at noon. He peered at you, bemused. After rounds, girls sat, sullen, or quietly weeping, or screaming in their rooms. Partly the weeping, the screaming, came from predictable sources: Dr. J. had refused a day pass, or revealed their weight, or informed them that their caloric intake was being bumped up. The screaming also came about because he was an unmitigated ass.

We specimens slowly filed down the hall to physical therapy and lay on the floor stretching (watched very closely). We made moccasin after moccasin from kits with dull, wide-tipped needles. And we crocheted and latch-hooked little poodle rugs, cross-stitched and knitted, and made collages from magazine clippings that were supposed to express our very deepest selves. Occupational therapy is supposed to give you a sense of effectiveness by showing you that you can actually do something other than starve. We had assertiveness groups, where we practiced asking for what we needed, and nutrition classes where we sat, rapt, learning that a piece of pizza counted as an entrée (one protein, one bread). We played role-playing games where we said something we really, really wanted to say to some member of our family, using I-Feel Statements. And we did our morning check-in (my Goal for the Day is to write in my journal, ask Dr. J. for a pass, finish my milk) and sat on our pillows on the floor, legs splayed, tendons jutting grotesquely from the backs of knees, coloring in coloring books, making little construction-paper cutout signs to hang in our rooms: SYMPTOMS ARE NOT AN OPTION, I HAVE THE RIGHT TO TAKE CARE OF MYSELF, I AM LOVED, TODAY I ALLOW MYSELF TO EAT.

I sat in the groups, not participating, partly because I was in a snit and partly because the topics seemed to have little to do with me. Passivity was not something that kept me up nights. My ability to state my feelings seemed perfectly well developed to me, considering how much time I spent on that unit, seething over yet another warning that my excessive temper, my language, my Attitude, were making Recovery difficult for everyone else.

My parents came to visit in the evenings. My father and I played gin rummy, double solitaire, crazy eights. We didn't talk much. We certainly didn't talk about what was going on. Periodically we'd fight, and they'd leave. Everyone on the unit talked about how nice my parents were, how well we got along. I nodded.

One night, my mother came alone. This was potentially dangerous. My father acted as a buffer between us, I acted as a buffer between them, my mother between my father and I. Classic triangulation. A house of cards depends on the stasis of each; pull one out, and ashes, ashes, we all fall down. My mother sat in a chair by my bed while I played solitaire on my bed tray. In therapy it had come to my attention, despite my adamant insistence that my mother was immortal and lived on Mount Olympus, that my relationship with her was perhaps less than perfect. It had been suggested to me, in therapy, that I might have picked up some of my neuroses about food from my mother.

I casually broached the matter with her. I mentioned that she was perhaps a bit overconcerned with her own body, her weight, how much she ate. She sat in her metal hospital chair, arms crossed, fingers flickering, smiling a patronizing smile. I pressed her. The smile turned nasty, and she announced that I had no business blaming her for my problems. I said, I'm not blaming you, I'm just saying I might have picked up some habits—

She said, *Sweetheart,* you didn't pick anything up. You just came this way.

She stood up from her chair, picked up her purse, and walked out. I lay on my bed, looking at my reflection in the night-blackened window. I turned my face into my pillow, then pulled the pillow over my head.

I had just come like this, with a peculiar tendency to self-destruct.

I went to individual therapy on Tuesdays. My family and I sat through family therapy on Thursdays. My mother was cold, sat back in her chair, legs crossed, one arm holding her waist, one hand flickering, twitching, touching the upturned collar of her shirt, the sharp lapel of her suit. She didn't meet my eyes. Pressed by the therapist, she would snap, eyes flashing, a quick stiletto to the ribs. My father was warm, concerned, leaned forward, elbows on his knees. When pressed, he would snap, voice rising, jaw clenching, a blunt fist beating steadily on his thigh. I tied myself into a strangle knot in the corner of my chair. Went for the jugular, swore. Hissed at my mother, uncoiled, snakelike, to shout with my father, face to spitting face.

At first we went in smiling. I was their little girl and I was sick. They were gung ho to get me all better. We talked a good game, their arms around my shoulders. My witty jokes. This ended quickly. Sixteen years of a bad marriage, and sixteen years of a fucked-up child, were swollen and pulsing under the skin, waiting to burst.

My parents were scared, but they were also new at this. They believed, then, that it was simply a matter of getting me fed. Things would return to normal. This is the Little-Bit-Overboard-on-Her-Diet Theory. This holds the real issue—the fact that you're dabbling in a fatal disease, on purpose—at bay and stalls any meaningful progress. You don't yet know that monsters larger than diet and weight will have to be worked through. Your family will have to look at you in a new light: not simply as their little girl—even the parents and spouses of older eating-disordered women often display this attitude—but a human with a history, a range of emotions, a person perhaps more complex than they perceive. And you will have to look at them as humans, fallible, who love you, rather than as either enemy or savior. You will all have to grow up a great deal.

Neither my family nor I was ready to do that yet. It was easy for us not to. They saw my eating disorder as just one more weird outcropping of my contentious, possibly crazy nature, and I saw them and their attempts to be supportive as one more example of their general awfulness. Both of us were very wrong. Neither had, at this point, any other way of looking at it.

Family therapy was spent fighting. Predictably, my mother said it was my father's fault, he said it was her fault. Then they changed directions, created an unprecedented Marital Alliance, and agreed that it was my fault. Oddly, I agreed with the therapist that it wasn't anyone's fault, and that we were wasting time with our endless fire breathing of blame. I did enjoy, however, having permission to tell my parents, without censor, what idiots they were. They, too, enjoyed the padded oasis, the hour a week that allowed them to rip each other apart, limb by limb. The sessions were beyond virulent. All the years of making it work for my sake, all the years fearing a dam break if only a word too many was said, fell apart. On a kamikaze mission, we flew at terminal velocity toward each other.

Things would never be the same. You cannot watch your child kick death's door and expect that you will forget. You cannot tear open family wounds and hope that they will heal without a scar. Everything changes. For better or for worse, the family fell apart.

A few friends from Edina visited me in the hospital. I sat on the bed, blanket over my knees, trying to laugh. It was my best friend's birthday, they had balloons. They were going out after visiting me. They brought flowers, filled me in on local gossip. We didn't talk about where I was. We hung in blank space and fell silent when the nurse came in to take my blood pressure, temperature, pulse. She returned with a cup of Ensure. I bit my lip. I could not ask why I was being given extra calories. I had to be normal. I could not scream or cry. I smiled weakly and, hands shaking, drank it as my friends tried not to watch. They hugged me, stiffly, one by one, and left.

I knew the night they came that they wouldn't be back. I didn't want them back. I was embarrassed, humiliated, and I didn't want to deal with anyone who would remind me of what a mess I was. My year-long absence had created an unbridgeable distance. My illness exacerbated it. What held me to a past I didn't want snapped very fast. I was free to go.

August: Vital signs stabilized, head cleared a little, I felt strong and restless. I ate when I was told, taking normal bites. I confessed, in therapy, a wide-eyed desire for health. Life, I said, beckoned. I feel so good about myself, I said. My charts noted that I made a complete and sudden turnaround. Treatment effective.

In the hospital, I did not get well. I got worse. I would've gotten worse anyway, I was so far gone. But the hospital became a haven for me, as it does for many of us. It became the Eden I longed for when I was out. It was as close to death—that still, silent, very safe place—as I thought I could come. Life stops. Time stops. You become a case, a study, a curiosity, a problem, a sickness, a child. You do the crossword puzzle all day long. You read countless books, undisturbed.

And when they let you out at last, you are far more scared than when you went in.

Out of the hospital, I slept around. Some guy from AA thought I was pretty, so we'd have sex in the back of a car. Cool night, fall coming early, mist on the glass, I thought how funny, the print of my toes on the window. I sat in an all-night diner, picking apart a fat-free muffin, smoking Camel straights.

I would later reflect, with morbid pride, on the incredible work it must have taken to craft so careful a lie. I would reflect on the seamless, smooth surface I must have shown: the magician pulls the endless scarf from his sleeve, the slippery silk snaking on, and on, and on. I managed, somehow, to convince my parents that I was in perfect condition to move to California. The salt air will do me good, I said. Plans were made. I would rent a room in the house of my father's ex-wife. I would attend the high school where she taught, where her son was enrolled as a sophomore. I would have weekly individual therapy, twice-a-month visits with a psychiatrist, a nutritionist, an M.D. I have a weight to maintain. I will be weighed. Nothing will escape the watchful eye. Or so the story goes.

At the end of August, I kiss everyone good-bye and board a plane bound for San Francisco. On your left, says the pilot over the speaker, are the Rockies. I am drunk on Bloody Marys. In the warm late-summer night air, I take a shuttle bus north, sit next to a man who tells me about his daughter, his money, his job. Hand on my knee, hand on my hand, my hand pulled to rest on his short, thick cock. Stuck in the back of a bus with nowhere to go and nothing to say that wouldn't be rude, I have silent sex with a married man in his wide, comfortable seat, my knee caught between the armrest and his hard clenched thigh. Afterward, he reads a magazine by the light of a full moon. I watch the shimmering hills, the wide swaths of tilled land where low fog clings and spins, blue and ethereal, the wild apple trees that hunch their backs and hover like vultures at the side of the road.

I breathe deep, press my head back into my seat as Highway 101 flies by. I smile. I've become the Artful Dodger. I have a new game.

5 "Persephone Herself Is but a Voice"

California, 1990–1991

Reach me a gentian, give me a torch!
let me guide myself with the blue, forked torch of this flower
down the darker and darker stairs, where blue is darkened on blueness
even where Persephone goes, just now, from the frosted September
to the sightless realm where darkness is awake upon the dark
and Persephone herself is but a voice
or a darkness invisible enfolded in the deeper dark
of the arms Plutonic, and pierced with the passion of dense gloom,
among the splendour of torches of darkness, shedding darkness on the lost bride and her groom.

—D. H. Lawrence, "Bavarian Gentians," 1932

It's a very dark house. Set far back from the main road, up a steep dirt driveway overhung with trees webbed with Spanish moss, down the driveway, past the chicken coop with the mad old rooster who crows at 2, 3, 4 A.M., up the driveway again. Ahead of you, the huge dark house, slipping slowly down the foothills of Bennett Mountain. Behind you, a valley, swimming in purple moon. Sky wide and cool. All around you, hills and trees and wild sounds, hisses through dry grass and whispering leaves and the quick pummel of hooves.

A sagging deck runs along the front of the house. Two chairs, a small table, an ashtray full of butts smoked only two-thirds of the way down. Up the stone steps with the wrought iron rail, you open the brown door. Inside the doorway, a stairway in front of you, a door to your right, kitchen to your left. Dark. Past the kitchen, a dining room, then living room, bedrooms you never enter. Woodstove, tall black pipe. You will, when winter comes, sit on the woodstove in your jacket, freezing cold, trying to get warm. You will melt your coat to the seat of your pants without noticing.

Become familiar with this kitchen. Stand in the doorway. Left: counter, microwave—you will need this, pay attention—sink, window over the sink, looks through the tall wild rosebushes, down the hill, into the valley. The coop, the old toolshed where a seldom-seen man named Ray lives and makes paper masks. Dead cars, burrowing into fallow ground, weeds sprung up around: Volvo, ancient green camper, occasional others, you will never keep close track. From the sink, you can see the garage, the overgrown garden, the hills.

On the counter: toaster, jelly, honey, peanut butter, butter, sugar in a blue and white bowl, salt. spices, cutting board. Bowl of fruit: apples, oranges, bananas, one kiwi on its last legs. In the cupboards: pots, pans, potato chips, rice cakes, bread, small crumpled plastic bags holding stale heels. A fish tank in the corner, piranha in the tank. Piranha will later commit suicide during dinner, leap in a macho show of belly-muscle right out of its tank to die gasping on the floor. Birdcage with a muttering green bird. Ancient cat who sleeps on the washing machine in a room off the kitchen. Two huge dogs, Rhodesian Ridgebacks, Tiska and Moe.

Refrigerator. So full and mysterious you will not detail its contents now. Suffice to say there is butter, cheese, milk, all of these things you will need. There is tofu, which you will buy and not eat. There are many leftovers, which you will eat. The cupboards to the right of the oven are for the man who lives down the hall from you. He plays blues guitar in the night. Eats potatoes, oatmeal, straight from the pot. Why dirty a dish, he says. Directly to your right—this is the important part—are the cupboards for crackers and cereal. Cornflakes, granola, boxes and boxes of health food cereal that has a scratchy texture and grates the throat on its frenzied way back up. There are cookies on the very top shelf, as if you were a little girl and could not climb up. Could not, if your need was enough, levitate. As if.

Go up the stairs and notice the spiderwebs in the corners above your head. At the top of the stairs, to the left, is the door to your room. Bed immediately to your left, window on the opposite wall. Long yellow couch below the window, desk to the right of the couch. Lamp on the desk casts a pale warm light. You knock out the window screen, sit in the sill, and smoke. Sometimes you climb out onto the broad, flat roof and lean over the edge. On the deck below you, very late, you will see the red end of a cigarette in the dark, moving by itself back and forth in bright streaks. You will hear a disembodied cough. Sometimes you climb the ladder to the next layer of roof, lie on your back with a boy you will meet, make grand and impossible plans, close together, edge of a blanket clutched in your hand. Counting stars and invisible deer rushing by.

Back in the hallway, at the top of the stairs and to your left, you find the bathroom. A long counter, three sinks, three mirrors over the sinks, three mirrored cupboards under the mirrors. You have the sink on the end, by the door. In your cupboard are diuretics, laxatives, various pills. In your mirror, you see only your face, chest, stomach, top of hips and butt. You have to stand on your tiptoes to properly see your butt. If you stand on the toilet you can see your thighs. A window by the toilet, a fan, a heater, the whir and tick of which are just enough to cover the noise. A shower. A scale. The scale is two pounds off. When you arrive, you weigh 102. You watch the needle falter toward that number, then fall back, as if in time elapse, fall back, back, when you step onto the scale each day, ten times a day. Give or take a few. When you wake up, when you get home from school, after you binge, after you purge, when you eat dinner, after you throw up dinner, before you pee, after you pee, before you gulp handfuls of laxatives, after they take their hideous effect.

There are two bedrooms at the far end of the hall. Your stepbrother, the son of your father's first wife, has a room full of masks and bongs. The other room is rented by the man who eats from a pot. Glancing in: two windows, a bed, a guitar in its open case.

You have been here before. You love this house. It has a certain magic to it, a certain creak and sigh in the wind, a smell of wood smoke and salt fog. The ocean at Bodega Bay lies thirty miles west as the crow flies. On still nights, from the top of the roof, you can hear it. You can always smell it. You can smell the salt and the sharp, high scent of eucalyptus that burns through your brain. This is the smell of home.

The house is owned by your father's ex-wife, whom you call your stepmother, and her husband. They have raised the people who you call your brothers. They are not technically brothers. They are the boys your father and his first wife adopted some twenty-odd years ago, the boys your father calls his sons, the boys with too many families, too many demands on their time and their love, the boys who taught you to roller-skate and ice skate and spit. These are the boys you ran after when you were very small, crying, Wait for me!, who trotted back and picked you up when you fell and tied your shoes and made you apple butter sandwiches (Paul) and ice cream sodas (Tim). The boys of few words, whom you adore but do not know. They are young men away at college who have always been an intermittent, shadowy part of your life. They weren't around long enough to see what had happened in the meantime, how the little girl became a hospital ex-con, curiously "cured" and yet thinner every time they came home from school, thinner and meaner and more and more withdrawn. You cannot look them in the face when they ask, as they do from time to time, "Are you all right?" Of course I am, you say, and smile.

The youngest boy, ten months younger than you, still lives at home, down the hall. You and he have a strange, bitter, tight thing that one might call friendship. You fight, you slap. Or you lie on a bed, stoned, beating out of time with music, talking of nothing in particular. Not talking, in specific, of what is happening to you. Arguing when you steal all his shirts, when he shows up for breakfast wearing your best red skirt. You share some friends.

You've known the woman who has welcomed you into her home and trusted you to tell the truth. She is the mother of three boys, and you are an almost-daughter. You have a tendency to firmly attach yourself to anything older and female, collecting mothers in a way. She is one. You are close. She loves you, and you her. You grocery shop together. You go to the coast and walk.

Late August. You take trips to Bodega, light bonfires in the dunes. Sand grass and ice plant, lost poppies, thorns. You wear Mexican ponchos, pocket in the front, Baggies of grass in the pocket, papers, lighters. You sit in circles, knees tucked up to your chests, arms around your knees. The ocean, black, below a deep-blue sky. The ocean, rushing up at the shore. The smell of wood smoke, sharp, and pot smoke, sticky sweet. The wind and roar.

Late August. You are pregnant. Again. You knew this when you left. You think, This is God's little joke. God will continue to play this joke for several more years, a cruel reminder that life happens, that the laws of nature will knock you on your arrogant ass no matter how hard you fight. You wait. When waiting is too much, you fall down the stairs when no one is home, an easy dive, belly down. Body still weak enough to fall for such an old trick. Flush the red matter away. No tears. The uneasy guilt and cringe in your chest are not for the baby, but for the breasts that are tender, a trace of blue veins, fat. They will shrink, you assure yourself over and over. Shrink.

These will be a strange few months. This is the only time in your life when it is safe to say you are crazy. Mad as a hatter. You remember things in random flashes. The days seemed a blur even then, not because of the smearing hand that runs over memory's chalk drawings, but because days ran, sleepless and liquid, into one another, swirling in a fascinating vertical descent, a helix of blood in water, dancing down.

Things will be skipped in this chapter because there is so much I don't remember. It burned off, I think, like dawn fog with the first hot burst of sun. This is what's left.

Late summer, drought. Hills dry, gold, like combed hay. Glinting. Trees still. I fed the chickens in the mornings, crunched down the gravel path, ducked into the cool, rank air of the coop, dumped a bucket of feed on the ground. I know for a fact that my first month there I was actually trying to Follow my Fucking Program, munching my afternoon snack each day precisely at three, drinking my milk. I know for a fact that I was dating young boys again because, of course, they never ask. Breathless and hot, tremble-bellied boys. I remember lying in bed with them, listening to the dark. I remember thinking as I walked down winding foothills roads, whistling through the tall weeds in the hills behind the house: *I'm home, I'm home, I'm home.* It was the smell. The eucalyptus leaves of *before, back then,* that time that seemed so purely mine, when my small legs seemed sturdy enough to travel just about anywhere, down Walnut Boulevard, down the mossy creek bank, over millions of acres of fields.

But my legs were weakened and something was wrong, though I didn't know what. The only particularly revelatory moment was this: I woke up before my stepmother and brother on the first day of school. I went downstairs, into the kitchen, still a pale gray with thin light. I reached for a banana, set it on the counter, took the cornflakes from the cupboard, went to the fridge for milk. Stood with the door open, staring blankly at the milk. I thought, quite clearly: I don't have to have any milk. I don't have to eat any breakfast at all. I shut the door. Put back the cornflakes. Took out a small knife, cut the banana in half. Ate the half in 120 bites: sliced into quarters, each quarter sliced into 30 small bits. Ate it with a fork.

It was so easy. It was so organized, so very much the same as I remembered it. All concentration reduced to the lowest common denominator, the brain switching over to the simple patterns of numerical logic, the tidy arrangement of bits of banana on the white plate.

Suddenly full of energy, I made my lunch: two rice cakes with a pat of peanut butter, an apple, a graham cracker, a diet Coke. Heart pattering with the sudden realization, amazed that it hadn't occurred to me before. How stupid! I thought. I've been eating all this time, and no one's even here to give a damn!

There was a sudden shift in my attitude toward starvation. Before, the not-eating had always smacked a bit of deprivation. The human body and mind rebel against deprivation. The fact that I was not allowed to eat—I was well beyond thinking that I just wanted to diet, I had developed the idea that I *personally* was not *allowed* to eat—had frightened me, made me twist my fist against my belly, writhing with hunger pains. But all of a sudden, it seemed perfectly delightful that I didn't have to eat if I didn't feel like it. And I didn't feel like it.

In retrospect, of course, that was part of the game. A test, to see if the lie detector really works, see if Big Brother is really always watching, or if he occasionally falls asleep in his chair. The hospital had sparked in me an infantile desire to dodge the rules, to gleefully watch the Very Caring faces tighten and whiten with irritation at their own impotence, at your uncanny ability to trip them, force their hand, fuck them up. You do not notice that this is, pure and simple, a bunch of crap, and you are still, as ever, fucking yourself up, not them. You let yourself believe that you are really at battle with Them, because it's easier. You have escaped Them, a fugitive running, and you are rather pleased with the discovery that you are a very good liar.

I didn't know, yet, just what a liar I would become.

We drive down a narrow rural road, turn into the gravel lot at school. On the right, fields, creek, tangled clusters of thin trees. We walk up a sloping hill and approach a little school, separate one-level buildings scattered in a semiarc across a wide grass field. Kindergarten through grade twelve. I go to the eleventh-grade classroom, set back among a small prickly woods, a picnic table in a tiny yard.

It is sunny and cool. A girl with a scarf wrapped about her head comes around the building, sees me, says, You must be Marya. I nod. She is Rebecca. Thin silver threads in the purple of her scarf catch light. We go inside, sit down. Eleven students in the class. The teacher is a beautiful older woman, fast talking, energetic. Sometimes, when the room is quiet, you can hear a rooster crow from a nearby farm.

Two weeks later, I will be sitting in my chair at the back of the class. I will get a funny prickly feeling in my feet. I will be looking at the back of a boy's neck. An odd boy. Julian. Julian Daniel Beard. I made him tell me his whole name one day, sitting on the grass at lunch. Gangly, awkward, wears a pressed white T-shirt every day. I have listened to his laugh. I have made jokes to hear him laugh. He's laughed, glanced at me quickly, sharply, shyly, then looked away. He is the kind of boy you want to make blush by telling him terrible bawdy jokes. You want to tease him, watch his funny bow mouth crook in a smile. You have ducked your head to follow his skipping glance. His eyes are the color of very old army coats, that worn green.

In class that day, I thought to myself, with no small amount of alarm: I'm going to marry that boy. I'm going to marry that geeky boy! He sat up, turned around hurriedly, stared at me as if I'd said the words out loud. I stared back at him. He swung back to his paper, curled himself over the desk like a fist, stuck his tongue out to the left side, scribbled madly away at a paper on the Industrial Revolution, as if he were slowing up America's progress, as if he had a railroad empire to build, right then, in the little wood-paneled schoolroom with fall winds ambling in through the open door.

Fall 1990: We sat on the steps behind Copperfield's Bookstore & Cafe, and grungy long-haired barefoot baby-hippy boys with pierced nipples played guitar. We smoked hand-rolled cigarettes and drank coffee. I rode in the back of a trundley blue pickup truck from somewhere to somewhere else, watching narrow dirt roads roll by beneath the wheels. Life was good, and I was giddy with freedom. That fall, without noticing, I had stopped planning my life. I became bohemian because I had nothing better to do. I was in limbo, and limbo is nice because no one asks you any questions, and no one wonders where you're going or where you've been, and life is one big dancing bear Grateful Dead sticker on the window of an old Volvo. People speak of karma, and it is very easy, very very easy, to believe all is inevitable, and all you have to do is lean back and watch your life go by.

It's just life, after all.

But a person like me, a person who needs a project at all times, a cause, cannot go for very long without one. This was, ostensibly, a year for me to kick back a little, loosen my grip on the need to race through my life and get everything done all at once and faster than anyone else, a year for me to "explore" my "psyche," "reconnect" with my "body," take "things" a little "slower," "ease up" on my "self." This was, I told my parents over the phone and in letters, a time of great "growth" for me, a time of simply "being," of "health."

Bullshit. This was, as I perfectly well knew, a stroke of sheer luck, a stellar opportunity for me to ease away from the real world, move deeper and deeper into the eerie childish singsong land in my head.

It started in earnest, I think, in October. I simply did not eat. I was tenacious this time. It was definitively not about "losing weight." That particular moniker for what I was doing seemed absurd, even to me. That term is external. What I was doing was purely internal. I was trying to starve. I was exploring the extent of hunger. The hunger was the thing, the heady rush. I ate cereal at breakfast and drank water all day. I carried a two-liter bottle around with me everywhere, filling it every hour. Sometimes I drank a little juice at lunch. I remember reading the label on a bottle of carrot juice, drinking one-third of the neon orange contents.

Rebecca and I went to the grocery store together one day in late fall. I was wearing a blue dress. We bought Oreos and dried apples. We ate the Oreos and drank wine in her kitchen that afternoon. She said: I'd never have guessed you used to be anorexic. I replied: Oh, well that's all over now. I tossed my hair. I ate the Oreos slowly, licked the cream from the middle. I walked home, said hello to the family, to the boyfriend who had come for dinner. I have to clean up, I said. I went into the bathroom and threw up for the first time since I was hospitalized. Stood up, looked at my face in the mirror. No puffiness, no marks like there used to be. A little watery around the eyes. I laughed, a terrible glee welling up in my chest. All of the Oreos had come up, all of the wine. I washed my face, my hands, I put on perfume. I was an expert. I could do as I pleased. Nothing could stop me. This was completely my own. I went down to dinner, picked and pushed the food around on my plate. Batting my eyes, making them laugh. The poor boy in love with me held my hand.

In my file at TAMS there are letters. There are notes, a packet of correspondence from Kathi and the doctor to the "team" of "professionals" who were "watching" me in California. There were specific instructions, things to watch for: Weigh her in a gown, *not in street clothes.* Please be aware that she has had an eating disorder for many years and will require close monitoring. She should see a medical doctor every two weeks, a psychiatrist monthly, a nutritionist and a psychologist weekly, check for the following things. They had taken every precaution. The bases were covered, the team in California assured them that they were professionals, they would do as they were told.

I think I saw the psychiatrist once. I did, at first, show up for therapy weekly. Stood on the scale in street clothes. I sat and told her how I was doing so well, how this move had been good for me, I was definitively (I leaned forward in my seat, wide-eyed, long-haired young girl, gesturing rapidly, pulling up tears and scattering them on her carpeted floor) on the road to health. I brought her poems about my health. My connection to the earth, my relearning of the rhythms of the blood and breath. Blah blah blah. I laughed as I wrote them. I was and am bored to tears by such schlock. Goddesses and wombs and the feel of new dirt in my hand, yah-da-yah-da-yah-da. She was deeply touched. "Have you been throwing up at all?" she'd ask. "Oh, heavens no," I'd say and laugh at the very idea.

After school, I'd come home. The stepmother and brother gone, house silent, save for the shuffling step of her husband in his office. Open the cupboard, get out a bowl. Pour cereal, sugar, raisins in the bowl, put two pieces of bread with cheese in the microwave, shovel the cereal into the mouth while the cheese melts, eat the bread and cheese with one hand while buttering graham crackers, eat the graham crackers while pouring more cereal, more cheese and bread, go to the freezer, get out the ice cream, shovel in ice cream while buttering bread, eat the bread while climbing up to get the cookies, eat the cookies while dumping cold rice in a bowl.

If the husband comes in while your cheeks are bulged, swallow quickly, smile, talk about school. Babble. Say: I'm just starving, we played soccer today. Make a show of shoving the bowl aside, picking up the paper while he makes his coffee. You will not be able to stop thinking about the cereal, so don't even try. You will begin to think about what else you can eat. Don't panic. He'll leave soon, you'll be able to keep going. If he asks: What, have you got a wooden leg? just laugh. Say: I guess I do. When he disappears into his office, grab a few pieces of bread, a few diet sodas, run up to your room, shut the door, stuff the rest of the food in your mouth, swallow, run into the bathroom, turn on the fans, the shower, the tap in the sink, click up the toilet seat, swig both sodas, vomit. And vomit some more, until your knees are too weak. When you stand up, they'll buckle, and you'll swing to the edge of the sink, holding on for dear life.

Dear life my ass. By November, you wish you were dead. You want nothing more. Every day, every fucking day, you run up the steps of the house, breathing hard, swing open the cupboards, thinking: You pitiful little bitch. Fucking cow. Greedy pig. All day, your stomach pinches and spits up its bile. You sway when you walk. You begin to get cold again.

You fall in with a boy a few years older than yourself. One night, after sex, you are standing in the kitchen, naked. He is getting you a drink, you are leaning on the counter. He comes to hold you. He pinches the skin of your upper arm and says, My God. You have, like, literally no fat on your body. You smile and ask, Does that bother you? He smiles, says, No. I like it.

You will not know until years later that he was saying that so as not to hurt your feelings. You will, years later, show up at his house—he's right where you left him, stoned on the couch—you will wind up fucking around, he will tell you how much more sexy you are now, with an ass to hang on to. He will smile. You will almost be proud of your health. But you, at sixteen, don't know this. You will, for years to come, pinch the skin on your arm, just to see if you've got any fat on your body yet.

In his bed, you will wither, quickly. Rebecca will begin to worry. Your pants are too big, she'll say, you look thin. You'll say: Too thin? She'll look at you—you're standing in front of a mirror—and say, Yeah, a little too thin. You will not be able to hide your smile.

And then one day in early November, you will be standing in the kitchen. Your brothers are home, everyone is home. People are eating. Your stepmother will hand you something, you don't remember what now. She'll say: Try this. You, terrified—when the hell am I going to have a chance to puke, with all these people around?—will try it. You will eat a pretzel, a carrot stick. You will become increasingly, noticeably agitated. Finally you'll leave, take a bus into town on the pretense of going to the library. You will walk, fast and hard, down the street, breaking into a run, it's a brisk day, it's sunny. You rush through the drugstore, thinking: ipecac, ipecac, ipecac. It's a syrup used to induce vomiting, that's all you know. You've never used it before, you don't know how it works, you don't give a flying fuck, you have to find it. You pace the aisles, pulling at the cuffs of your shirt, your hands rough and cold. You can't find it. It's nowhere.

You are wearing overalls. You arch your back and stick your stomach out as far as it will go, put your hand on your faux pregnant belly. You sidle up to the prescription counter, put on your face, smile, and calmly ask the pharmacist if he has some ipecac? You'd like to have some in your first-aid kit at home, you know, in case the kids swallow something awful. You, sixteen, praise God for the time-elapse aging process of your face. You look old enough to have kids and be pregnant. He nods, Oh yes, he says, those kids'll eat anything. You both laugh. As he rings it up, you can't take your eyes off the little brown bottle on the counter. How old are your kids? he asks pleasantly, taking your money. Two and three, you say. It rolls off your tongue, you pat your belly, say, "And zero." He laughs, congratulates you, and you pocket your change and the ipecac, take your receipt, thank him, he thanks you. You walk, casually, out the door, duck behind the building, and swallow the entire bottle of vile, gag-inducing syrup on an empty stomach.

The label reads: One spoonful, to be followed by eight ounces of water or milk. *Do not administer the entire bottle.* In case of overdose, call your poison control center IMMEDIATELY.

You stroll down the sidewalk, calmer now. You have visions in your head of stopping at the gas station, leaning over, throwing up like you do every day. This is under control. This is fine. You'll be fine.

You can't stand up. It's sudden. You reach for the wall of a storefront, the sun is spinning horrible crazed circles in the sky. You think: I'm dying. I'm having a heart attack. You try to walk, but you can't. Passers-by stare at you. You try not to care, you try to breathe. You stagger into a little café, order a bowl of soup, thinking, maybe I didn't have enough in my stomach for this to work. You feel pale, covered in a film of cold sweat, and you can't steady your hands. You sit with your head on the table. Soup comes, you take a sip. Shove back from the table, napkin on your mouth, push people aside on your way to the bathroom. You don't even get the stall door shut. You vomit in insane, ripping heaves, blood spattering on the seat. You throw up a carrot stick, a bite of something, a pretzel, quarts of water, blood. When you're done, you pull the door shut and get down on your knees. Your hands will not do as they're told, you have to use both hands to get toilet paper, wipe off the seat, the walls, the floor. You sit on the floor, shaking, for an hour. Finally, you stand up, wash your face and hands, walk slowly to the library, where your brother will pick you up. You lie down on a bench. When he comes, you say: I don't feel very good. He takes you home. You go to bed in the middle of the afternoon. You sleep fitfully, woken by the sudden lurch of your stomach toward your throat. Sheets soaked in cold sweat.

You go insane about now. You understand, it just happens. Crazy isn't always what they say it is. It's not always the old woman wearing sneakers and a skirt and a scarf, wandering around with a shopping cart, hollering at no one, nothing, tumbling through years in her head.

No. Sometimes it is a girl wearing boots and jeans and a sweater, arms crossed in front of her, shivering, wandering through the streets at night, all night, murmuring to no one, nothing, tumbling through the strange unreal dimensions in her head.

Bedtime, and the house falls darker still. I sit at the window, waiting for the mutterings and shufflings to slow and stop. The clock counts its minutes, small change. I hold the back of the chair with one hand, do exercises endlessly, waiting for one o'clock. Only four hours till morning, I think, after one. Until then, the exercises. Organizing sweaters, pants, clothes on their wire hangers, by color, by pattern, by size. Writing. I write a series of poems about a woman dying. Voyeuristic poems about watching a woman dying. I write about her silence, her face turned away, her still and patient biding of time, a war bride waiting for her dead husband to return. About her pushing her rowboat away from shore, oarless, floating toward invisibility. I read: *Once asleep—who knows if we'll wake again?/. . . Don't sleep! Be firm! Listen, the alternative is—/everlasting sleep. Your—everlasting house!*[1]

At 1 A.M. I'd pull on my coat, my boots. Walk down the stairway, out the door, down the long driveway to the road. Sometimes, I'd go to the stoned boy's house. We'd sit and watch TV. We'd have sex, sometimes. I remember only that the bedroom had two windows through which blue light spilled, and it smelled sticky sweet. His guitar leaned against the wall. Sometimes, I'd just walk. Down roads and up roads, through hills, through the neighborhoods, cold. Counting the small squares of lamplight in the houses where someone was still awake. I wondered who they were, and what kept them up. I went down to the little strip mall, the all-night 7-Eleven a single glow beside the dark bluegrass bar, the dark deli, the dark beauty salon, Acrylic's Only $19. I bought a thirty-two-ounce cup of coffee, black. I sat outside on the bench, smoking, holding the cup in both hands.

I remember what my hands were like: birdlike, papery, blue and numb. They did not grip so well anymore. When the cup got a little lighter I'd stand, keep walking. Wait outside the Safeway across the street until dawn light began to come over the hills to the east. I'd walk through the aisles awhile, pass by the cigarette stand, stuff three packs up the sleeve of my coat. Buy a pack of gum, a pack of cigarettes. Walk a while more, up the narrow road that hugged a steep outcropping of the hill. Sometimes in the narrow ditch between road and hill, sometimes on the other side of the road, along the barrier that held the cars in, the flying cars that whipped my hair up as they passed, headlights skimming by me, missing my figure there in the shadow. Sometimes I stood on the

[1] Marina Tsvetaeva, from "Insomnia," 1916.

railing above the little town with its scattered lights, above the steep drop, wondering if the wind would come up and lift my feet and throw me into the swimming fog that hung over the valley.

One night, standing by the side of the road, just past a little roadside market, I found food on the ground, crusts of an eaten sandwich, a few scattered chips. I bent down and began picking it up, putting it in my pockets. I remember only that I did this. I do not remember why, or what I thought, or felt, or if I was there. Crouched, a beam of headlights came around the bend. My face flew up, I'm sure startled. I was wearing thin clothes, winter had come. I had forgotten my coat, wore only a thin T-shirt, hanging loose on my frame. Did the headlights catch the shadowy cage of ribs? Did they catch the hollows under my cheeks, the sockets of my eyes? What did the driver see? The car screamed to a stop. A man stepped out. He held a hand out toward me, maybe ten paces away, Are you all right? Don't be afraid, I just want to help. He took a step toward me. Ma'am, can I help? Ma'am, I just—

I bolted.

Some nights I tried to sleep, I truly did. I'd lie down, pull the covers around me. Look into the shadows and hills through my windows. Shut my eyes, think: Sleep, sleep. But as I neared sleep, I swear I would feel something in my chest, something far stronger than my body, pulling away from me—how do I explain this without sounding completely absurd?—something lifting out of my body, straining toward the window, toward the hills. I do not believe in God, but I do believe in some human center, and I believe that mine, having had enough of me, was trying to leave. I lay there, concentrating on pulling it back. *Don't go!* I thought. *Don't leave, not yet!*

But some nights I just concentrated on the feeling of it pulling away and thought nothing at all.

I did not speak of this to anyone. Or of anything else. After school, on cold bright days, I would run down to the parking lot and jump into Julian's car, and we'd drive. Anywhere. We'd sit in small cafés, drinking sour lemon tea, suddenly shy. Climb up onto the roof and watch the sky and talk about music and God. We'd walk through the hills at the edge of town some mornings, at dawn. He'd wait at the end of the driveway in the dark, and my footsteps, crunching through the frost and dirt, would shoot out into the mist. We'd watch the sunrise over the hidden lake, sitting close together but not touching. We'd talk, very softly, of time. We said, how incredible, that two people could be such good friends, and we lay close as lovers without touching, even once.

I was very much in love with him and it hurt like hell. Because it was too honest and horribly innocent, because he was a boy from a small town who lived right and believed in the world and his power to change it, believed in love and forever, believed in people. Because I was not what he saw, and because I could not show him what I was. I wanted to tell him, but I couldn't.

Years later, after we're married, we will cry about that time. I should have seen it, he'll say, I was such an idiot, how could I not see? We will put our foreheads together, and I will tell him, again and again, that he could not have seen.

No one saw. Not the people I was living with, not my teachers. My parents, trying to keep an eye on me from afar, had no way of telling what was going on. My medical "team" was incompetent. My life was day and night: the day, the light, I spent with Julian, laughing, suddenly human and flush with life, a sixteen-year-old girl in love. The night, I spent watching someone who looked like me having sex with someone else in a dark room that reeked of pot, or wandering, literally crazed with starvation and lack of sleep, through streets that were not safe for a girl.

But that kind of girl is not a girl, quite. Madness is not what it seems. Time stops. All my life I've been obsessed with time, its motion and velocity, the way it works you over, the way it rushes you onward, a pebble turning in a brook. I've always been obsessed with where I'd go, and what I'd do, and how I would live. I'd always harbored a desperate hope that I would make something of myself. Not then. Time stopped seeming so much like the thing that would transform me into something worthwhile and began to be inseparable from death. I spent my time merely waiting. I knew this even then.

At Christmas, I took a train to Portland to meet my parents on neutral ground. I wrote during the ride, avoiding sleep or food. I stepped off the train. I was beginning to have a hard time walking, my motion had slowed somehow. I would watch my hands struggle to close, or open, or move from pen to paper to coffee cup. My parents were standing at the station, side by side. They did not smile. Years later, when asked what she was thinking, my mother would say: You looked like an escapee from Auschwitz. We went to my aunt and uncle's house. We had dinner, spaghetti and French bread. I remember buttering the bread. I ate, then threw up. In the evening, I sat on my mother's lap, leaned back against her chest, sleepy and finally warm.

I didn't know this, but my parents called TAMS in Minneapolis the next day in a panic. My mother told Kathi that I was skeletal. My father was furious. What the hell is going on here? What the hell happened? She's lost at least twenty-five pounds! I went about, cheery. I began to refuse to eat with anyone, swore I ate better alone. I leaned over the balcony of my grandmother's apartment and scraped my food off the plate, watched it fall twenty-four stories to the ground. I can't eat bread, I said, or meat, or cheese, I can't have milk. I'm doing really well, I said, I truly am, I've been working really hard in therapy.

How the hell did this happen? I'd been rigging the scale at the therapist's office. Easy. Got there early, it was just a regular bathroom scale. Moved the little dial, hopped on. Good, she'd say. I'd hop off. At the nutritionist's office, the medical scale made it a little harder. After the last class at school, I'd start loading up my pockets while the other students in my class laughed at my bizarre routine. Every bit of jewelry I owned, cans of soda, into my pockets. I wore shirts with extra pockets, rocks in the panties and bra, sometimes a couple of books in the baggy part of a sweatshirt. Three or four layers of clothes, fisherman's sweaters over the sweatshirts, T-shirts, then a coat. Several layers of pants, long johns, tights. Then water. As I lost weight, I had to drink more and more water, four, six, eight liters of water, and then hold it until after the appointment. She was a nice nutritionist. I used to be an anoretic, she offered, so I understand. I nodded sympathetically. We'd go over my food charts for the week, my tidy little notations, three well-rounded meals, snacks, multivitamins. She'd congratulate me on any special little "extras," a cookie, a candy bar. I'd gotten very good at filling out the sheets, did it during lunchtime on the day of my appointment. Tried to remember what regular people ate. Wrote it down. Immediately after our session, I'd run to the bathroom and pee like a racehorse.

In the letters from TAMS:

> Weigh Marya in a gown, NOT street clothes, always AFTER voiding. Check the specific gravity of Marya's urine frequently. If it falls below 1.006, she is water-loading.

Christmas was a lovely vacation, I'm sure. I remember it only in terms of what I ate, when and where I threw up. I remember, also, the most macabre Christmas gift ever given: my collection of recent work, given in such astoundingly blind faith to my parents. Entitled "Health." Suicide poems. The series called "Alex," the dying woman. In the last poem, she kicks off. They aren't about me, I insisted. Are you sure? my father asked. Oh, no, I said. I made them up.

Train ride back to California. Car ride back to Santa Rosa. The day after I leave Portland, my relatives' pipes break, spilling my undigested dinners, in their spaghetti entirety, all over the floor for any and all to see. My parents are still there. Their pipes had broken before. They call TAMS, Kathi says get her back here, *now*. My parents call the people I am living with. Bear in mind here, I am completely unaware of any of this. I am doing nothing in particular but contemplating death. I wait, pacing through downtown in the night, shaking off the hands of the vagrant acid-fried men with gray beards. The people I am living with argue that I am doing better—for all they knew, I was—and that it would only disrupt me again to ship me back to Minnesota when I'd only just begun to put down roots. My parents say fuck roots, she's dying. She's not. She is. She's not. My parents call my stepbrothers. I sit on the living room floor of my friend's house, stoned out of my mind, climbing out on ten-foot ledges because I think I am a cat. Getting the munchies, spending three hours trying to cut a bagel, turning it in circles and circles until it is a shredded mess and I give up. Drinking instead.

My brothers come back from school without warning. I am informed that I am in deep shit. I am, within two days of departure, spotted by a highway patrolman, running down Highway 101. Where are you headed, Miss? Mexico. Oh? Excuse me, I have to go—fall asleep in the backseat of a cop car, comfortable ride. They drop me at the end of the driveway, I say

I don't want them to wake my husband, they give me emergency numbers to call should I need help. Sure thing, I say. Somehow it registers that I am going back to Minneapolis. I say good-bye. Night before I leave, I binge wildly in the kitchen of my boyfriend's house, ice cream sundaes, cheese sandwiches, deluding myself that I can gain enough weight to keep myself out of the hospital. My boyfriend says gently, Don't eat *too* much. I laugh. Sex a nauseated lurching, belly distended, head pounding. Next morning I wake up, throw up the night before. Realize I cannot digest food anymore. After my last day of school, Julian, Rebecca, and I drive to a croissant shop. I drink coffee. I swear I'll be back. Soon, I say, very soon. I just need to get my weight up a little, nothing big, I'll be back next month. In the car, Julian and I cry. I want to tell him. I tell him only that I love him. He, the only sane part of my life anymore. I hold on to him so hard I think I'll break him in half. He doesn't know what's going on. Watches me walk up the driveway, slowly. Stopping to rest on my way. He realizes, for the first time, just how thin I am. I didn't bother to hide it that day. No use.

Brothers on the front porch, unsmiling. I say hi. They say hi. The last thing I remember is one of them saying, very simply, that he can't stand to watch me do this to myself. He stares out over the valley and shakes his head.

Next thing I know, I'm on a plane. Takeoff, my blood pressure hits the floor and I—it amazes me even now to realize how utterly oblivious I was—am surprised. I lean my head back, trying to will my heart to beat, wondering what they'll do with me if I have a heart attack on the plane. A steady scream rolls through my head, some voice: *I'm only sixteen! But I'm only sixteen!* I sleep or pass out. I am getting off the plane; mother, father, aunt, uncle, two cousins await my arrival, stand in a tight little knot, tense. I say hello. My cousins say, Hey, Mar. My aunt says, angrily, So we hear you've been puking again. I am too tired to flare. I just nod.

Next day, I walk up the stairs in TAMS, up to Kathi's office, gripping the rail. In her doorway, I ask brightly, "So how do I look?" I hold out my arms, as if showing off a new dress. She looks at the medical evaluation I've just had, sitting on her desk, and says, "Sit down." I stand there, blankly, stupid. "So how do I look?" I repeat. She snaps her head toward me and hisses, *"Sit down before you drop dead."*

I sit. She stares at me. She says, "Jesus Christ."

Methodist Hospital, Take II. I am freezing cold. I am wearing my coat. They dump out my purse, my bags. I slide down to sit on the floor while the nurses, who know me well, assign me a room and a primary nurse. Someone comes over, pulls my arm out of my sleeve, does the usual blood pressure pulse temperature thing, takes me into the main room, sits me down on the couch. You're hurting my arm, I say. My hands in the pockets of my coat, I rub the edge of the box of laxatives I've stashed. They don't search my pockets. I sleep in the main room that night, on emergency monitoring. The light from the nurses' station keeps me awake till near dawn.

As I lie awake I think about Dr. J. What he will say to me when he sees me the next day. I think about something he'd said to me the last time I was in. Sitting in his chair one morning, he'd said, with a patronizing smirk on his face: Well, it's not like you're a sixty-pound anoretic or anything.

Seven months later, I returned, grinning in triumph. Not sixty pounds but closer than I was, in the low eighties. I lay in bed, pressing the bones of my knees together. Tapping them together, a steady singsong rhythm: clickclickclickclickclick.

MARYA JUSTINE HORNBACHER. F. DOB 04-04-74.

I. AXIS I:

A. 1. Anorexia nervosa, 307.10
   2. Malnutrition secondary to severe starvation.

B. 2. Bulimia nervosa, 307.51

C. 3. Major Depression, recurrent, 296.33

II. AXIS II:

A. 1. Mixed personality features.

NOTES: BRADYCARDIA, HYPOTENSION, ORTHOSTASIS, CYANOSIS, HEART MURMUR. SEVERE DIGESTIVE ULCERATION.

Interlude

November 5, 1996

You know, sometimes I get sick of writing this. I wake up in the morning, I lie in bed awhile, mentally conducting my heart, *one* two three four, *one* two three four. I look at the light coming in through the blinds. The cat stands on my stomach, glaring at me. Julian hogs the pillows. All things are in their place: The paintings are still on their hooks, no one has come in the night and taken my stuff, no one has left me, nothing is missing, nothing is wrong.

I try on three shirts, two pairs of pants. I smoke and put on my eyeliner. I stare at my face from all angles. It isn't right. It never is. I stand and look at my butt, my hips, my thighs, the way my upper arms look when I press them as hard as I can against my side. Are they bigger? Is the left side of my rear end bigger than it was two weeks ago? Julian comes in with coffee. Do I look like I've gained weight? I ask. He says no. This is a tired routine. I always ask, he always says no. I say, You're lying. He says, No I'm not. I look at the right side of my butt in the mirror. He sits down in my chair. I say, You always say that. He says, Well, honey, I don't know what to tell you. I ask, So, seriously, I don't look like I've gained weight? He says, No, you don't. I say, But I don't look like I've lost weight? He says, No, you don't.

This seems impossible to me. It seems biologically impossible to stay the same size, although I must. It seems one must always be either bigger or smaller than they were at some arbitrary point in time to which all things are compared. The panties that are possibly tighter than they were. When? You can't say when. But you are *absolutely positive no question* that it's true. It ruins your day. You get into bed that night with your husband, your lover, your friend, your boss, whoever, and roll over, facing the door, curled fetally into yourself. The hand snakes over to your side of the bed. You say: I'm tired, don't touch me, I have a headache, I feel sick, stop it, go away, leave me alone. Because you, in the course of the day, have ballooned to the size of a small hippo. You are sure of it, your skin is too tight, you wish to take it off, you're hot.

This is the very boring part of eating disorders, the aftermath. When you eat and hate that you eat. And yet of course you must eat. You don't really entertain the notion of going back. You, with some startling new level of clarity, realize that going back would be far worse than simply being as you are. This is obvious to anyone without an eating disorder. This is not always obvious to you. But this stage, when it is effectively Over, is haunting in its own way. Your closest companion is now, as ever, the mirror. You could detail, if anyone asked, each inch of your skin, each flaw amplified, each mole, bulge, wrinkle, bone, hair, pock, except for your back, which has always bothered you, not being able to see yourself from behind, watch your back, so to speak. This is the pitiful stage where you do not qualify as an eating-disordered person. And you feel bad about this. You feel as if you really *ought* to count, you ought to still merit worry, still have the power to summon a flurry of nurses, their disdain ill hidden, your skeletal smirk.

But you are in the present tense. Your husband sips his coffee, saying, But dear, I don't really *care* if you've gained weight. And you, triumphant, logical as the Red Queen, shriek, You see? I *have* gained weight! I knew it! And he sighs. You ask again, Do I look fat? No. Plump? No. Round? Well, you're a woman. What do you mean? I mean—I mean—

I picture husbands all over the world, hovering in doorways, caught in a terrible tangle of language, feet and hands bound by these slippery words, glossy and meaningless as the pages of a magazine.

6 Lockup

Minneapolis, 1991

Oh there is no use in loving the dying.
I have tried.
I have tried but you can't,
you just can't guard the dead.
You are the watchman and you
can't keep the gate shut.

—Anne Sexton, "Letter to Dr. Y," 1964

January 1991. As my parents sat with me in the hospital, holding my shoulders, I sobbed. I wanted out. I wanted to go back to California. The television in the main room sent out loud bang-pow sounds of a war in Iraq. I wanted Julian and his eyes and his funny laugh. The piercing hospital lights hurt my head. I wanted my dream world back. In the night, dark bringing me the familiar dissolution of object and angle and boundary I craved, I wrote wild, manic poems in the dark, scrawls across the page, complete nonsense, a series of some random sort, one hundred poems of delusional wandering. I wanted to die, right then. I had this idea in my head that dying would be lovely, a simple loosening of the ankle shackles that held me to the ground. I would lift off into the sky, float over the iced white streets, yes, that was death, and I was a princess trapped in a cage, dying of a broken heart. That was death.

I did not yet understand that the gasp and wheeze of my heart was death. The wild skittish flitting of my eyes and my hands working themselves together, trying to get warm, was death. The absence of any understanding that my body was falling away from me like a pair of old pants was death. I did not understand. It did not occur to me that I'd gone crazy. It did not occur to me that I would either be dead or locked up for good in the near future. I know that while I was in the hospital, I requested a pair of scissors and cut my waist-length hair to my chin. Someone's boyfriend, visiting, said I looked like a model. I was of course thrilled and failed to register the obvious and extremely sicko ramifications of that comment. I was throwing up every meal in my suitcase, or out the window, during free (unsupervised) times. I know that one day, sitting on my bed, I had my one-on-one time with a nurse. She told me, slowly, that I wasn't speaking clearly, wasn't making sense. She was wearing a red-and-white striped shirt. I was wearing a blanket. I began to cry. I said, You just don't understand. But there was a terrible fear that took hold then, when she said that. It hit me that I might have destroyed my life completely. They weren't going to let me out this time. And the one thing that remained—my mind, for better or for worse—was going. Or gone.

In the last week of February, my vital signs stabilized and my insurance pulled out. I was discharged on grounds of noncompliance and insufficient coverage. Eating disorders are regarded, by insurance companies, as temporary and cured once the heart speeds up a bit. I was returned to my parents' house, batty and sicker than when I'd gone in. The tiny bit of weight I'd gained in the hospital scared me, and once discharged, I just stopped eating altogether. I enrolled in the high school where my mother was assistant principal, fell the second day I was there, went into the nurse's office. I tried to eat lunch in my mother's office, couldn't, didn't eat. People stared at me in the halls. It took me several days to realize that they were staring at me because I was so thin. It made me feel better to realize that, because it meant that something, at least, was right, something in this total mess was good. In the evenings, I sat at dinner with my parents, staring at my plate. I remember the night when I literally, honest to God, could not figure out what the hell to do with the fork. I picked it up. I held it. I started crying. I can't eat, I said. I felt terrible. I actually wanted to eat, if only to erase the ghastly horror on my parents' faces, if only to get them to laugh once or twice, or yell, or speak at least a little less softly, as if I were not about to break. I was not used to this gentleness. It cast a funereal pall over the dining room table, hovered over the plates of food like fog. There was no fighting, nothing at all, only my parents staring at me (in agreement, for once: our child is a lunatic) sadly, and me staring in panic at my plate. Catching my reflection in the mirror to my right, seeing my face parsed into Picasso-esque pieces: cheeks and chin out of proportion, eyes pasted on at random. At long last, I was completely alone.

My father says of that time: You were very sweet. It was almost as if you were saying good-bye. I expect my sweetness, my apologetic smile, must have struck them as strange and as frightening as theirs struck me. It was almost as if they, too, were saying good-bye.

My father sat awake, all night, at the side of the bed in my childhood room, the air heavy with that smell that hangs in hospital halls. No twitch of pulse at temple or wrist. The white sheet over my body did not rise or fall. And so he pulled a loose thread from the quilt and held it over my mouth. He sat there, waiting for the thread to sway, if only a little, all night, every night during that interminable month. Some nights, I'd feel myself being pulled up through the waters of sleep, hear the dim bubbling voice of a man, Marya, wake up. WAKE UP, PLEASE, honey, come on. My body would rattle, a marionette, someone shaking me, my head too heavy to hold up. Marya, say something. (Groggily: What?) Nothing. Go back to sleep. His voice dim and distant, my bedroom dark, I sank back, felt sleep wash over me, a wave heavier than God.

Dizzy, walking slowly out of class, back to the nurse's office every day in school. Weighing in at TAMS. Within a week of discharge I was readmitted on emergency notice, twelve pounds lighter than when I went in. They suspected laxatives. I tried to explain to them that I didn't even have the presence of mind to pick up a book, much less get myself to the drugstore to steal laxatives. I just wasn't eating, and my body had just quit. I remember sitting in Kathi's office with my father holding my shoulders so tightly they bruised while he called my mother at work to tell her I was being readmitted. I remember his voice, suddenly calm: Judy, don't cry. Come on, pull yourself together.

I remember thinking: It's her birthday. We were supposed to go out to dinner.

I remember thinking: I've never seen my mother cry.

Never in my life, before or since, have I felt such profound guilt.

Methodist Hospital, Take III. I went into dinner, sat down in front of my half-a-peanut-butter-sandwich, looked away from it, huddled into my coat. All the other patients were staring at me, of course. I'd just left. A girl I'd gotten friendly with leaned over and said, Marya, eat. You were eating fine last week. I said, Yeah, well.

It's not very polite to say, at dinner, that you only ate to get out to stop eating all over again. No good giving away tricks. People on eating-disorder units are notoriously supportive of one another's recovery. Less competition.

The next thing I remember is at the end of the stay. The rest of it is gone. We were sitting —me, Dr. J., primary nurse, Kathi, my parents—in the conference room. They were discussing what would be done with me, as I was beyond their control at this point. I was staring out the window, tapping my foot as hard as I could, thinking: Butter, butter, butter, butter, trying to work off the butter I'd eaten at breakfast by wiggling and shifting and scooting around in my chair. Gray foggy day, dirty snow outside on the streets eight floors down. I remember they were talking about the unlikelihood that any eating-disorder unit would take me, given my history of total nonresponsiveness to treatment. Voices and voices. Dr. J. throwing his hands up, my parents shaking their heads, my mother with her head in her hands. Kathi's calm low voice, voice of reason. Butter, butter, butter, butter, butter, Marya? (MARYA.) I come to attention. Hmm? (Do you want to get well?) I'm not sick. Buzzing in my head. Habit of taking my own pulse, cold fingers pushed under the cuff of my coat, laid on the thin skin of my wrist. Still beating. Lose track while I'm counting, start over. Lose track. A small and private giggle. I can't count. Ugly winter's end, gray snow and city soot on the streets, bare trees. (MARYA.) Hmmm? (You see what I mean? someone says, not to me.)

Willmar.

The word shoots out into the room, cracks through the haze like a bullet. I sit up in my chair. Did someone say Willmar?

Silence. They all stare at me.

I start screaming.

Willmar. Minnesota State Institution. For the legally insane. Where you are left to die in the kind, soft-spoken care of nice men in white coats. Never promised you a rose garden! screams this little girl, all eyes and bags of clothes. Fuck you all! she screams. I won't go, I won't go, I won't go!

She turns frantically to her mother, Are you out of your mind? You'd let them put me away? *Fuck you!* She runs out of the room, flings herself onto her bed, waits for the heave of sobs. Nothing but numb. Realizes that she no longer knows how to cry. Fascinating. No one watching. Scoot over to the side of the bed, lift the lid of the rancid suitcase. Throw up the butter.

Scoot back. Now *that* would be interesting, she thinks. The state pen! Well, fuck it. Nothing I can do about it now.

Kicked out of the hospital, a few days riding, half-asleep or half-dead, in the back of the car while my parents bang on the doors of treatment centers, pleading with insurance companies. A few meetings with doctors. I remember only their faces in shadow. I remember the light coming in through a window. I do not remember what I was asked or what I replied, only that we left each time, turned down.

Kathi works some magic to keep me out of Willmar, and it is March 19, 1991. I am standing outside the door of Lowe House, the Children's Residential Treatment Center. It looks like a 1950s apartment building, square and brick with weird baby blue panels on some of the windows, on the south side of a high-crime square with a scraggly park in the middle.[1] It's sleeting. I'm shivering. My mother is crying and wearing a green coat. I have, as usual, not the faintest idea what's going on. Just another hospital, I think. Figure a way out of it soon enough. A woman comes out the door. I hate her on sight. She introduces herself to me with a most ingratiating tone. I say nothing. I look at the leafless shrubs around the building, bundles of black sticks. I say bye mom dad. See you later. They cry and hold on to me for a long time, tell me they'll be here to visit soon. I stiffen against them, shut down my heart like a window. I cannot stand to see them like this. I cannot stand that I'm doing this to them. I cannot stand any of this and I shut down. Click. I follow this woman upstairs three floors to Unit B.

---

[1] I will, three years later, move into an apartment building (crack house) catercorner from Lowe House. This is where I will find my first measure of sanity. I am convinced at some level that the daily reminder, as I looked out of my kitchen window at the loony bin from which no shred of sound ever escaped, the reminder of my own tenure in the diagnostic netherworld of madness, acted as a constant reality check for me, turned me away from the window and to the cupboard, to a bowl of cereal, an apple, or to the phone.

MARYA JUSTINE HORNBACHER. F. DOB: 04-04-74.

1. Life-threatening weight loss. Laxative abuse. Orthostasis, dangerously low BP. Irregular heartbeat. Severe and rapid deterioration of physical signs.

2. Enmeshed father-daughter relationship. Detached mother. Stressed marital relationship. Daughter triangulated in marital system.

3. Fear of abandonment. Fear of intimacy. Distances self through hyper self-control and food issues. Uneasiness around males.

ADMIT FOR LONG-TERM RESIDENTIAL TREATMENT. CAUTION: HAS BEEN HOSPITALIZED ON FOUR SEPARATE OCCASIONS FOR HER EATING DISORDER. BUILDING RESTRICTION UNTIL FURTHER NOTICE. TWENTY-FOUR HOUR WATCH.

Three triple-lock soundproof doors fired their rounds behind me, salute to my arrival in Wonderland. I stood there blankly looking down the hall. Nothing but a hall, brown carpet, rooms on either side, all doors open. At the end of the hall, another door with a red EXIT sign. I am relieved for no other reason than the comfort in knowing there's a way out.

Suddenly, crashing into the silence, from one of the rooms whirled a dervish, a tiny wind, a small boy hurtling down the hall at warp speed. I caught a glimpse of his face: Coke bottle glasses, mouth curled into an animal sneer, little arms and legs pumping like pistons. He flung himself into the wall, fell, stood up, flung himself, fell, stood up, flung. From another door came men, big men with a gray mat. They tackled the little being, rolled him up in the mat, carted him past me and out the door. From inside the mat came a muffled shriek. The door clicked shut. Silence again.

I turned to the woman.

"Who was that?" I said.

"Duane."

"Where are they taking him?"

She, hand on the small of my back, pressed me not-too-gently down the hall.

"The Quiet Room."

The Quiet Room? Mary, mother of God. What in the HELL was I doing here? This was not an eating-disorders unit. This was not a hospital. "Treatment center," they'd said. Lowe House was an asylum. Last stop before Wilmer. You fail here, the game is over. I paced in my room as she dug through my bags, two little piles.

"Please sit down, Mara."

"Marya."

"Please sit down."

"Why?"

"Do you want a time-out?"

"A WHAT?"

"I'm going to have to ask you not to be abusive."

"EXCUSE ME?"

She glanced up at me. She had bad hair. Bad, bad hair. "Mara, you are making a choice."

"To do WHAT?"

"All right, that's five minutes after lunch."

Lunch? No one had said anything about lunch. I turned to the window, tried to open it.

"The windows are locked to keep clients safe," said Miss Manners.

I rattled the window. Unbreakable Plexiglas, sealed at the edges. Definitively locked. I looked down at the street below, the park across the street where dogs ran randomly about, uncollared. I watched them bark. I realized that Lowe House was soundproof. I leaned my head on the window.

In one pile on my bed—hospital sheets, flat hospital pillow—were clothes, books, shoes. She took the high-heeled shoes. They were placed in the other pile, with earrings, pictures with glass frames, several bottles of pills, matches, lighters, cigarettes, switchblade, Swiss army knife, mace on a key chain, all keys, things with hard plastic, anything sharp, anything with a rough edge. She took the pencils and pens. I debated each item, I said: But I don't cut myself, I'm not suicidal, I swear to God, I need the pencils and pens, take the keys, I don't care, but for Pete's sake, leave me my earrings, my eyeliner, GIVE ME THAT PICTURE OF JULIAN, *please* don't take Julian. I started crying, JESUS CHRIST, what IS this place?

She said nothing, bad hair falling over her flat face. She turned to me, searched my pockets, asked me to take off my coat. I refused. Mara, we just want to keep you safe. (FUCK you.) You do not have the right to abuse me. (The HELL I DON'T.) That's ten minutes. (Doing WHAT?) Sitting on your bed, after lunch. (AS IF YOU WERE GOING TO LET ME DO ANYTHING ELSE, you BITCH.) She frisked me, rifled through my pockets as I stood there, about to explode.

She did not check my shoes.

I stood there, grinning in my head. I had laxatives in my shoes. Little pink ones, they'd been there all day. I'd been rolling them under my heel through the intake session, the meeting with so and so. I'd been gripping them with my toes while my parents gripped me saying good-bye. I'd walked up the stairs with them, sworn at the nurse with them, sworn at the unit manager with them, stood there, shivering in my shoes, holding the laxatives close with my toes, my Christ, my companion, my suicide attempt, just in case.

She stood too close and suddenly something snapped. I bolted, out the door of my room to the left, a manic rattling of the door. It didn't open. I ran the other way, down to the blessed red EXIT sign, flew through the air at the door, weightless and bare as a plucked bird, threw myself against it, it held fast, I jiggled the handle. I screamed, threw all my weight into my shoulder and slammed it against the door, which stood steady and solid as a tree. I sank to the floor, curled into myself, sat staring at the wall. Miss Manners came and took me back to my room. She said: I understand. I said: Like hell. She said: That's fifteen.

Now about lunch, she said. Are you going to eat lunch? I shook my head. She said: You understand that if you don't, you'll be making a choice.

I turned facedown on the bed and waited for lunch.

I thought: No Exit. I thought: This is what hell is like. Bad furniture and no mirror anywhere, stupid smiling women who perpetually say I Understand. Locked in a room with other people for eternity. Damned to an inferno of asinine conversation, I Feel This and I Feel That, and no one knows how to say your name, and your days pass on a timer, ticking out five-ten-fifteen minutes of penance for your sins.

My first weeks in Lowe House were primarily a series of days through which I floated, stunned. On Unit B you woke up in the morning, you made your bed, you waited in line for a shower. The bathroom door of course was locked, but for a different reason than in the hospital. At Lowe House, the Clients were at much higher risk for self-injury than your average eating-disordered person (no, I did not connect the fact that I was your average eating-disordered person *and* a Client) and Staff wanted to keep an eye on you at all times, lest you try to drown yourself in the shower. I was not allowed to go into the bathroom by myself, but at least they let me shut the stall door. And listened.

We sat in the main room, a petri dish, and were watched from the office while we waited for breakfast. The TV was on, cartoons. I read the paper, sitting with my feet tucked under me on the couch. There were several couches, a table, cupboards full of Legos, crayons, paper, toys. There was a routine: One was expected to get up on time, shower, dress, and make one's bed. It alarmed me to find that each of these ostensibly simple activities posed problems for some of my compadres; when John and Peter woke up, they were wont to punch Staff in hypoglycemic rage, and so waking up was a problem. A good half of the patients flat-out refused to get out of bed and began their days arguing with Staff about the Point of It All. Then there was a problem with showering, because there were those among us who did not, for their own reasons, care to shower. Dressing, too, seemed most useless to many, given that there was nothing to do all day but contemplate the crappiness of one's own life, and pajamas would do just as well for that. Making one's bed turned, many mornings, into a battleground for control, and shrieks of fury were heard down the hall as infinite philosophical reasons for not making one's bed were thrown out and shot down by Staff, with a patience and kindness I had thought was reserved for saints.

Meanwhile, I was already getting into trouble for keeping my room too clean, my bed too tightly made, my makeup perfect, even in *sleep*—"Wears lipstick to bed. Often sleeps fully dressed, including shoes"—and I sat on the couch trying to ignore David, who stood in his doorway in his Jockeys and a fishing hat, casting an imaginary fishing line at imaginary fish, laughing horribly and hollering, from time to time, "Bitch!"

When the chaos had been moderately organized, we lined up at the door, went down two flights of stairs, walked through an echoing basement hall, into the cafeteria, sat down at a table. Staff sat down with us, talking cheerfully. There were two tables. At the other table, across the room from ours, sat Unit A, which lived one floor down from us and was, as far as I could tell, a little less fucked up than Unit B. In one corner of the room, there were institutional refrigerators, a small work area for the cook. The cook, a small woman with a raspy voice and a not-insubstantial belly, piled serving dishes with food.

My first morning there I sat in my chair, looking around the table. There were twelve empty plates. One of them was apparently mine. The cook came over, put a bowl of scrambled eggs, a plate of English muffins, and a plate of bacon on the table. All around me, the other kids were talking, pouring themselves orange juice as if they had nary a care in the world, as if orange juice was not liquefied *calories*. Chris, a small and temperamental boy with a sharp tongue, was scowling, and hurled a sarcastic comment at David. The Staff said, not harshly, "Chris, why don't you push back for a minute until you're ready to have breakfast with us." Chris shoved his chair back overvigorously, tipped over backward, and everyone started laughing. Chris started hollering, was sent to the hall, stormed into the hall in a cloud of obscenities. A Staff hopped up and dashed after him, the other kids whispering that he'll have like a *major* time-out.

The food *stunk*. It smelled terrible. I passed the bowl of eggs to my right when it came to me, sat rubbing my hands under the table. They were cold. I stared at the bacon. Ben got in trouble for hogging the bacon. I tried to imagine how anyone could possibly be capable of taking bacon voluntarily, let alone too much of it. My plate remained empty. It was explained to me, the day before, that "we eat family style here," and I had no idea what that meant. Staff suggested that I take some food. I shook my head. I was still in limbo, I had not been given my treatment plan yet, and I was baffled by the fact that I had to serve myself. I was absorbed in trying to figure out how much fat is in eggs—bacon being utterly out of the question—how much butter is on the English muffins. I asked the cook, "Is this skim milk?" She shook her head, no. Therefore milk was out of the question. I had eliminated all items. I would sit there and eat nothing. I wanted some tea. I asked Staff if I could go upstairs and get tea? He said, cheerfully, no. I liked him. He was a ruddy-faced, tall fellow with long red hair pulled back in a ponytail and a good sense of humor. He made the other Clients laugh. It occurred to me that he was the sort of guy I would've had coffee with, talked books and music with, had I been on the outside. I wondered how he could sit there and be cheerful with all those lunatics around.

I was painfully, suddenly aware that I was one of those lunatics.

I watched the boys scarf down their food, I listened to Staff tease them for talking with their mouths full. I watched the girls eat, talk to one another. My roommate, a tall girl named Joan, tried to make conversation with me, told me what the day would be like. I tried to smile, tried to speak. I watched the other anoretic across the table from me serve herself, eat slowly, but eat. She watched me not-eat with a palpable, ambiguous look of jealousy and anger on her face. She said to me finally, in a low voice, "They're going to make you eat eventually, you know." I said nothing. Staff said to her, "Sarah, you are only responsible for yourself," and he smiled at her. She looked at her plate.

The nurse arrived with a tray of small paper cups, like those taster cups at yogurt shops, only they were full of pills. Everyone said, Hi Shawn, and Shawn, a woman in her fifties with a pleasant face, said good morning to everyone, and passed out meds. She got to me, set a cup full of Prozac and multivitamins in the center of my empty plate. I swallowed them with the smallest possible sip of milk. I tried to picture the size of the sip: a tablespoon? Twenty calories, maybe? Maybe just ten? One-eighth of a gram of fat? More?

I liked this business of having the freedom to serve myself. It seemed just right to me. It had the desired effect of empowering me to make my own choices, and I thought to myself in a grandiose voice: I choose not to eat at all. I suppose, in retrospect, that only a rather disturbed person could find a locked institution liberating, which I did, for just under a day. They weren't making me eat. They were waiting to see what I did, but I didn't know that. I found that out after breakfast, when Shawn took me upstairs to her office, put me on the scale, and found me hovering at about eighty pounds. Then I got a treatment plan.

It entailed this: Either eat, and stay here at Lowe House, or don't eat, and go back to the hospital, where you will be forced to eat, and then return to Lowe House.

No exit.

Can't I just go back to the hospital and then go home? No. But all the food here is fattening! That's not a very accurate perception. Yes it is! Well, the food we have is the food we have. I won't eat it! Then you'll go back to the hospital. Fine, at least the food there isn't DRIPPING WITH FAT! That's all right, but then you'll come back to Lowe House. Are you telling me I'm STUCK HERE? Yes.

Stuck there, yes. But I still had my laxatives, therefore I still had my eating disorder, and therefore I still had myself. In a little satin jewelry bag in the back of my closet, I kept the laxatives between two sweaters folded neatly on their shelf. I would never, during my stay, *consume* the laxatives. I would, however, keep them in a corner of my mind as they were kept in the corner of the closet, picture them there, picture reaching between the sweaters, taking them out, tipping my head back, swallowing them all, should the need arise. I would hold on to this small comfort, a pharmaceutical security blanket, calming myself with their mere presence, my modicum of control over me.

Think back to the fact that children, in their early years, teach themselves how to regulate moods, slow the careening train of anxiety as it clatters through the brain. It's not so uncommon for a person to simply teach themselves the wrong thing. Like me.

By the time I got to Lowe House, a horrible paradox was running my life, and to some extent runs it still: My only means of self-regulation was self-destruction. To give up a long-standing eating disorder, one that has developed at precisely the same pace as your personality, your intellect, your body, your identity itself, you have to give up all vestiges of it; and in doing so, you have to surrender some behaviors so old that they are almost primal instincts.[2] I had to give up the only tried-and-true way of handling the world that I knew, turning instead to things untested, unproven, uncertain. I am a suspicious person by nature. I could not simply take as gospel that I would "someday" learn to live without the eating disorder. I was not absolutely certain that I could do it: I had no "normal" life to return to, no prior experience of eating "normally," being "healthy." So I kept the eating disorder—small reminders, the uneaten laxatives, the patterns that organized my eating of carrots and peas, the little thoughts that got me to sleep (I can always go back, I can always do it again when I get out)—as backup, just in case. That was a mistake.

It took Staff a few days to get the idea that I wasn't going to serve myself. They revamped my treatment plan. At breakfast the next day, there were eleven blank plates and one plate full of food, covered with cellophane. It was lukewarm, the plastic steamed up with what I was sure was straight fat. A glass filled too full of milk sat next to it. I was informed that if I chose not to finish my food, I would be given a can of

---

[2] "The root of masochistic conflict," Zerbe writes, "probably stems from the earliest time in development when the establishment of a body self is disrupted" (167). The equation of self-protection with self-destruction—or of pleasure with pain—can be viewed as a psychological fissure in the psycho-physical boundary previously discussed. It has been speculated that many eating disorders have at least some basis in an early childhood trauma, however minor, usually occurring in the first year of life. This is why I use the term "primal" in describing the depth of conflict that an anoretic may experience, and to highlight the profound difficulty she may have in giving up her behaviors. It is primal not in the sense that it is innate, but in the sense that it may be *experienced as innate.* Lacking language, an infant can only express her needs through physical behavior; later in life, this developmental gap may manifest itself in an eating disorder, wherein needs and emotional states are both expressed and regulated by a physical "language." It is notable that well over half of all eating-disorder patients are considered to be "alexithymic," that is, unable to effectively verbalize emotional states, even as they are often exceptionally verbal (in my case, diagnostically "hyperverbal") in expressing intellectual concepts. Even now, during my hours of therapy, my articulations are limited to the intellectual. I will intellectually inform my therapist that I have, for example, sliced up my arms with a razor blade (see afterword) and then quote medical textbooks as an explanation for why such behavior might arise in a theoretical person. "How do you feel about this?" my therapist will ask. "Well, I think it has its primary etiology in blah blah blah—" "But how do you *feel?*" I stare at her blankly. "I don't know."

Ensure after the meal (a whole can? Yes. But that's WAY more calories than the food! Then finish the food, Marya) and another can at snack time in the afternoon. They tried this for a while, but I was still losing weight. The cans of Ensure became mandatory, whether I finished my food or not. Nothing was fair. Everything was falling apart. There was nowhere I could go.

And so there was really nothing to do but try to get well.

Except that I didn't really know what was wrong. At Lowe House, the focus was not on food, or body image, or anything of the sort. They treated you as a person whose life and emotions had somehow made you very sad, and this was an approach I did not know how to handle at all. It was an approach that seemed entirely reasonable for the rest of the Clients, whose problems were, in all objective reality, far more serious than mine; some were victims of unspeakable cruelty at the hands of their own families, abandoned by parents, shuffled from foster home to foster home for years, like my roommate and Duane. Some were victims of rape or childhood sexual exploitation. Some had severe personality or thought disorders, from depression so severe it was mitigated only by a battalion of hard-core antidepressants, to multiple personality disorder or possible schizophrenia. Some had deep and probably chemical emotional disorders that had gone completely out of control, leading them to multiple suicide attempts, massive sexual promiscuity, and drug use. A few were, as far as I could tell, just plain old criminals who had somehow ducked into treatment instead of jail, and probably wound up in jail anyway later on.[3]

Whereas I was a big question mark. A victim, primarily, of myself, which makes victim status very uneasy and ultimately ridiculous. My family messy, but hardly psychotic. The specifics of my diagnosable disorder, beyond the obvious eating, unclear. I appeared to be some form of

[3] It is notable that there were no black patients at Lowe House. Several years later, working on an article about the racial imbalance in juvenile detention centers and residential treatment centers, I would return to Lowe House on assignment and find myself talking to a number of administrative brick walls. Ultimately, the article would question the judicial pattern of "referring" young white criminals to treatment while "referring" young criminals of color to the penal system.

depressive, though this would later turn out to be inaccurate (I'm manic). I showed, noted my shrink in his notes on our meetings, no signs of a personality or thought disorder. I seemed, he also noted, a relatively well-adjusted, if emotionally blank, severely eating-disordered young woman exhibiting "the ideas and behaviors of a person ten years older than her chronological age. . . . She is pleasant but condescending and intimidating. She makes the examiner feel as if he is asking stupid questions that he should know the answer to or that certain [questions] have foregone conclusions that anyone would understand."

I was condescending because I felt like a serious idiot, a royal fuck-up, and a general lost cause. It became apparent very quickly that I was light-years away from understanding my Issues. I understood that what I was doing was not, by any objective standards, healthy, and I understood that there were reasons I was doing it. It was not my opinion, however, that those reasons were anything serious, anything complex at all. I assumed, though I did say this, that there was something innately wrong with me, that I was *a priori* flawed in some way. I was not sad, I was not angry, I was not depressed, I was not bipolar or schizophrenic, I did not have a personality disorder, there were no events in my life that were overly traumatic, nothing external was wrong. What was wrong was *me*, therefore no amount of therapy would make me well.

All of us have theories about the world and about ourselves. We will go to great lengths to prove ourselves right because it keeps the world in our head coherent and understandable. My theory was simple: I was a screwed-up person. The phrase "self-fulfilling prophecy" comes to mind.

Eating disorders are different, in some ways, from most forms of depression or other "mental illness." It is important to note that many people who get eating disorders have a preexisting chemical depression or other biological predispositions that lead to eating-disordered behavior, but then there are also many people who get eating disorders without that predisposition. I was, to the best of anyone's knowledge, of the latter set. Furthermore, the chemical imbalance that malnutrition induces may lead to depression, which in turn is dealt with through eating-disordered behavior, which is what probably happened in my case. The point I'm getting at here is that while depression may play a role in eating disorders, either as cause or effect, it cannot always be pinpointed directly, and therefore you never know quite what you're dealing with. Are you trying to treat depression as a cause, as the thing that has screwed up your life and altered your behaviors, or as an effect? Or are you dealing with a screwed-up life and disordered behaviors that are simply *depressing?* Will drug therapy help, or is that a Band-Aid cure? How big a role do your upbringing and family play? Does the culture have anything to do with it? Is your personality just problematic by nature, or is there, in fact, a faulty chemical pathway in your brain? If so, was it there before you started starving yourself, or did the starving put it there?

All of the above?

I was not, the month before my seventeenth birthday, dealing with any of this. I was sitting at the little table in the main room, reading schoolbooks. We had school every day from just after breakfast to just before lunch. We sat in three tiny rooms, grade levels abolished altogether, doing whatever assignments the three harried teachers figured were appropriate for our age, using whatever ancient schoolbooks the Minneapolis Public Schools threw our way. They just fed me books, at first. I developed an academic plan for myself to lessen the manic anxiety I felt about being out of school, which was a great hindrance to my Future. I had a book of Trigonometry, a book of history, and several books of American literature. I read voraciously as much Whitman and Emerson and Thoreau as I could get my hands on, swooped through trigonometry (and promptly forgot it), read all of ancient history, Greek, Roman, Chinese, then into the Middle Ages, then started in on the early American short story, wrote paper after paper for a teacher who just wrote "Excellent!" at the end of every one. Hair pulled back in a bandanna, glasses propped on my nose, no shoes, cozy as a bug in a rug, reading. No one to bother me, "No deeds to do, no promises to keep," I began to compulsively take down my favorite quotes. I have four fat three-ring binders full of spiral notebook paper, scribbled over with quotes from e.e. cummings. Whitman I thought a bit mushy, very fond of the Modernist approach. This was my favorite: "What's madness but nobility of soul/At odds with circumstance?"

What's madness but nobility of soul
At odds with circumstance? The day's on fire!
I know the purity of pure despair,
My shadow pinned against a sweating wall.
That place among the rocks—is it a cave,
Or winding path? The edge is what I have.

—Theodore Roethke, "In a Dark Time," 1964

Give me a break, I was sixteen. At sixteen, locked in a mental ward, who would not want to believe in some level of nobility? In all truth, I thought I *did* know the purity of pure despair. I firmly believed that I was *living* pure despair, wronged by fate and at odds with circumstance, the innocent man falsely accused and incarcerated for life, the martyrdom of the misunderstood. I felt *terribly* misunderstood. It was simply not *fair*, this cruel punishment. I was not mad! Certainly not, not like the rest of them! No no! I was able, quite able, to maneuver my mandatory conversations with Staff away from any discussion of my problems, onto the neutral ground of the problems of the theater, the problems of politics. I worked the conversation back to the war in Bosnia, the attempted coup in Moscow, the dreadfully repetitive musical format of Andrew Lloyd Webber's musicals. I danced happily through my days, writing long esoteric letters to Julian filled with quotes and contemplations, never once telling him that I was writing from a locked ward. As far as he knew I was writing from Mars. I was reading and reading, sitting patiently in the alternative world in my head throughout group therapy, picking my nail polish, refusing to sleep, sitting down at dinner, standing up and screaming at the top of my lungs to the cook, *You bitch!* I screamed, *You gave me too much MILK, what the hell is the matter with you, are you trying to make me FAT? This is like, AT LEAST an INCH too much milk, I'm only supposed to drink EIGHT OUNCES, this is AT LEAST TEN*, tipping over the table, kicking and screaming all the way back to my room. Later that night, when I was supposed to be Processing the Incident, getting sidetracked on a concept in *Walden*, jabbering on and on. My parents came to visit. We sat having stilted conversations in the main room while Staff unobtrusively sat in a chair across from us, observing. We talked about books. They brought me books. I sat at the table, behind my battalion of books, peering over the top, half-reading, half-talking to them, telling them about my books.

Then Staff took away my books.

I went to my closet one day, pulled on the handle. It didn't open. I ran to the main room, looking for the pile of books on the table, the pile I'd left on the windowsill, the pile on the floor. My books were gone. They'd taken my books. I ran into the office—one desk, a long counter, cupboards, a refrigerator, a bunch of chairs, Plexiglas windows for walls, eyes on our little world—and said, trying to be calm, "Why is my closet locked? Where are my books?" My primary counselor, Janet, began: "Your treatment plan—"

"WHERE ARE MY BOOKS?"

"Marya, can you lower your voice?"

"WHAT THE HELL HAVE YOU DONE WITH MY BOOKS? DID YOU THROW AWAY MY BOOKS?" I had suspected, even accused them, of trying to make me stupid before. It seemed entirely plausible to me that they, not comprehending at all the *absolute necessity of books,* might have thrown them away.

"No, we didn't throw your books away. We feel that it will be a positive experience for you to deal with your emotions for a while, instead of distancing us through books."

"When do I get them back?" I asked, twisting the cuff of my shirt in my hand.

"As soon as you choose to deal with your issues."

"WHEN?" Clenching my fists.

"That will be your choice."

I lost it altogether. I started tipping chairs, screaming at the top of my lungs, hollering that I wanted my books, how was I supposed to GET ANYTHING DONE without my books, throwing coffee mugs. I hollered that I couldn't deal with all these STUPID CRAZY FUCKED-UP PEOPLE if I didn't have SOMETHING TO DO, I was going CRAZY in here, it was BAD ENOUGH without them TAKING MY BOOKS, and I was led down the hall, shrieking and kicking the walls, kicking my closet, kicking the heater and punching anything solid, then flopping down on my bed, screaming once more into the pillow, taking a deep breath, and then I started to bawl.

I cried for three weeks, more or less without stopping.

They were very impressed. I was dealing with my Issues, from a psychological standpoint. From where I lay, it looked like I was going to cry for the rest of my life. Of course I didn't. Eventually the tears dammed. And I started feeling a little better.

In Lowe House, something happened. I've been trying to figure out exactly what it was. A loony bin is a fairly low-action place to be, not a lot going on, a whole bloody lot of time to sit and think. What I know is this: I went in with no emotions, no will to live, no particular interest in anything other than starving to death. I came out eating. Almost normally.

From the beginning, I tried very hard to keep the whole thing at bay. Being institutionalized is a major blow to the ego, no matter how you cut it. My entire identity-being was wrapped up in (1) my ability to starve, and (2) my intellect, I had a complete identity crisis when I realized neither of these was impressing anyone. I had a lot invested in not being one of Them, those other kids in there—I was patronizing, bitchy, mouthy, aloof as a goddamn queen on her royal throne. I was restless, anxious, didn't want to Connect with any of the other patients because that would mean I was no better than them. And God, how I needed to believe I was better than them. I needed to believe they were fucked up beyond all hope, and I was simply an erroneous guest in their midst. They were children, I was an adult; they were needy and I needed nothing.

Duane, not much more than four feet tall, ruined everything.

Hair sticking up in tufts, glasses so thick his eyes were two inches big, tiny little pants perpetually falling down, Duane was eleven. He was a car thief, a truant, an abandoned child, and a ward of the state. He'd been there a year by the time I arrived. He was the one who came hauling ass down the hall on my first day.

He climbed up onto a chair at the table where I sat reading, before they took my books. He pushed his glasses up on his nose.

"Hi," he said, staring hugely at me. I glanced up at him. "Hello," I said, coolly.

We sat awhile.

"You wanna play Legos?" he asked.

"Not really," I said. He nodded.

"What do you want to do, then?"

"Read," I said.

We sat.

"So," he said. "What are you in for?"

"Nothing," I said. He nodded sagely.

"You're skinny," he said.

"I know," I said.

"Is that why you're in here?"

"Kind of."

"You wanna play rummy?"

I wavered. I was a card addict.

"Come ON," he bellowed, grinning. Wheedling: "We can play with four decks."

We sprawled out in the hallway and played rummy for the whole afternoon, stretched the rows of cards out down the hall. When Staff called us for dinner, we started clearing them up. His tiny body crouched over the cards, he said, "Hey." I looked up. He pushed his glasses up on his nose, said, "How do you say your name?"

"Mar-ya."

He nodded. "Okay." We sat separating decks, my twig legs splayed, his miniature tennis-shoed foot tapping my socked one absently. Without looking up, he said: "Marya."

I said, "Yeah."

He asked, "Will you be my sister while you're here?"

I smiled. "Yeah." He looked up at me and gave me the goofiest, most wonderful grin. I felt like I'd been offered the Nobel Prize for Normalcy.

Nights, before bed, Staff read to us. We brought our pillows into the main room. They turned down the lights, the kids sprawled out on the floor, jousting for couches. I sat, bolt upright, in a stiff-backed chair, still dressed. They were kid's books. I didn't complain. I tried not to let my eyes flutter shut. I tried not to let myself be lulled. But the voice, the quiet, the kids who spent their days screaming in some inarticulate pain that was all too real, all too recognizable to me, all of them laid out, dozing, giggling. The fact of Staff giving a damn about any of us was painful. I looked out the window at the treetops with the beginnings of buds, the city just north of us, and tried not to cry. I had no idea why it hurt, why the hand of a Staff on my shoulder made me flinch, why the nightly, sudden peace of the reading set off tiny explosions of longing in my chest. I didn't know what I was longing for.

Worse yet, after the reading, there were Hugs. People requested, very politely, hugs, from each other and from Staff. There was a milling about of huggings, and for those who did not do hugs, or were in a fight with the proffering hugger, there were handshakes. I thought it was penultimately bizarre. At the end of the reading, each night, I shot from my chair, as if from a slingshot, bolted down the hall, dove into bed fully dressed before anyone had the chance to touch me. It didn't take long for Staff to start teasing me about it, hollering after me, THERE SHE GOES! GOOD NIGHT, MARYA! DON'T LET THE BEDBUGS HUG YOU! I'd holler back, NIGHT! And bury my head under the pillow.

But the night after Duane and I played cards, he caught me. He ran me down in the hall, blocked my door with his wee body, and said, staring at the floor, "I know you don't usually give hugs but I was wondering maybe if I could give *you* a hug, you don't have to hug *back* or anything, but I thought maybe since you've been here a while and you haven't had any hugs at *all* in like *weeks* maybe you need a hug."

I leaned down and stiffly hugged him. He held on to my neck so tightly, the contact was so startling, and his small self so warm, that I took a sharp breath inward and started to cry, and he said, patting my back, "Hugs are very good for you. I'll give you another one tomorrow, if you want."

And I just held on for dear life.

When I was a small kid, there were plenty of hugs. My parents are big on hugs. My father gives bear hugs, tight and quick. My mother usually puts her arms around your shoulders and bangs on your back, as if she's trying to burp you. My friends and I had always hugged. It wasn't as if I'd never been hugged, as many of the Clients had not. But at the same time, physical contact has not come naturally to me. It seemed, and seems, laden with significance, so laden that one might like to avoid it altogether. One might, in fact, over a few years, begin to avoid it like the plague, begin to claim such absolute ownership over one's own body that contact itself—the brush of a hand, even, let alone the startling number of emotional and physical nerve endings jangled by an embrace—begins to seem a threat.

Sex was different. At first, sex had been a sudden shock, a jolt that brought me, if briefly, back into my body, and I had initially wanted that. But as bulimia gave way to anorexia, sex became a study in dissociation, a physical shutdown, the brain splitting off and watching bodies from above. As I've mentioned before, bulimia is a more physical form of eating disorder, anorexia more cerebral. For the bulimic, sex is an attempt to fill the void with something like passion, even though the aftermath brings the disorienting sense that you are spilling out of your skin. But for the anoretic—for me, at least—the usual pleasurable blitzkriegs of the bedroom become a losing battle, a terrifying onslaught of synapses shrieking at a terrible pitch, a feeling that your heart is about to burst, your body itself shatter like glass. And so your brain defects. Sex is not experienced so much as it is seen, and this translation of physical experience into intellectual exercise had made sex tolerable.

Hugs are difficult, however. Kissing is perhaps more intimate than sex itself. Similarly, hugs imply emotional, rather than sexual, intimacy. They are a gesture from one person to another of nonsexual caring, and the idea of being cared for in a nonsexual way was not something I could understand. Contact with another person reminds you that you are *also* a person, and implies that someone cares about you as such. This felt to me profoundly false, and I felt I did not, in any way, warrant such care, such contact. Contact with another body reminds you that you have a body, a fact you are trying very hard to forget.

Duane was the first to pick his way into my brain. Beyond the simple fact that he hugged me, and made me laugh, he did something that I believe was ultimately more important: He made me care about someone other than myself. The exaggerated attempts I had been making to protect myself were, in great part, diverted into a desire to protect him.

The extreme pain I felt was put into perspective by the fact that his pain was far, far worse than mine—and that, at eleven, he was dealing with it a hell of a lot better than I was. Until he left Lowe House the following summer, we were an odd little pair. I sat with him when he fell into one of his long silences, mentally trying to shed some light on what dark lurked in the back of that small brain. He sat next to me on the couch and tried to make me laugh when I was crying, after a screaming phone call with my parents, or after a bad day trip home. I knew, and told him, that he was going to make it, that they would find a foster family for him. He believed no one would ever take him. "I'm too mad," he'd say, "I'm never going to find a family 'cuz I get so MAD," he'd bellow and wind himself up to throw a fit—and I would say, "Don't be mad, you'll find someone and they'll love you because you're wonderful."

And he'd say, "I'm glad you're my sister." I'd say, "Me too." He'd say, "I think you better eat today." I'd look away.

They charted my Issues, intimacy being the big one. I wanted none of it; no attachments, no physical contact, no displays of emotion. They noted that I knew of only two emotions in myself: pissed and fine. "But fine isn't an emotion," they'd say. I'd sit there, blank, completely lacking any affect, trying to come up with a parallel word to describe how I felt.

I felt flat. I felt two-dimensional, front and back. This wasn't right, either. They gave me a list of emotions with corresponding faces. I studied it with some devotion. In community meetings (CM, twice a day) I would crow, very pleased with myself: I feel indifferent! They gave me an elaborate program to take up the time left over from the loss of my books. I had mandatory playtime every day. I had to play. I found this very confusing. Staff pointed out to me that I, like most of the kids on the unit (I bristled at the comparison), had never really been a child and needed to make up for lost time. I disagreed, staring at the crayons set before me, as confused about what I would do with them as I'd been about an empty plate. But what does *play* mean? I pleaded at the disappearing back of Staff. Play *what?* She'd smile at me, I'm sure you can think of something, she'd say. And there I'd sit, wishing passionately for a book.

Eventually they assigned Duane to play with me. Things improved. Soon we were making collages, building elaborate Lego castles, constructing houses of cards, though the latter activity had a tendency to conflict with our Issues of frustration and occasionally sent Duane into his furies, spinning down the hall, or put me into a catatonic, blank-eyed stupor for a few hours. I was assigned to twice-daily one-on-one time with my counselors. I was assigned, to my delight, a journal.

But one-on-one time, which had at first allowed me the verbal contact I craved, a chance to have my version of human connection—cerebral, removed, a soliloquy of complaints or a means of picking fights with Staff—soon began to open doors I would've preferred to leave shut. Staff was not stupid. They stopped taking the bait and started calling my bluffs sooner than I'd expected. They simply wouldn't fight. I'd make some searing, brilliant observation on the infinite flaws of the program, the Staff, the food, the touchy-feely bullshit approach they were taking, and they'd just sit there, waiting for me to deal with the fact that I was mortified to have gotten myself into this situation. They held up a mirror and made me look.

I didn't want to look. The very simple fact that I'd been avoiding all along became, in the quiet hours, in the patient presence of people who bewilderingly cared about me, unavoidable: I hated myself and did not believe that I deserved to live.

In my journal, too, which at first had seemed so comfortable and familiar a thing, it soon became impossible to avoid myself. There were only so many ways I could describe, in my frantic scribbles, all the ways in which everyone was wronging me, all the ways in which I was certain I was right and they were wrong, before it became painfully obvious even to me that I was lying. All of my grandiosity, my arrogance, my holier-than-thou attitude, my loud voice, my hard-edged don't-touch-me-fuck-you sneer, was a lie. Everything about me, in fact, was a lie. I'd finally been caught and exposed for the farce that I was.

I didn't know what lay beneath the skin I wore. I didn't want to know. I suspected it was something horrible, something soft and weak and worthless and stupid and childish and tearful and needy and fat.

I started cutting my hair. Of course, what else would you do when your repertoire of emotional skills is limited to the random, the pointless, and the bizarre. Every week, when my parents came to visit, I had less hair. I requested permission for the scissors, requested accompanied access to the bathroom, sat in the sink, pulled a fistful of hair away from my face, cut. And cut. I caught sight of my face one day, in the mirror: a vicious sneer, a mouth twisted and white. I kept cutting until Staff gently pried my fingers loose, took the scissors, returned me to my room, sat at the edge of my bed while I lay facedown, fingers playing in the rough edges of my hair. Up to the ears, then close to the scalp. Then one side shaved, then the other, then the whole head. I sat at dinner, watching David play with his bald peas, laughing maniacally to himself. The night I shaved it off altogether, a Staff named Mark, whose take-no-prisoners approach I respected and feared, pulled me aside, looked me hard in the face, and said, Marya, your hair. I said, Yeah, so? crossing my arms in front of me. He said, It's *harsh*. I said, Yeah, well. He leaned down and whispered to me: No matter how thin you get, no matter how short you cut your hair, it's still going to be you underneath. And he let go of my arm and walked back down the hall.

I didn't want it to be me underneath. I wanted to kill the me underneath. That fact haunted my days and nights. When you realize you hate yourself so much, when you realize that you cannot stand who you are, and this deep spite has been the motivation behind your behavior for many years, your brain can't quite deal with it. It will try very hard to avoid that realization; it will try, in a last-ditch effort to keep your remaining parts alive, to remake the rest of you. This is, I believe, different from the suicidal wish of those who are in so much pain that death feels like relief, different from the suicide I would later attempt, trying to escape that pain. This is a wish to murder yourself; the connotation of *kill* is too mild. This is a belief that you deserve slow torture, violent death. Without being entirely aware of it, I had settled on starvation as my torture of choice. When people think about killing themselves, they usually think about killing themselves with the least amount of pain, the briefest period of suffering. This is different.

There was a girl on Unit B, an incredibly sad girl, who cut herself with anything she could get her hands on. Bits of glass she found on the street, she saved these for her private moments under the sheets. An accidental, overlooked sharp edge on a windowsill. In group, the rest of the patients tried to understand, tried to say to her: But why? She shrugged and looked at her hands. I told my father about her. I remember his face, worried, mortified; he said: My God. Self-mutilation. And he shook his head. I just don't understand that, he said.

I understood.

I understood so well, in fact, that I would begin to do that very thing a few years down the road. After my eating disorder was "over," I would go in blind search for something else with which to tear myself apart. I found a razor blade worked quite well. In Lowe House, what this girl was doing to herself made perfect sense to me. It seemed to me that only our means were different; our ends were very much the same. Carving away at the body to—symbolically and literally—carve up an imperfect soul.

I didn't talk about the mortifying revelations I came to in my moments alone. I talked about my relationships with my parents, to some extent. I felt then, as now, that my parents were only one part of a larger complex of issues. I talked more and more, as time went on, about the role of my own personality—the need to feel powerful, the desire to be successful at all costs, the usual culprits like perfectionism, innate sadness, anger. Even in Lowe House, I was aware that there was something larger that had sparked this in me. Even then, the easy excuses of low self-esteem, bad parenting, media images, didn't seem sufficient. They were related, certainly. But the part that kept lurking, unarticulated, in the back of my head wasn't discussed. Because there isn't a good way to discuss it.

That part was me. The interplay of my upbringing, familial and cultural, with my own character, was not something I either understood nor did I really want to. I didn't want to deal with the fact that there was something about me that had made this possible. I didn't want to deal with the fact that I may have, if not just "come this way," then come with some traits, some tendencies, that led me to do this. There was simply the issue of my brain. There was simply the issue that, despite the love my parents did give me, the support I'd gotten all along from friends and other people in my life, I had an insatiable curiosity about the limits of my own self. Combined with my self-hatred, that curiosity was dangerous. I could never quite explain to people that, in addition to all the other more obvious factors, I also just wanted to see what would happen.

That curiosity had yet to be sated.

While I was in Lowe House some things did change. I began to piece my life together, stitch together memories into a patchwork quilt that made a chaotic sort of sense. When I arrived, I could not tell them anything about myself. Long periods of my life had been erased, events were lost and out of order. When you cannot say who you are or where you've been, when you've reduced yourself to no more than a skeleton with a bunch of puzzling awards, you cannot even begin to have a sense of yourself as a whole person. I asked my parents to bring in all their old photo albums, quizzed them at length about their lives, their marriage, my childhood, what they'd been thinking at this point, at this point, what happened here and here and here.

They, slowly and awkwardly, began to remind me, asking often: You don't remember that? My mother saying, bitterly, as she looked out the window: How quickly they forget.

But I began to remember. For better and for worse.

The better part was that, while I was living within the safe confines of an oversize padded cell, remembering gave me some insight into the hows and whys of what had happened, and I was in a place where I could feel relatively secure in looking at my problem, if only with tentative glances. It gave me a sense of who this person was that they referred to when they said my name, and while this was painful—I came face-to-face with a profound and nauseating hatred for the child I had been, the subhuman creature I suspected myself of being, and understood that I would have to come to some sort of reconciliation with her in order to be whole—it also gave me something I needed: the beginnings of order. The brain craves order, and I leapt upon the missing pieces with a hunger that can be credited only to a resuscitated survival instinct. I wanted to understand, and I kind of wanted to get better.

This had a down side. The self-knowledge I gained scared me to death. The unknown order I was approaching seemed more dangerous than the disorder I knew. And when I left Lowe House, and got sicker than I ever believed possible, it was all the more sad because I did it with a constant, horrible knowledge that I had come so very close to health and chickened out.

The snow melted, the leaves sprang out overnight, as they always do. I was taken off building restriction and began to go along with the group on outings, to the hospital pool a few blocks away—I swam, like most of the girls, in a long T-shirt, embarrassed about my body—to the movies, or on a drive. My parents remember that I began to have more affect, laughed a little, began to take notice of things—a child on the swings in the park, a woman in a funny hat in the café where we were allowed, now, to have unmonitored time together. I was allowed to go on passes, home first for a few hours, then overnight, then for the weekend. I remember it only very vaguely. I mostly remember that I was beginning to feel strong, and I was beginning to feel almost happy.

My roommate, Joan—suicide attempts, abusive mother, abandoned by father, repeated foster homes—and I, both rife with Intimacy issues, had managed to push past a few of them and had become friends. It is noted on my charts—under "Positive Gains"—that we were both getting in lots of trouble for talking after lights out, laughing too loud, acting, essentially, like teenagers. She laughed at me when I stood on the bed, shrieking, "My butt!" She said, Yes, Mar, you have a butt! It's there so you can sit down! *Sheesh,* she said. Some people. When we were falling asleep at night, both buried under piles of stuffed animals we'd had since birth, she'd say, Night, Mar. I'd lift my baby blanket off my nose and say, Night, Joan. And then it was very peaceful in our room. The soft shadow of the night Staff stretching over our tiled floor. The occasional scream and hush of a nightmare down the hall.

I wasn't gaining much weight. I hovered just under my goal weight of 101 most of the time. The closer I got to it, or the days when I stood on the scale in Shawn's office and actually *was* 101, I cried. But for all the emotional "work" I was doing, one step forward and two more back, and for all the good effects it was having on my relationships, my sense of personal worth, and all that, I was not wholly convinced that I would be able to go on without an eating disorder, so I didn't throw myself headlong into recovery. I think I had the idea that if I could just get a little *happier,* my eating disorder simply wouldn't *matter* anymore. Maybe I could just have a *moderate* eating disorder when I got out, but not be so *miserable.* Just "diet normally" like "everyone else." Good luck. Basically this is the equivalent of a binge drunk deciding to be a social drinker, or—as I recently, ludicrously, attempted—a three-pack-a-day smoker deciding to smoke only at parties. Of course it was utterly terrifying to me to relinquish, even for a short period of time, some token eating-disordered behaviors. What if I forget *how*? What if, God forbid, I completely lose all control and decide not to *want* to have an eating disorder? I pictured myself, as we say in our catty little culture, "letting myself go," messy-haired, laying around being *relaxed* all the time. I would not, until many years later, notice that "letting myself go" might have other connotations: freeing myself, for example, from a fatal disorder and a compulsion to wear eyeliner at all times.

It took them a while to realize that, for several months, I'd been waking up at 5 A.M., moving as quietly as I could to the sink in my room, turning the tap ever-so-slightly, just enough for a trickle of water to slowly slide down the side of one of those big plastic cups, a Minnesota Twins cup. I drank one glass, then another and another, glancing over to Joan's sleeping figure as I silently gulped, drinking probably a gallon or more of water every morning, then lying in bed, waiting until it was time to get up. I held it until after my morning weigh-in, then asked during school to go to the bathroom, my bladder about to explode.

One day in school, Staff beckoned to me during class, pulled me out into the hall, and handed me a pee cup. I argued. It was a lost cause. My pee was so diluted it almost didn't qualify as pee. That was the end of that. My weight that afternoon magically dropped back down to my admission weight, and I was back on building restriction.

When I got my privileges back, I went on a pass and came back six pounds lighter than when I'd left. In truth, I have no idea what happened. I expect I just wasn't eating enough and probably walked too much. When you're in shaky medical condition, you often lose weight at the drop of a hat, as my present-day doctor will tell you. At any rate, they suspected laxatives, which I shrieked and hollered, honestly, that I hadn't taken. I told them: Take a blood test, for chrissakes! They did not. They ransacked my room. And found, of course, my stash of laxatives.

It didn't look good.

I cried. Because laxatives could have killed me, I might as well have had a loaded gun sleeping between sweaters in my closet. Staff put me on the highest level of restriction, worse than building restriction or room restriction or anything. Back onto twenty-four-hour watch I went. I sat, crying, in a blue plastic chair in the hall outside the Staff office. They brought me food on a plate. I remember trying to eat it and crying so hard I couldn't swallow the food, my bite of mashed potatoes soaked with tears and falling off the fork with a salty sad splat. No one was allowed to talk to me. All the other kids just walked by, trying to wave imperceptibly, trying to catch my eye and mouth: Hi. Duane had several fits in a row. I was furious with myself. I knew perfectly well that I'd just extended my stay by several months.

By summer I was getting very antsy. It was a good summer. I was healthier, beginning to eat pretty normally, in part because I wanted to go on the summer trips the unit was planning. We went hiking in Taylor's Falls, southern Minnesota. I have pictures of me in my father's old fishing hat and a backpack, almost smiling at the camera. David scowls, my roommate Joan looks scared, Duane is grinning madly, the Staff looks pleased, it's a bright day, we're standing on a big rock. We went to camp. I feigned superiority about the whole affair—camp, indeed—but nonetheless ate and ate and ate in the weeks before we went so I would be allowed to go. We went sailing and hiking and had campfires and ate pancakes at breakfast. I remembered then how much I liked pancakes, and put syrup on them with a little rush of abandon. I remember afternoons, between horseshoes and swimming, debating at length with a bemused Staff as to whether I ought to drink a regular soda. Will it make me gain weight? I worried. She said she doubted it very much. And besides, she said, popping open a Coke and grinning at me, Why does it matter? I took slow fizzy sips of Orange Slice, telling myself over and over that it was just sugar. Nothing wrong with that.

I have pictures of that trip, too; me sitting at the wheel of a boat, hair growing out a little, almost a crew cut, wearing a life jacket, a pair of shorts, my legs looking, to my present-day gaze, painfully thin. I am definitely smiling in this one, a great big I'm-steering-a-boat grin. We went to a Dairy Queen across the lake, where I had a very brief fit because there was no nonfat frozen yogurt. Then pulled myself together, smiled at the glowering Staff and Joan, who was pinching my arm, and ordered a Mr. Freeze in a loud voice. And slurped it up. I have a picture of me sticking my tongue out, cherry red, at the camera.

I was getting better. It scared me something terrible. But I felt safe. I felt like I could maybe deal with life. I actually had made friends with people who had no reason to like me. I'd actually gotten attached to my counselors. There is a picture of me and Joan curled up on my bed, looking like the teenage girls we were, a blanket over my knees, Joan giving me rabbit ears, a teddy bear tucked between us.

I both wanted to leave—with that same sort of cranky agitation you feel when you've been sick in bed awhile—and stay. Because I was happy. And because I was scared to get out. I'd never felt good about myself before, not really, and I was beginning to. I was actually working in therapy, trying to get a grip on who I was and why that was enough. In late summer, I began to page through the course catalog for the University of Minnesota's fall classes.[4]

I remember, one day in early September, sitting on a window ledge looking out at the street. I was journaling. For some reason it just hit me like a baseball in my stomach: I was going to have to give this up. The eating disorder. I was just going to have to let it go. Not part of it, all of it. No leaving Lowe House and just "dieting" a little here and there, no counting of units or calories or fat. None of it. I was going to have to keep eating on the outside the same way I was eating on the inside: normally.

I was patently aware that I didn't think I could do it.

---

[4] I have never technically graduated from high school. I acquired enough credits at Interlochen to graduate but was waylaid from my lifelong plan to start college at fifteen by fleeing the hospital for one year and spending the next locked up. I started college at seventeen and was granted a number of credits for the compulsive reading mentioned above. I got into the university by enrolling in a Post-Secondary Enrollment Option, a program for high school students who have run out of high school classes to take, and somehow just proceeded with college.

And then I did something I have regretted ever since. One day, in the evening group, a girl was talking about a frightening experience she'd had that day: A man had approached her in the park, scared the hell out of her. This brought up everyone's issues with abuse and fear and inappropriate behavior, etc., so the unit was in a bit of chaos. I got up and walked out of the room, sat down in the hall, and started bawling. A Staff came after me. After a few minutes I told him, through tears and gasping, that I'd been sexually abused by men in my father's theater when I was a child.

It was a lie.

It was not premeditated. It leapt into my brain and I spit it out. The subconscious is not always an ally with the better parts of the self, not always that kind "intuition" that magically leads us toward sunny rainbowed health. Sometimes it is pure id, pure unmitigated base need. In this case, a base need to hang on to my eating disorder at all costs. Just after I spit it out, I realized the effect it would have: The remainder of my time in Lowe House was spent dealing with this non-issue. It was a nightmare. My parents were completely torn apart—briefly, until they figured out that it couldn't have happened. All of the therapists were proud of me for dealing with this difficult issue. Everyone was almost relieved that there was a nice, pin-pointable reason for my total disembodiment, my selective amnesia, my sleep disturbances, my promiscuity, my fear of men, my issues of intimacy, my issues with trust, the whole nine yards. It all came back to the abuse, which never took place. In essence, I lobbed a firebomb to the right, and while everyone was chasing the firebomb, I disappeared stage left. Absolved. I created a straw man and he took all of the blame.

In truth, I do show all the signs of having been sexually abused, a fairly classic case of "post-traumatic stress disorder." In truth, I think therapists had suspected abuse and were waiting for me to "disclose" it when I felt "safe" enough. They had plenty of reasons to believe me—I showed the clinical signs—and no reason not to. My parents, for reasons known only to them, did not tell the therapists that they thought I was lying. But as was often the case with me in Lowe House and elsewhere, my oh-so-honest-and-open revelations were, at best, distractions—my teary-eyed attempts to end the bulimia at Interlochen that were purely an excuse to starve, my "genuine" interest in health in Methodist intended to speed up release, my "heartfelt" exploration of embodiment in California that was meant to keep my therapists, family, and friends focused on my "journey to wellness" rather than on my progressive deterioration. This time, though, I took distraction to a new level, from the realm of irrelevant truths to the realm of mirage.

I have never forgiven myself for doing this, and I doubt I ever will. It was purely self-serving, unbelievably short-sighted, inarguably another in an endless series of manipulations that were designed to keep me, and my eating disorder, away from prying eyes. And it worked.

I didn't have to deal with any of my real problems for the rest of my stay. I did this to get out. In late September I started school at the University of Minnesota, which seemed like the most fantastic thing that had ever happened to me. I left Lowe House every morning, took a bus to the U, took my classes, bused back. It was five hours of freedom. I remembered how much I loved to think, how much I loved work. I remembered that I was actually good at something other than starving and puking. I began to believe that I'd make it on the outside, that things would be all right. I was soaring through my classes, high on adrenaline, proud of my progress, hopeful about life.

I began to believe I was "well." At least well enough to leave. At least not crazy anymore. I plowed over my own fears about leaving and started pushing hard for release. It was granted.

Leaving was hard. I said good-bye to people I'd come to care about and trust, such as I trust. On November 5, 1991, after dinner, my father arrived at the door, helped me carry my things. It was dark out, the snow was deep, the air was sharp. We got into the car. I lit a cigarette, he pulled out a cigar, and we sat puffing away, grinning, smoke swirling blue around our heads.

We drove home.

On my release chart, the last notation is this:

"Recovered?"

7 Waiting for Godot

Minneapolis, 1991–1992

Vladimir: We're waiting for Godot.
Estragon: *(desparingly)* Ah! *(Pause)* You're sure it was here? . . . And what if he doesn't come?
Vladimir: We'll come back to-morrow.
Estragon: And then the day after to-morrow.
Vladimir: Possibly.
Estragon: And so on.
Vladimir: The point is—
Estragon: Until he comes.
Vladimir: You're merciless.

—Samuel Beckett

Winter 1991. I loved life. It was a very strange time, and I loved my life. Mornings, living in my parents' house, I'd wake up, put on my robe, step out onto the deck to smoke. Still dark, just beginning to get purple, breath coming in thick cold clouds. The silence of northern dawn broken only by the patter of a cardinal's wings, the crunch of my feet on the snow, the scratch of a fox's paws as it scooted in shadow over the frozen pond. I would get dressed, go upstairs, eat breakfast, make my lunch, walk up the hill to Valley View Road, catch the number six bus to Minneapolis, watch the suburban ramblers give way to the skyline of the city. I'd read the paper, review for classes. I loved college intensely. I was taking political science classes, getting into heated debates with teachers and classmates, writing papers, spending hours on end in the library. I got a job at the university's daily newspaper, on the environmental beat, which by sheer luck happened to be incredibly busy that year. At the end of the day, I'd take the bus home in the early dusk, eat dinner with my parents, go downstairs to study and work.

And study and work. And study and work some more. There was no sudden transition this time. It went slowly, so much so that I didn't see it coming. Gradually, the night just got longer. Gradually, it seemed, there were just more things I had to do. Gradually, breakfast shrank. And lunch. And dinner. There would not be a dramatic moment, this time, not for a while. In a way, I was starting over. Easing my way down.

Nights, at about eleven o'clock, I'd go upstairs to get my evening snack: a bowl of nonfat granola, covered with nonfat yogurt, honey, raisins. A big bowl of mush I'd mix up well. I'd flip off the kitchen light, carry the bowl downstairs again, sit down at the desk with my book, holding it open with my left hand. With my right, I performed my elaborate nightly food ritual: I picked out all of the raisins first, eating them one by one. Then I ate the yogurt—avoiding a single granola oat—licking it from the spoon, not taking whole spoonfuls, just enough to coat the spoon with a thin sheen of aspartame pink, and licking it off. This took some time. When I had gleaned all the yogurt that I could from the bowl, I ate the granola, completely soggy by this time, in tiny bites. This took about two and a half, three hours. When I was finished, I smoked my last cigarette and went to sleep. I would wake up a few hours later to get ready for school.

I didn't actually stop eating. I just started eating strange things. There aren't very many anoretics, actually, who flat-out do not eat. That's not a sustainable system, and even we know that. You have to eat enough to subsist. This time, I really believed that I was eating enough. I believed I was eating so much, in fact, that I had room to cut back. I cut back. Breakfast dwindled from cereal, fruit, and juice, to cereal, period. Then I stopped eating the cereal, grabbing an apple on my way out the door, hollering to my dad that I was late, no time for breakfast, I'll get something at school. Tossing the apple in the garbage can at the bus stop with a hollow *thunk*. Lunch went from being a normal sandwich and fruit, to low-cal bread—it tastes exactly like air and is about that filling—with nonfat mayo and mustard, a tomato slice, and a piece of nonfat cheese. I did keep eating dinner, since I was eating with my parents and couldn't get out of it. I began, of course, to lose weight. Not fast. Just enough to stop getting my period again, just enough to feel a little cold. And a little more obsessed with my weight.

Saturdays, I stayed at home, sat at the kitchen table, staring at huge bowls of microwaved frozen corn and peas, drowned in salt and butter-flavored powder that looked like pollen. I ate the peas first, then the corn. One at a time. With a fork. Sometimes I ate a piece of melted non-fat cheese on a piece of low-cal bread. But I was eating. My parents were worried and tried not to say so. I told them, Hey, but I'm eating! And they nodded and tried to smile. I stared into my bowl of corn and peas, chasing the peas, stabbing them with the tines of my fork, one by one.

I ate, certainly, even was "committed" to eating. I was halfway under the impression that I was, in fact, trying to stay well. I just wanted to see if I could cut back a little bit. On eating, on health. The meal plan they'd given me at Lowe House underwent a few alterations, the most notable being the complete elimination of fat. I was willing, perfectly willing, to eat. Just no fat. Ever. Not even a trace. This often happens in eating disorders: caught, you change tactics, you change tempo or type of obsession. I slowed down, stopped focusing on calories, and became obsessed with fat.

I was thin when I came home from Lowe House, and I didn't notice myself getting thinner. At my weekly appointment at TAMS, I was surprised when another pound or two had fallen away. Kathi worried, but not too much, not yet. I was doing good work in therapy, my tears genuine, my laugh quicker to surface, my enthusiasm for life more real, more lasting. I was making plans for the future that weren't so terrifying, now that I was doing better. I applied, in late winter, to a number of colleges, none of them in Minnesota. We all believed I would be ready, the following fall, to leave again.

I was dating some, nothing serious, mostly nice guys I'd met in classes or in cafés off campus. I was beginning to get some feeling back in my body. My experience of myself was still primarily visual—what do I look like, am I attractive, what is the power of my body over others—but there was also a small, creeping element of the experiential, a tiny thrum of pleasure here and there. I remember one night, standing at a bus stop with a man I was seeing, when he pulled me close. I remember the feeling of his wool sweater against my cheek, the sound of his heart beating layers below. I remember a warmth seeping through me, and the cold fingers of wind pulling through my hair.

Now, with all these things milling about in my memory, I do not understand, in retrospect, what happened. I should've known better, I should've called myself on all the lies I was telling myself—I'm eating enough, I'm doing all right, I'm healthy. I was happy. I had learned, or thought that I'd learned, that I was a valuable person. I understood that I needed to eat to live, and I wanted to live. I said to myself: It takes time, it's not that easy, you can't expect yourself to be perfect this soon. There are altogether too many "empowering" things that the professionals tell you that can be twisted around and turned against yourself. I had heard a few too many times that if I threw up, it was just a "slip," if I stopped eating for a little while it didn't *really* mean I was relapsing. How long is a little while? It stretches out, one week, two weeks, three, and you're back where you started. Professionals give anoretics and bulimics way too much credit for having their brains in order: You have to be patient with yourself, they said, you have to be nurturing to yourself, be nice to yourself. And so, as I went through another day without food, as I crunched over the snowy bridge crossing the Mississippi, mittened hands held to my frozen face, I said to myself: I have to be patient, I'm being nurturing to myself by not expecting too much of myself, I will not push myself too hard today, so I guess we'll just have some coffee for lunch. I sat at the long tables in the student union, smoking, bent over my coffee and books, watching the people around me laugh and eat, and I thought, It's okay because I'm giving myself a break right now.

We all do this. I've never met an eating-disordered person who could not come up with an astonishing battalion of solid-sounding, intellectualized reasons why they can't eat. I listen to my friend Connie say to me over the phone, indignant, "But I just CAN'T eat as much as they're telling me to eat. It's ridiculous, this business of *three* meals a day," she huffs. I ask, "How much can you eat?" She says, with finality, "One meal." In the hospital, women shriek and holler about how much they're eating: "But NO ONE eats this much!"

Unfortunately, that has some truth to it. There are precious few women who eat normally. You get out of the hospital, look around at what other people are eating, and realize the nice little meal plan you're on—though you need it to stay healthy—is not the norm. You start cutting back. And back. You forget that you have a habit of cutting back until there's nothing left to cut. I said to my family and therapist and friends: I really am eating, I really am doing better, of course I'm still a little weird about food, I'm working on it, *dammit.*

And I thought, sometimes, about the day in Lowe House when I'd sat at the window and realized I had to give all of it up. I knew very well that I was not giving it up. I was hanging on, as so many of us do, to some small part of it, to a part so small it seems a mere token, nothing dangerous, a talisman of sickness, kept in the pocket, rubbed between finger and thumb. I told myself it would be all right, just hanging on to this little bit. And I knew, in the back of my mind, that it would not.

The year rolled over on its back and died. Midwinter, I stopped sleeping. After dinner, I'd drive back over to the university district, sit in a grungy all-night café, the name of which changed often. Dimly lit and noisy, tables that rocked on their stands, chairs with ripped vinyl seats, the wood of the tables scarred deeply with carved words, poems, epithets, signs, the bathroom walls covered with graffiti from floor to ceiling, mirror obscured with paint. A strange crowd came and went: students and vagrants, dealers and runaways, regular joes and complete loonies. Coffee was seventy-five cents and refills were a quarter. I brought a stack of books and a notebook, packs of cigarettes, and sat coiled in a chair in the corner, rubbing my eyes, red in the almost tangible haze of smoke, swallowing coffee so thick it left sludge in the bottom of the cup. Reading Bertrand Russell and John Stuart Mill and Marx. Eyeing the cases of muffins and cookies. Getting hungrier as the night wore on. The music they played, grating, banging, throbbing, crashing music, fading into the back of my mind as I read, occasionally looking up from the pages of my book to watch people shouting at one another over the cacophony, or staring intently down at their chessboards and cards, lighting cigarettes behind cupped hands, bodies bumping into bodies in the crowd. I gave cigarettes to those who asked, pocketed their proffered quarters and used them for refills, spoke briefly to the various figures who stopped at my table, Whatcha reading? What's your name? You've got nice eyes, turning my page and wrapping my foot in the strap of my purse under the table.

When I got too hungry to read anymore, thoughts turning repeatedly to food—Should I get a muffin? Just a muffin, no big deal. Should I? Should I? Blueberry or raspberry? How much fat in a muffin? They're big muffins, how many calories?—I slammed my book shut and left. Out the door, onto the street corner where a small throng watched each midnight passer pass, this in the early phases of grunge, ragged clothes hanging loose on the thin figures of middle-aged men and teenage girls, boys in their twenties and very young women with babies and toddlers who hung on the cold metal stalks of the street signs, NO PARKING, SNOW EMERGENCY ROUTE. My breath appeared, white against the dark, and I walked in small steps over the icy sidewalk back to my car. I drove down Riverside, down Cedar, then hit the freeway back to the suburbs, 35 South to 62 West, taking the curves too quickly, light from the freeway lamps running in sheets over the windshield, over my hands. The freeway mostly empty, the houses clustered near off ramps asleep. I drove my father's red car, a stick shift, cup of coffee in my left hand, cigarette in my mouth. Tired. A little lightheaded, six, seven hours since I'd eaten my last minimeal.

The roads in Minnesota, in winter, are very slick. This was a winter of black ice. Black ice is what happens when it snows heavily, then warms up a little bit in the afternoon. At sundown, the temperature drops and the melted snow on the freeways freezes into thick sheets. You can't see that it's ice because it's too smooth, it just looks like the road ahead of you. Black.

After midnight on a night with snow in the forecast. Cloud cover. No moon, no stars, little light. Jittery on caffeine. What I remember is this: I was bent forward over the steering wheel, trying to see. I had thrown my cigarette out the window, had both hands tightly wrapped around the wheel. Shaking. My head wouldn't clear. I shook it, as if trying to get water out of my ears. I shifted to a lower gear. I was in the right lane. Coming up on an entrance ramp, I saw headlights coming toward me from behind. I swerved into the left lane. And blacked out.

There was an incredible grating sound, deafening, and then I was thrown into the steering wheel, over and over and over again, and something was hitting me hard and everything was spinning and the median kept coming at me. Then it stopped. I sat there. A few cars sped by. There were cop lights, an officer pulling me out of the car by the arm, asking me questions I didn't understand. I was sitting in the cop car, looking at the wreck. My father's car was completely totaled, each corner of the car shoved back into the body. I didn't have any idea what had happened. Looked like I'd hit the median with one corner, bounced back, spun, hit, spun, hit, spun, hit. I sat there thinking about the muffin. I should've gotten a muffin, I thought. My neck hurt. Smoke rose from the folded hood of the car, very white in the dark. The cop shook his head. You're a lucky kid, he said to me. I said, My father's gonna kill me.

A tow truck took me and the car home. The headlights must've woken my father, because he was standing on the front porch in his pajamas, looking very fierce. The conversation that ensued gave us fits of glee later, but it wasn't funny at the time.

I hopped out of the truck and stood there. He hollered: WHAT THE HELL DID YOU DO TO MY CAR?

I hollered: I'm JUST FINE, thank you!

He hollered: Well, I FIGURED that, you're standing there, aren't you? Now WHAT in the HELL did you do to my CAR?

He bought a new car. He told me later that he had a sinking feeling I'd crashed because I wasn't eating enough, probably because I was light-headed or blacked out. We didn't discuss that. I turned away and said, Back off, leave me alone.

Very shortly after that, everything fell apart. Again. I'd been able to pretend, up to that point, that nothing was really wrong, not seriously wrong anyway. That ended.

It was January. A cold spell hit. One of my stepbrothers and his girlfriend came to visit. My parents went up north with them for a long weekend. I stayed home because I wanted to get some studying done for classes that were starting soon. It started as if it had never stopped: I unlocked and opened the front door one day after spending an afternoon at the library. I walked into the kitchen, set my bags down, went to the cupboard—the dangerous cupboard, the one by the door, wherein lurked the bad foods, cereals and crackers—opened it, took out the cereal, poured a bowl, and started eating.

And eating. I ate until there was no room left, went to the bathroom, puked my guts out, washed my face and hands, returned to the kitchen. Time must've passed because outside the window it was dusk, then dark. I turned on the kitchen light, blazing and bright in the yellow room, the rest of the house still dark, the dogs in the basement still whining to be let out, and I stood at the counter, shoveling cereal into my mouth on automatic pilot. I ran out of cereal and moved on to bread, ran out of bread and moved on to eggs, leftovers, ice cream, crackers, stopping every so often to puke in the dark bathroom, staggering back to the kitchen, bumping into door frames and walls that suddenly stuck out in strange places, moving onto the soup that my father had made for me to eat over the weekend. I ate all the soup and threw it up, whole noodles and carrots and peas flooding the toilet bowl, spattering the walls, spinning away when I flushed.

By midnight or so, I'd eaten everything in the house except the lime marmalade that had been sitting at the back of the refrigerator for as long as I could remember. I didn't eat the dog food, either. But I thought about it. It occurred to me to let the dogs out, so I did, then fed them, picked up my keys, got in the car, and drove to the grocery story, intending to buy all the foods I'd eaten so no one would know.

No coat, no hat, no gloves. Freezing cold and short of breath, dizzy, I got out of the car and went into the store. The lights were blinding. I squinted and went from row to row with my basket, desperately trying to remember what I'd eaten. I had no memory of the event whatsoever except that I'd gone to the refrigerator for the millionth time, opened it, and realized with horror that it was empty. I couldn't remember what my parents kept in their house. Blank. I couldn't even remember if I'd ever seen them eat. I wandered up and down the aisles. This, I will later read, is known as "cruising" and is often the precursor to gastric rupture, which is fatal. Suddenly I am at the checkout counter with a basket full of food. I'm paying. I'm loading the bags into the car. I'm driving out of the parking lot.

Less than a mile away from the house, I have no idea how to get home.

I panic. All I can think about is my need to eat. Now. This minute. I need to eat, fast, I need to eat a lot of things very fast. My mouth needs to be full, I need to be chewing on something, something salty. I pull over to the side of the road, crawl into the backseat, and start digging through the bags, pulling out things I don't remember buying, finally landing on a bag of potato chips, getting back into the front seat, ripping open the bag, stuffing a handful in my mouth, pulling back onto the road, driving aimlessly around until I recognize a road and follow it home.

In the house, I dump the bags on the kitchen table, the floor, the counter, and clear a space for myself. I keep eating. I mix up blueberry muffins and let them cook while I suck down everything in sight, run to the bathroom, desperately wanting to rid myself of the feeling of fullness, throw up, run back, frantic to get the fullness back. I stand there eating until all the food is gone. All of it. Gone.

I look up from the empty bowl in front of me and catch sight of my bloated, hideous face reflected in the dark window over the sink.

I lean down and throw up.

Flip the garbage disposal switch, rinse out the sink. Turn off the kitchen light, feel in the dark for the staircase's handrail. I make it most of the way down before I feel that weightlessness creeping through my body, the dark getting darker, before I feel myself start to pitch forward and take flight, soaring into a black hole.

I woke up in the morning, rancid at the foot of the stairs, rumpled in my clothes. Sitting up, my head pounded, I held my fists to my temples. I went upstairs and looked at the wreckage. Empty boxes everywhere, wrappers and cartons and dishes and brown paper bags. The morning-after effect was not lost on me. I felt like I had the worst hangover in the world and really couldn't remember the night before.

Absolved by amnesia, I did it again. For the next three days.

There are two ways to answer why, after a year without bulimia, I fell right back into it when my parents left. Maybe it was because I needed them there, I wasn't ready to be on my own, I felt abandoned. I doubt it. I think it was something else, something so long established that it didn't occur to me *not* to reboot the bulimia. To this day, I cannot stand in my parents' kitchen without thinking about all of the possible foods I might eat. This doesn't happen in my house, or in anyone else's. It is only at my parents' home. I think my eating disorder by that point in my life was pure habit, a habit more deeply ingrained than I or anyone else had thought. I think that merely being alone in my parents' kitchen flipped a switch in my head, and a glaring neon sign started to flash: BINGE.

It didn't scare me until Monday, the first day of classes. I went into the bathroom during a break to take a dump. When I stood up, there was nothing in the toilet but blood. It wasn't my period. I hadn't had my period in years, save for a few short months in Lowe House. I tried to ignore it. It kept happening all day. At the end of the day, scared, I went into a phone booth and called a medical information line. I didn't manage to mention the probable cause. I was told to get to a doctor immediately.

I did not. I decided the safer course was to stop eating. Eating was too dangerous. Obviously I couldn't handle eating. Clearly I was too weak and spineless to be eating. I sat in the bathroom stall with my head in my hands, willing my insides to stop bleeding. I came out of the stall, splashed water on my face without looking at it, checked the size of my ass in the mirror. Fat. I was sure I'd put on weight over the weekend. Lots of it, tons of weight. I stopped at the pay phone again, called my dad to say I'd be home late, I had a lot of studying to do.

He told me the sewer had backed up. Again. All over the basement, it backed up, Marya, do you care to explain this?

I said: I had the flu. All weekend. Terrible flu. Gotta go. Bye.

I have never been so mortified in my life. If my stepbrother and his girlfriend hadn't been there, it wouldn't have been so bad. Their opinion of me mattered a lot. And here I was, clogging the sewer, flooding the bathroom and basement with my vomit, disgusting my sister-in-law-to-be so completely that she asked my mother, very nicely, for some new towels in case theirs had been inadvertently splashed with puke.

But we didn't talk about it until they left. My parents put me through the inquisition, Come on, honey, just tell us the truth. (I AM, I swear to GOD I had the flu!) But honey, I don't mean to be gross, but that's an awful lot of vomit for someone who just had the flu. Honey, there were noodles and peas from the soup that I made. (Well, of COURSE there were! I thought maybe the soup would stay DOWN, but it DIDN'T, I'm SORRY, why doesn't anyone fucking TRUST me?) Well, if you're sure . . .

In my charts for therapy that week:

> 1/16. Reports she had the flu over the weekend. Sewer backed up. Appears thinner.

To appear thinner in a week's time, you have to lose a fair amount of weight. In my eyes, I looked like the pig I thought myself to be. Bulimia scared the hell out of me. Anorexia is so disembodied, so imperceptible for such a long time, so socially sanctioned, that you can go a long time clinging to your belief that there's nothing wrong with it. The minute you stick your fingers down your throat, you know damn well something's wrong. You know you're out of control. The first time you ever eat without stopping, the first time you ever feel that sudden wave of need crash over you, feel your face tighten in desperation for food, any food, *now*, you know something's wrong. And let me tell you, the first thing that comes to mind is *not* "Gee, I must be really upset about something. Let's sit down and think about that." The first thing that comes to mind is: more food. And then, the horrible, nauseating realization that you are, in fact, as uncontrollable, as needy, as greedy, as you've always secretly suspected.

Once you realize that, there's no reason to stop. You say: Fuck it, then. I'm a fat cow ugly bitch weak slug lardass and I might as well keep eating.

But like I said, bulimia has always scared the hell out of me—precisely because of the inevitable horror that hits you midway through a binge. I have been known to go to great lengths to avoid pain of any sort. The pain of feeling like you are, truly and eternally, a filthy, bilious, greedy slob is intolerable. When I became seriously anoretic for the first time, it was the first time in my life when I was not afraid of myself. Fucked up, sure. But from then on out, I would always connect my ability to get control over my rampant needs and desires to my ability to starve.

The following weekend, my parents were gone again. I had been working all week, trying to talk myself down, trying to reassure myself that I'd be fine, I wouldn't binge, I just wouldn't eat at all if that was what it took. That seemed to be what it took. On Friday, after classes, I went home, let the dogs out, sat stiffly in a kitchen chair, reading the paper, trying not to think about food.

There are reasons people binge. One of them is malnutrition. That's what was going on, and I knew it. I knew perfectly well that I'd been eating way too little for a couple of months and was now paying the price for it. It did not cross my mind that a surefire way to stop obsessing about food was to eat properly. The only way I could do this, in my mind, was to keep myself away from food completely. I hung out with the dogs for a while, then got back into the car and drove to my little café with a mammoth pile of books, intending to stay all night.

Which I pretty much did. Until near dawn, anyway.

It was 1 A.M. when he swung around a post, long hair hanging down onto my table, dangling dangerously close to my coffee. I moved my cup. The noise was deafening. It was always packed in there on weekends. Minneapolis being the land of ten thousand treatment centers, the coffee shops and cafés are often jammed like San Francisco bars, standing room only after 10 P.M., bass pumping through the floor so hard your table throbbed and your books shivered. I was reading Bertrand Russell's *Unpopular Essays*. His hair was blond and I heard him holler over the din, "HI!"

I glanced up and said HI.

He asked: CAN I SIT?

I answered: NO.

He said: MY NAME IS DAVE.

I said: GOOD.

He sat. He leaned close to me across the small table, stuck out his hand, and said, What's your name?

For the next few hours he talked. And talked and talked. I decided that I would sleep with him. I did this, went about mentally seducing men just for kicks. The point was never the sex. I hadn't ever enjoyed sex much, and wouldn't for several years. The point was the game, and the game was not simply to get someone into bed. Men are embarrassingly easy to seduce. The game was to get them to fall in love with you first, or get them to think they were in love with you, think you were the most astonishing woman they'd ever met in their entire lives, and if things went according to plan, fuck them up forever.

By about 4 A.M. he had decided he was in love with me. Which, though a little strange, since I'd barely spoken, was fine with me. It's always nice when someone's in love with you. Gives you leverage. I took him home. We made a fire, lay on the floor making abstract plans, lying to each other because we could. We went to bed and stayed there for the weekend. I don't know what happened, precisely, but something did, and I found myself rolling around in the sheets with a man I knew only as Dave and having, arguably, the best sex of my life. Certainly the most startling sex. The most raucous, noisy sex, shocking me in the moments when I would see myself from the outside, unrecognizable, bare and laughing and crying out and who the *hell* was this woman, falling back into a deep, deep sleep, content and deliciously sore?

Sunday I dropped him off at the café, told him not to call me again. It was fun, I said, but you know how it is. Take care, see you around. I drove off on my way to work. I remember it now as a film clip, a voyeuristic sort of memory, watching from the door. I remember it as the blue curve of a woman's back lit by moonlight through the window, the box of condoms spilled by the side of the bed, the ring of a wordless voice shooting out through a silent house.

It was too much for me. It was too intense. It made me too hungry, afterward, too easy in my body, too careless as I sprawled on the floor eating apples and cheese. It made me want more, and that wouldn't do. Sex and women with eating disorders are strange bedfellows. We approach it in different ways. Some women avoid it like the plague, much more than I did. Some women seek it out as a source of marginal intimacy, an oasis of companionship in a desert of isolation. Others, like me, use it as power, but that's a little different: The power game is the mental foreplay, the sex itself is almost irrelevant, and when the sex takes over your body, makes you lose control, you've lost the game. Some women, as we laughed about it in the hospital, use it simply to burn calories, but then there's the bummer of having to be naked and seen in the flesh. Some use the limited pleasure it brings as a fleeting reminder that the body can, in fact, feel something, anything, other than hunger. But that, too, backfires, because the desire for sex is a hunger in and of itself. Some, and this was me, too, use it as just another form of self-destruction, throwing the body around like an old coat, into bed and out of bed with whoever comes wandering by. When I slept with Dave, I had a hard time understanding what was happening. Wait a minute here, this isn't what sex is. Sex is staring at the ceiling and saying oh-baby oh-baby and thinking about the size of your thighs. What the hell is this? I was used to sleeping with people because I endlessly found myself in identical situations where it was easier to just fuck them than to say no. Obviously I was in those situations because it gave me a rush to get there. I never really cared for the follow-through. What happened that weekend was altogether different. I didn't know why I'd done it. It didn't occur to me to just grin and say, Why not? All the times I'd slept with people I didn't care about, didn't enjoy sleeping with, I never once felt guilty. This time, I felt like a slut. All that moaning and eating naked. Good lord.

My father found the condoms. There is, of course, the question of what the hell my father was doing, digging around in my drawers. There is, furthermore, the question of what the hell my father was doing, getting pissed off that I was having sex rather than being at least marginally relieved that I had the brains to *use* condoms. We got in an incredible fight. I screamed at him for invading my privacy, he screamed at me for breaking the rules, betraying his trust, having sex in his house, having sex at all. I screamed at him for being such a blind fool that he'd missed my growing up. I screamed at him for being so fucking overprotective. He screamed that I was too young to be having sex.

At the time, I felt that he was being utterly unreasonable. In retrospect, I can't say what "too young" for having sex is. I was seventeen. I'd been having sex for a good long time, so it didn't seem too out of the ordinary to me. Maybe he was right. He tried to ground me, but I think it seemed a little ridiculous at that point, even to him, given the fact that I was a full-time student with a full-time job. What was notable was the virulence with which he attacked my choices, and the measure to which it was painfully clear that the problem was not that I was too young to be having sex, but that he was afraid of my growing up, and that he would do anything in his power to prevent that. The problem was, I had already grown up.

As was his way, my father flipped out about it. This is a subject my father and I have never discussed in any depth—because it is such a delicate issue, because I don't know that he understands it any more than I do—so my thoughts on this are speculative and subjective. The easy part is understanding the fear he seemed to feel about my leaving him with no one to take care of. The hard part is trying to figure out why he was so incredibly angered by my involvement with men and with sex. Say it's because he didn't want me to grow up too fast. That's reasonable. He wouldn't be the first father who felt that no one would ever be good enough for his little girl. Say it's because he wanted me to stay a little girl, say he had a few problems with women, say he was threatened by women, say he was angry with women, say he had a bit of a problem with their independence from him, their control over him. Say he didn't want me to become one of them. Say he needed me to need him. Say he wanted to be the most important man in my life. He wouldn't be the first father to feel threatened by the entrance of other men into a daughter's world.

And he wouldn't be the first to feel more than a little threatened by the advent of a daughter's sexuality. The child is developing a side of herself to which he has no access, and over which he has no control. I have spoken before of the highly idealized relationship between some women with eating disorders and their fathers. That relationship balances precariously on the daughter playing a dual role: that of innocent child, and that of companion. When the innocent child part disappears, when she becomes a rebellious, foul-mouthed teenager fucking strangers in your basement, the relationship dissolves. The child you loved and were loved by has disappeared.

Ideally, a father can come to terms with his child becoming a woman, can come to accept the other men in her life. Eventually my father did this. It just took a while. During my short stay at home—my father's growing hysteria over the loss of his child, and his attempts to reverse the course of nature—I was completely confused. It sent me into a state of equally hysterical self-defense. This also put my mother in the horrendous position of mediating what looked too much like a bad breakup. As has always been the case in my family, my father and I loudly fought it out in the living room, the kitchen, the dining room. My mother and father fought it out behind closed doors, and I honestly had no idea what was going on. Nor, I think, did they.

I shut down. My father needed me to need him, and I could not. I had grown up (normal), and decided I would never need anything again (not). And the last thing I needed, I thought, was some bastard trying to hold me back. I hated my younger self with an intensity that frightens me even now. Of course I resented and deeply feared anything that threatened my chances of escaping who I'd once been. My father became my nemesis, the symbolic focus of my fury at everything I'd ever been and never wanted to be. After the Condom Incident, I doubt there was a day we did not go head-to-head on the issue of my independence. We both became incredibly desperate people. He was desperate to keep me. I was desperate to get the hell away from him.

Conventional wisdom says that eating disorders are a means of stopping time. The line goes, halting physical development at a prepubescent stage gives the eating-disordered person a symbolic sense of safety: safe in childhood, safe in the bosom of the family, safely at a remove from the big bad monster of sexual maturity and its implication of adulthood and responsibility. I do not think this is always accurate. I have looked at this long and hard, trying to fit my life, my personality, my experience of eating disorders into this framework. My life and I just keep spilling out. We don't fit. Maybe, if we stretch it, we can say that in the year before I was to leave home (again), my eating disorder reappeared because I subconsciously wanted to stay at home with my father (who drove me bats) and mother (who barely spoke), in the warm and comfortable womb of childhood (which was shitty), avoiding sexual maturation (which I didn't much like but wasn't afraid of) and responsibility (which I craved). But that's really stretching it.

The only thing I can come up with is that maybe, in some small way, my anorexic body was an apology to my father for having become a woman. Even that is problematic. It's far more plausible to me that my anorexic body was a confused statement directed more at the world than at my father, both an apology for being a woman and a twisted attempt to prove that a woman can be as good as a man. There are many women who get eating disorders primarily because they're afraid of adulthood, so afraid that they will do anything to prevent it. But I was so afraid of being dragged back into childhood that I would have done anything to avoid it. The reading of eating disorders needs to be more complex than the rather Freudian analysis that sees the anorexic body as symbolic of regression. It is equally possible that the anoretic is attempting to demonstrate—badly, ineffectively, narcissistically—a total independence from the helpless state of childhood, from the infinite needs that she recognizes in herself and will annihilate in any way she can.

I remember childhood, even now, as an embarrassing time, a time of weakness and need. Being put in Lowe House, however much it helped me recognize the acceptability of some basic human needs, was a setback in my grand plans, and having to live in my parents' house was even worse. My father's need was palpable and painful and suffocating, and I'm sure that my hell-bent race toward adulthood was equally painful to him. But he was not in a very good place just then, and had a very difficult time separating himself and his needs from his expectations of me. My mother had a tendency to float off waving her hands whenever my father and I got into conflict. I know that they fought about this. I know that my mother was trying to get my father to back off and just let me grow up, and I also know that my father felt that we were ganging up on him, as he always had and always does, despite the fact that my mother and I did not share a single conversation on the matter.

My mother once told a therapist that she felt like she was living with two crazy people. My father and I were both very hurt by this. In retrospect, I don't blame her one bit for feeling that way. And even as I write, I know that my father will read this and feel like I'm siding with her. He always has. My mother always feels like I'm siding with him. I felt stuck in the middle, of course, but more than that, I felt sorry for both of them. They were both running around licking twenty-year-old wounds, grabbing me, pulling me between them, pointing at their emaciated, manic daughter, and saying, "See?"

As if I proved anything. They both had the rather self-important assumption that the world revolved around them, and that my problems were their fault. I had pretty much tired of thinking about their Role in my Problems. I was tired of their endless petty bitching, tired of my father's neediness, tired of my mother's facile peacemaking, and wanted to get on with my life.

Here we find another turning point. I'd had my eating disorder for nine years. The causes were endless and cross-referenced and footnoted and referred to other causes. The major etiology was, by that time, my personality, and the very simple, inescapable eating disorder itself. It was habit by then. My parents could've been the sweetest, most understanding of parents, my culture could've been the most feminist and egalitarian of cultures, and I would still have gotten worse because my eating disorder had become a part of me, the way I dealt with my own brain, my emotions, the world I was living in, my daily life. Everything was filtered through the lens of anorexia and bulimia.

Did my family set it off again? Did my father's neediness and my fear of it spark relapse? My mother's distance? An article I read? A woman I saw? Not likely. What probably happened is that, faced with a number of things in my life that I didn't like, I turned to my eating disorder because I had never, ever figured out how to fucking *deal*.

Similarly, it was tough to say whether my teeth-bared, hissing demands to be left the hell alone—"Get OVER it," I'd holler, "I'm FINE, back OFF, I JUST want to get ON with my LIFE"—were a normal stage for any ambitious seventeen-year-old. Perhaps it was just a normal desire for a little breathing space after the microscopic scrutiny of the hospital and loony bin. Maybe my desperation was more complex. My desire to leave Minneapolis, and my family, may actually have been a desire to leave me behind and become someone else.

I suspect it was the latter. A pattern was well established by that point: I'd spent the last several years plotting escape routes, using them more to escape a persona than a place. Even way back at my intake interview at TAMS, when asked what I would change about my life, I had replied, "I would move." Not the usual reply—make new friends, take up a hobby, get along with parents better, improve my grades—just "move." Not until I was nineteen would it occur to me that the old adage is true—everywhere you go, there you are—and even then I didn't stop moving.

At seventeen, I was under the strong impression that everywhere you go, you'll find a brand-new you, the way you happen to bump into a friend in a café. In each new place, I always turned out to be someone I liked better than the old me. Someone without a past following her around like toilet paper stuck to the heel of her shoe. Someone who spoke less often and less rapidly, smiled without showing her teeth rather than grinning lopsidedly, wore sunglasses and had cool shoes. Who was known neither as that-silly-kid or as the-incurable-crazy-sick-person; a woman who was not known at all.

The year I moved home, some switch flipped in me, cutting off the lights in the rational part of my mind, shutting out the self-knowledge I'd gained in Lowe House, and leaving me with a blind, desperate desire, more virulent than ever, to get rid of the self that I hated and make me new. Success, I firmly believed, was the key to my salvation. It would absolve me of the sins of the flesh and the soul, lift me out of the life I hated. "Success" meant a perfect career, perfect relationships, perfect control over my life and myself—all of which depended on a perfect me, which depended in turn on me living inside a perfect body. I did not stop to think about the drawbacks of forfeiting youth and health for the sake of success. There was no contest. The fact that I did not examine the connection I made between success and self-annihilation would, in the year to come, nearly kill me.

I spent less and less time around my parents. I stopped bingeing almost as soon as I started and switched back to starving. By February, I was practically living at the newspaper office, pushing for more assignments, covering as many stories as I possibly could. My job technically demanded only thirty hours a week, but I began spending most of my time in the newsroom, on stories, tapping away, phone tucked on my shoulder, racing off to cover a story, grabbing frozen yogurt on my way back to my desk, letting it melt while I worked. I loved the job. I was covering several major statewide issues, getting friendly with the state legislators and U.S. senators who were involved, making "connections," doing lunch with so-and-so, filling notebook after notebook with my scrawled notes, scooping the major Twin Cities newspapers and roaring in delight with the rest of the staff early mornings, newspapers flying, when we beat out the big boys for a good story. I went to therapy, quite consciously constructing a picture of myself that would convince TAMS that I was getting better. We began to taper off my Prozac and my appointments in accordance with my verbal assurances that I was on the right track.

> 2/5/92: Near recovery. Marya indicates a desire to terminate weight monitoring.

A note is submitted to TAMS from me: "I have had no difficulty in continuing a healthy lifestyle and maintaining my weight."

I sat in the stairwell of the news offices eating the tomato out of my sandwich, throwing the rest away, smoking and guzzling coffee while I flipped through pages and pages of morning notes. Scribbling questions in the margins, chatting with the other reporters, laughing a lot. I was high on life. I'd just gotten early admission to Reed, the only school I'd applied to for early admission, and the rest of the admissions were starting to roll in. I'd see them in a pile on my desk when I stepped in late at night, and read them, grinning: It's working, I'm going to make it. Life was good.

I sat in a café early mornings, reading papers, drinking coffee. One day I remember vividly: I was wearing a short skirt and a green blouse and spring was beginning. I tossed my jacket over my shoulder and sauntered down the sunny street. Buds on the trees. I walked into work and sat down at my desk. There was a kick-ass photographer on the staff who sometimes appeared at my desk, spreading out negatives for one of my stories, bending over them, our heads close together, gesturing wildly, and then he'd shoot off to the darkroom again. His name was Mark. He showed up at my desk that particular morning and hollered (he was always hollering), HI! I laughed and he stood there a minute, looking befuddled. I said, "Yes?" And he said, "You look very nice today." I stammered. We sat there looking at each other for a minute more, dazed.

The spell broke and he was in motion again. I had a major story running the next day, what did I want him to shoot? He crouched down next to my chair and we jabbered and waved our hands and he tapped my shoulder lightly as he left and I stared at my blank computer screen for a while and thought, Oh, no.

It was not a good time to fall in love.

Nights got later and later. I'd come in the back door quietly so as not to wake my parents, and I'd sit down at my desk, keep working. My father and I had a final blowout and I left, moved into a friend's house until I found a place to live. I went to therapy less and less often. Mark and I began seeing more of each other, leaning against each others' desks and talking a mile a minute, maniacs both, skipping out for coffee, just the two of us or with other reporters, heading back to the office in a dark that got warmer daily. We went to dinner one night, alone. We drank a lot of wine. We lay on the living room floor of his house. I read him some of my work. It was very late. When I was done, he took my hand, turned it palm upward, carefully traced the lines. Threaded his fingers with mine.

> 3/4. Marya refuses to be weighed. Blood pressure orthostatic, very low temperature. Body fat 14.5% (in Lowe House, BF=19%). Feels bony! Suspect reemerging eating disorder.

Mark and I fell horribly, horribly in love. I was bouncing back and forth from friends' houses to my parents' house. My father screamed at me about Mark's motorcycle, about Mark in general, said he was too old for me (he was twenty-five). He was wild, my father said, I was growing up too fast. I spent my days in classes and the newsroom and all over the city. Mark and I drove anywhere and everywhere, talking of politics and the world and journalism and facts and thoughts and anything at all, crashing at the Motel 6 and laughing and rolling around until daylight and then heading back to work. I ate a carton of yogurt, sprawled belly down on the bed while we pored over magazines, saying, Listen, listen! and reading heatedly to each other all night until the magazines were kicked to the foot of the bed in our haste for motion and heat.

The plan had been that I would transfer to Reed. It was where I wanted to go, I'd been very clear about that, it was my first choice. Julian and I had been planning, in our letters, to go there together. They had an excellent political science program. But then I got a letter from American University offering me an obscenely large scholarship, larger than any I'd been offered. My parents said, Just think about it. Consider it. I considered it and said I wanted to go to Reed. They said they would pay for me to go out to Washington, D.C., just to look. Just to see if I liked it. I remember one evening, I was staying with them that night, painting my nails. I remember my red nails, my father asking, Have you thought about it? I had. Washington, D.C. It was the top of the line, the *Post* there, infinite internships, connections. I knew a few politicians, it was tempting. I said I'd go. Just to look.

The trip changed everything.

There is something wrong with Washington, D.C. For all the time I've spent there, I've never quite been able to put my finger on what it is—there are the obvious things, of course, the palpable greed, the thrum of excessive power, the unbelievable racism, the city itself a total political and social shambles. But beyond these, there is something *wrong* with Washington, D.C. There is a tight-faced look, a haggard and driven look that people wear as they race down the streets, shoving past one another on the subway, bashing one another in the back of the knees with leather briefcases as they push and jostle their way up escalators, into cabs, in restaurants. I have since wondered if there is something about the city itself that clicks with people like me, fosters the hunger for power and success to such a degree that the people themselves become hollow, sucked dry of simple humanity. But maybe I'm just imagining things.

It surprised but did not bother me, how naturally nastiness came to me. I waved down a cab outside the airport, face frozen, voice brisk. I watched the Capitol city rise up in front of me as the cabby careened toward my hotel. Spring of 1992, dark falling and the lights coming up, reflecting in leftover rain on the pavement and buildings. I checked into the hotel, headed up to my room, bought stale Skittles and a Coke from the vending machine—a real Coke, not diet. I was impressed with myself, telling myself that I needed the blood sugar. It was 11 P.M., and I hadn't eaten since my minimalist breakfast in Minneapolis.

I looked around the room: the usual TV, bed, chair and small table, ashtrays, wide mirror over the dresser. I flipped on CNN, undressed in front of the mirror, admiring myself from all angles, standing up on the bed to get a good look at my legs. Thin. Very thin. I put on my robe and sat back against the head of the bed, smoking and drinking my Coke. Arranging my Skittles by color, eating them one by one, red ones last. I stared at myself in the mirror, glee and a sugar rush bubbling up in me, thinking: Alone in a hotel room in Washington, D.C. Thus began my love affair with hotels, which has yet to end. The anonymity of it all, the just-another-woman-in-Washington, the solitude, the smoking in bed, the TV as late as I liked, the palpable proximity to speed and power, within spitting distance of the Real World. I could almost reach a hand out and touch it, this nameless thing I wanted so badly.

I stood at the window, looked at an imploded building across the street, and then at the Washington Monument rising up, white and ethereal in the distance. I decided to stay.

The next morning, invisible in my suit, I went down to the hotel restaurant for breakfast. Crisis. It was a buffet. There are few things so attractive to a bulimic as a buffet. "All you can eat" takes on new meaning when you know you could eat the entire buffet a few times over. I sat down at a table, opened the *Post* in front of me, looked at my watch, and gave myself ten minutes to calm down. If I hadn't calmed down by then, I would leave. Scrambled eggs danced in my head and I read about the primaries, glancing up at the television. Larry King's first interview with Ross Perot. I calmed down. I got up, grabbed a french roll, four packets of jelly, two strawberries, a sliver of melon. I stood over the platter of minimuffins for an embarrassingly long time, debating about the calories in a muffin the size of a nickel. Too complicated. I skipped them. Melon first, followed by the strawberries, the crust of the roll with jelly, the middle of the roll. This took me an hour. I timed it. And I went the rest of the day on 160 calories.

Subway to the American University campus. I loved the subway, the clickclick of my ticket in the ticket taker, the crush of the crowd hustling to the yawning doors. I loved the escalator out of the underground, light widening above me. I loved the walk to campus and the campus itself. Interviews and tours. That night in the hotel bar, I ate carrot and celery sticks and drank a screwdriver, watching CNN, writing maniacally in my notebook.

The strange thing is, the poems I wrote while I was there are all about the sadness of cities. The desperation I sensed. The incredible, terrible speed.

This seemed to be separate from me, somehow. I took a cab to a movie, went to a crowded café afterward, drank coffee, spying and eavesdropping, writing and writing. It was all very glamorous. The next day, I walked through the city, street by street, stopping once to buy a pair of tennis shoes when my good shoes wore out. I was high as a kite, trying to think of the city as a place I could live. I wandered through the vaulted halls of Union Station, basking in the deafening noise, the bodies rushing by me. I went to the basement food court, read every single menu, finally settling on a bag of orange sugar-free candies in a candy store. I sat on a bench, popping them into my mouth, glancing from newspaper—*Roll Call*—to people, thinking of internships and jobs. I decided I could live here just fine. No one even noticed me. I was invisible. It was perfect.

I have since wondered if some part of my brain had decided it would be a good place to disappear completely. Take my exit, leaving nothing in my wake.

Back in Minneapolis, I said I would go to American. I have a remarkable ability to delete all better judgment from my brain when I get my head set on something. Everything is done at all costs. I have no sense of moderation, no sense of caution. I have no sense, pretty much. People with eating disorders tend to be very diametrical thinkers—everything is the end of the world, everything rides on this *one thing,* and everyone tells you you're very dramatic, very intense, and they see it as an affectation, but it's actually just how you *think*. It really seems to you that the sky will fall if you are not personally holding it up. On the one hand, this is sheer arrogance; on the other hand, this is a very real fear. And it isn't that you *ignore* the potential repercussions of your actions. You don't think there *are* any.

Because you are not even *there.*

When you reach legal age, your parents and your treatment team lose their power to make treatment decisions without your permission. In other words, you have to be a voluntary patient, or they have to obtain a court order for your therapeutic care. Three days before my eighteenth birthday, I walked—head up, confident, extremely thin—into TAMS and terminated treatment.

That done, I packed up my things and moved into an apartment in Minneapolis with a friend from work, Sibyl. Full of independent gusto, I went grocery shopping for supplies. Anoretics have strange shopping lists:

Fat-free muffins (1 doz.)
Sugar-free jelly (strawb.)
Low-cal bread (wht.)
Fat-free sugar-free yogurt (12 crtns.)
Fat-free granola
Carrots
Mustard
Celery
Lettuce
Fat-free dressing (French)

And that is what I ate for the next three months.

Except for the nights when I would come home late and find Sibyl reading on the couch, saying casually, "Hey Mar, we ordered pizza. You can have the rest if you want." I would eat the pizza. And barf. And weigh myself on the creaky old bathroom scale. Sibyl, one of the healthier beings on the face of the earth, pulls no punches. Tells me I'm being ridiculous when I stand in front of the full-length mirror, as I do every day, worrying about the size of my butt. Suggests I get my shit together before I leave town.

May: Mark and work and road trips. Ninety-eight pounds. The LAPD is acquitted for the beating of Rodney King. The newspaper staff huddles in front of the television the day the acquittal is announced, the normally raucous newsroom stunned to an eerie silence. Someone breathes, "Jesus Christ." Then knocks his chair over backward and screams, "Jesus *fucking* Christ," and slams out the door. The newsroom explodes in chaos, people saying, over and over, "How the hell can we cover this?" staring at their computer screens, turning around and screaming, "I CAN'T COVER THIS," and walking out. People writing in jerky spurts, hands shaking on the keyboard, stopping suddenly, putting their heads in their hands. Three people quit in fast succession. The editor yelling at people to pull themselves together. I walk out and sit down against a wall outside, staring at the sky, an unbelievable blue. I'm shaking and nauseated, thinking about God's perverse sense of humor, sending such a blue, blue sky on a day when moral reason has become a charade. Mark and I can't sleep that night. We get out of bed and go sit on the swings in a park, talking, a few words between long ellipses of shaking breath. I wonder aloud if I have the guts to be a journalist after all. Mark leaps off his swing and says, You have to. Whether you do or not. You fake it. I nod and look at the sky.

June: Mark and warm weather and road trips and ninety-two pounds. Mark and I in bed, talking about politics. I leave the paper to write my own stuff full-time. My days are this: Wake up, sit down, write. I decide that I am learning discipline. I eat nothing but yogurt. We take a trip with my family to our lake house in northern Minnesota, go to a bar with my stepbrother Tim and cousins, play pool and get plowed. Freed from the usual inhibitions, we get home and I snarf down pasta salad right out of the Tupperware container, knowing I'll regret it in the morning. Mark is drinking too much. I am drinking too much. Back in Minneapolis, I see my parents occasionally, usually separately. My mother and I have coffee. She reads my poems and I almost explode with pride when she looks at me, smiling, and says, "It's good." My father and I have breakfast weekly. I order one fat-free muffin and spend an hour dissecting it, compacting infinitesimal sections (bottom, sides, top, middle) with my fingers, dunking them into my coffee, smoking between bites. He says, You're getting too thin. I say, It's just because I'm biking everywhere. Really, I'm fine.

July: Mark hits a bad depression. Every morning I get out of bed, shower, dress, read the paper. Poke my head into the bedroom. Mark wrapped in blankets, facedown in the pillows. Mark, get up. MARK. Go away, he says. I go away. I worry. When he finally drags himself out of bed, we don't mention the fact that it's three o'clock in the afternoon. We don't talk about his depression, we don't talk about my jutting bones. Maybe we don't talk about them because we don't want to believe they're a problem. Maybe we don't talk about them because maybe Mark likes them. We don't talk about the fact that a silence has crept between us. Neither of us knows whether it is my silence or his. We are both slipping away. He takes pictures of me, asleep in the grass, naked at the window, driving the car. I write constantly, trying to avoid the dull pain of gradual loss, trying not to think about the fact that I am leaving soon.

August: I go back to Washington for a two-week journalism seminar at American, pounding the pavement to the rustle of the East Coast rat race. The heat is oppressive and the flies swarm, the sun is blindingly white. I wear suits and sensible shoes and shake hands and interview and call my father from a senatorial building one afternoon and we giggle about the fact that I am on Capitol Hill. In a workshop about representations of women in the media, I get into a virulent argument with a cocky little bastard about advertising, my face flushed, both of us standing up and leaning our hands on our desks, hollering excessively articulate epithets at each other. He spits out, *Feminist*. The room explodes in laughter. He turns beet red and storms out of the room. I sink into my seat and stare at my notes, trying to keep my hands from shaking, embarrassed at my own unchecked fury. That evening, back in the dorms where the participants are being put up, three young women come to my door to talk about the seminar. We discuss, in cerebral and theoretical terms, eating disorders. One of them asks me point-blank if I am anoretic. I say, Oh my goodness, no. We all laugh and talk about the presidential candidates. When they've left, I stand naked in front of the full-length mirror, certain that I've gotten fatter since I've been there, holding up a little compact to see myself from behind. Saddlebags, I can *see* them. I sit down on the floor and cry. Then turn out all the lights, sit at my desk playing solitaire on my laptop, the sounds of people coming and going and shouting and laughing floating in through the open window, my hands blue in the computer screen's light.

Mark picks me up from the airport. In the car it occurs to me that he's slept with someone else while I was gone. I ask him, he denies it. I can see that he's lying. We are distant. In bed that night, we decide that it's over. I go to the bathroom, stand on the edge of the tub to see myself. I get down and stand on the scale. Eighty-seven. Hands counting my bones, I stare at my face and think: I don't need him. I'm thin. I'm thin. What do I need him for anyway.

I leave.

At the end of the month, my parents and I go to Oregon with my mother's side of the family—my three younger cousins, aunt and uncle, grandmother who has Alzheimer's (no one knows it yet because she's too polite to tell anyone she doesn't know who they are or where we're going). On the plane I wear a long pink dress, a hand-me-down from my mother. I think that I look exactly like her in this dress. It hits me that I am thinner than my mother. I gloat. My father tells me, as we drive from the airport to the coast, that I am too thin. He stares at the road. I ignore him and read my book. In the cottage at the shore, the girls and I play games and go for walks and have a grand old time. Sitting on the living room floor, my cousin Johanna reaches for a cracker, spreads cheese on it. My grandmother, who is sitting on the couch looking into space and humming to herself, grabs Johanna's wrist and says, in her high flutey voice, "Oh, *no,* honey, you mustn't eat that! You eat too much, you're going to get fat!" She pinches Johanna's arm and says, "Honey, look at this! You're getting fat!"

Time stops. No one moves. Johanna, who is twelve and quite thin already, starts to cry. I stand up and walk out of the room. I go to my bedroom and sob, my mother comes in after me and tells me my grandmother doesn't know any better, and I say I don't give a damn if she knows better, this whole family is totally *fucked up* about food. Later on, the girls and I go for a walk. I talk to them about anorexia, that they need to stay away from it, it ruins your life. They have the good grace not to mention the fact that I am grotesquely thin and a hypocrite to boot. They nod and promise me they'll stay healthy. We eat saltwater taffy together. That's all I eat the entire trip. My oldest cousin eats nothing but salad with fat-free dressing. No one talks about it. A picture of me from that trip shows me lying facedown on the sand on a sunny day, emaciated limbs akimbo, pale as bones. I look like a corpse.

The week before I leave for Washington, D.C., I stop by TAMS to check in with Kathi. They have no power to admit me to the hospital or prevent my departure. I have nothing to lose.

> Extremely thin. Says, "I'm ok now."

I leave Minneapolis at eighty-five pounds, touch down at Dulles, and lose what remains of my mind.

Interlude

Present Day

A simple thing: I get my wisdom teeth out. I go to the doctor, I sit in the waiting room, filling out the medical history forms. *Have you been hospitalized for a serious illness?* Yes. *Do you have a heart condition?* Yes. It doesn't ask specifics, so I don't elaborate. I take the form back to the blond woman at the counter. I am perpetually nervous in any establishment where needles and drugs lurk in small cabinets waiting to bite me. The smell of antiseptic makes me sick, the scrubbed pink hands of the nurses look like those wet tropical toads. Three people are standing in line behind me. The nurse says, loudly: Major illness? I say, not knowing what she's asking: Yes. She, impatient, says: What? I say: Oh. Anorexia.

She looks up at me for the first time, sharply. The nurse standing next to her looks at me. The woman in line behind me leans around to look at me, just enough so that I can see her move from the corner of my eye. I am thinking: Why didn't you just put it on the damn form? The nurse says: Heart condition? I say: Murmur. I say: I don't think you should give me a general anesthetic. She doesn't respond. She scribbles *Anorexic* on the form. I mentally beg the doctor not to say, when he looks at my charts, Well, you don't *look* anorexic.

He does. They always do. Unless you are so emaciated that you can barely walk, people don't think you "look" anorexic. You sit in your chair, gritting your teeth. He calls me Mayra. I don't correct him. I tell him: I don't think you should give me a general anesthetic. I have a heart murmur. He says, Oh, no, I'm going to give you GA, it'll be fine. I say: I really don't think it's a good idea. He says, Oh, no, you don't want to be awake for this. I say, trusting as any old idiot: Are you sure? He says, Oh, yeah. It'll be fine.

I come back the next day, I sit down in the chair. I say: Use my right arm, there aren't any veins in the left. They say: No, no, gotta use the left. (Why? No one explains.) There are several of them in there, I am getting more and more panicky by the minute. Someone wraps a tourniquet around my left arm. I say, louder: The veins in my left arm are all collapsed. They say: Make a fist. I make a fist. They poke around in my arm with the needle. I say: *The veins are collapsed.* A nurse says: No veins. (Whaddaya know, no veins!) The tourniquet comes off my upper arm, they wrap it around my forearm, pinching tight the four-inch-long, half-inch-wide purple scar that seams down the center. They say: Make a fist. I say: Don't use my hand. *Please do not use my hand.* They say: Make a fist. I make what fist I can, the muscles of my left arm long since torn by a razor blade and atrophied by time. Tighter, they say. The needle slips into my hand and I listen to my protests fade.

By the middle of the week, my heart is pattering a strange sort of tune: *Tha-thum thumthumthum. . . . Tha. Tha. Tha-thum thumthumthumthum.* I fall easily, I'm dizzy. They give me penicillin to fight the infection in my mouth. It makes me throw up. In two days, there is no food left in my stomach, and I begin to throw up blood, or rather, pieces of my esophagus. The penicillin shoots my immune system to hell. Two weeks later, my mouth has not healed. I wake up in the night, lean over the bathroom sink, spitting fat clots of blood. I have a bladder infection, a yeast infection, a bad cold, routine scratches on my arms that refuse to scab and break open at a touch, bruises that paint my body a funny shade of mottled blue: a hip tapped lightly against a door frame, a shin that bumped a chair. Two weeks later, I have lost fifteen pounds. I press my fingers to my sternum: an old habit, a private gesture, an attempted wordless reply to the nervous chattering of my heart.

In the mirror, my ribs thrust themselves forward through the skin, proud. In the mirror, my hands play them, a hollow instrument. My hands make their way to the sway of my back, snake down to press the twin knobs at the base. My hands, shy as hands meeting up with an old lover, touch lightly, in that breathless disbelief: Are you really here? Have you come back to me at last? My wedding ring loosens and spins on my hand.

In the bed, my husband pulls the sheets back in the moonlight, moves his hands wordlessly down my body. He bumps into the sharp rise of pelvic bones; he holds them, thumbs resting in the hollow of my belly. I wait for him to say: You've lost weight. I wait for the rush of stubborn pride it will bring, the release of being caught red-handed in bed with someone else.

He says nothing. He lies down at my side, turns his back. His stillness fills the room.

8 "Dying Is an Art, Like Everything Else"

Washington, D.C., 1992–1993

Dying
Is an art, like everything else.
I do it exceptionally well.

I do it so it feels like hell.
I do it so it feels real.
I guess you could say I've a call.

—Sylvia Plath, "Lady Lazarus," 1966

Washington was very exciting. I remember it vaguely, for the most part, because I was dying. Dying is also very exciting. It's a pity I didn't notice it sooner. I imagine it would've been good food for thought, as it were, to consider the process of one's own dying at the age of eighteen. But I did not notice. I was very busy. Very busy indeed, very important, no time at all, my days measured neatly by the clock on my wall, the ticking of the watch I wore on my wrist, translucent skin-cloaked bone. I kept having to punch new holes in the band of my watch as it slid up and down on my arm, tapping and tapping at the small pale jut of wrist bone as my arm swung when I sped down the swarming street, jaw set.

I knew that I was thin when I got there. I took this knowledge as progress. I had never before been able to see, consistently, that I was thin, and now, as I looked at myself in the full-length mirror inside my closet door, fifth floor of Hughes Hall of American University, I could finally see, as I pulled on the panties that hung on my hipbones as if my hipbones had grown more prominent for the sole purpose of having hooks on which to hang my panties. Now I could see that I was thin. Pretty thin, I thought, smiling a proud smile at myself in the mirror, good girl! It did not occur to me that I was too thin. After all, what is *too* thin. After all, you can never be too rich or too thin. But I stood in front of the mirror, saying, Maybe. Maybe thin *enough*.

This was a miracle. The absolute truism of eating disorders is that you never believe you are thin enough. Whereas most people set out to lose a few pounds—say five, ten, fifteen—and stop when they get there, the anoretic sets out to lose ten pounds and then says, well, maybe fifteen. She loses fifteen and says twenty, loses the twenty, says thirty, loses thirty, says forty, loses the forty and dies. Oops. She hadn't really meant to die. She just wanted to see what would happen. Wanted to see how far she could go. And then couldn't quite bring herself to break the fall.

It didn't matter at all, whether or not I was thin enough, and no, I was not sure, I couldn't be sure, who can be sure? Who's to say what's truth and what's perception? Where is the absolute standard? It didn't matter anyway, because I did not eat.

The near-total cessation of food happened very quickly. I had not necessarily intended to cut back on eating; when I left for Washington, I was already at such a low intake level that it did not occur to me that I could, or should, lower it further still. But I did, eliminating what seemed a few superfluous bits of food. On the surface, I did it as catharsis; food suddenly seemed to be a burden, a strain on my limited time, and I pruned my diet just a bit, a few nips and tucks here and there. In reality, I did it as a test of my own endurance. I wanted to see how long I could go, running on fumes. I wanted to find the bare minimum required to subsist.

Remember, anoretics do eat. We have systems of eating that develop almost unconsciously. By the time we realize we've been running our lives with an iron system of numbers and rules, the system has begun to rule us. They are systems of Safe Foods, foods not imbued, or less imbued, with monsters and devils and dangers. These are usually "pure" foods, less likely to taint the soul with such sins as fat, or sugar, or an excess of calories. Consider the advertisements for food, the religious lexicon of eating: "sinfully rich," intones the silky voiced announcer, "indulge yourself," she says, "guilt-free." Not complex foods that would send the mind spinning in a tornado of possible pitfalls contained in a given food—a possible miscalculation of calories, a loss of certainty about your control over chaos, your control over self. The horrible possibility that you are taking more than you deserve.

But systems, like corsets, keep shrinking, tightening around the body, pressing the breath out of you. They tighten further still until you cannot move at all. Even then they do not stop.

This is how my system of eating had worked when I was in Minneapolis: Food was divided into units. A unit consisted of eighty calories, the equivalent of your average slice of bread. Of course I made this system up in my head, and do not, to this day, understand why this particular system held such significance for me. This is how we work, we all have our systems. A friend of mine used to divide food arbitrarily into liquids and solids—solids including soup, bread, pasta, rice; liquids including chocolate, vegetables, and chicken—and would've argued with any rational being who tried to explain to her the alternative nature of "liquid" or "solid."

It's just a pattern we have, and we need it fiercely. I would have a hard time putting into words the passion we have for our systems. They are as near and dear to us as any saving God. We know them better than we know the alphabet, we know them in the deepest part of the brain, the way the hand knows how to write, even in the dark. They are the only things that stand between us and total disintegration into chaotic, needy softness, the only things that keep the uncertainty of things at bay. We take a certain sick pride in the fact that we know the caloric and fat content of every possible food on the planet, and have an understandable disdain for nutritionists who attempt to tell us the caloric content of anything, when we are the gods of caloric content and have delusions of nutritional omniscience, when said nutritionist will attempt to explain that the average woman needs a daily diet of 2,000 or more calories when we ourselves have been doing JUST FUCKING FINE on 500.

When I got out of Lowe House, I was (1) quite thin at 101 pounds, and (2) eating a consistent diet of 31.25 units, according to my calculations. By winter of that year in Minneapolis, I decided that 16 units would suffice. I cut my caloric intake in half and deleted my intake of fat altogether. By the summer before leaving for Washington, I was down to 10. When I got to Washington, I decided immediately to cut two units—just two, what difference does a measly two units make?—putting me at eight. By October, I went to six units, and by December, I was down to four.

Four units. Line up four apples and think about how you'd feel after a few days of eating that and nothing else. Or four slices of bread. Or one carton of yogurt and an orange. Or two bagels. Or a pile of carrot sticks and a bowl of cereal. I was eating 320 calories a day.

The term "starvation diet" refers to 900 calories a day. I was on one-third of a starvation diet. What do you call that? One word that comes to mind: "suicide."

Factor in, here, that most people have a funny habit of sleeping. I did not have this habit. Certainly not in Washington. I was afraid I'd miss something. I was manic, and starving, and starving explodes mania into a sort of psychedelic passion for wakefulness, a deluded disdain for such base needs as sleep. Most people sleep seven hours a night. That's seven hours where their bodies are essentially at rest and don't require as much energy in the form of food. Most healthy people can go seventeen hours on, say, 2,000+ calories, putting them at about 117.64706 calories per waking hour.

Put me, and a lot of people like me, at, say, twenty-one hours awake, three hours tossing in half-sleep, at 15.238095 calories per waking hour.[1]

By the way, I also became a little obsessed with numbers in Washington.

So guess what happens next.

It was 1992 in the Capitol city, an election year with candidates who had the nation up in arms. I hit the ground running because when in Rome, you do as the Romans do. It was a hell of a year to be in Washington, with Clinton promising to save the economy and spread youth and vigor over the land, Bush looking old and taking the heat for all national ills, the city sent into turmoil with the promise or threat, depending on which side of the aisle one sat, of a Democrat back in the White House. It was a hell of a year for an ambitious would-be reporter, with no sign of a personal life to hold her back, to break in. I was work-

[1] The medical research will tell you that people who simply eat a *low-fat* diet, with a relatively normal number of calories, have a higher rate of: depression, anxiety, mood swings, difficulty concentrating, difficulty communicating, and freak auto accidents.

ing for a small wire service as managing editor, which meant I started at forty hours a week and in short order decided that that was simply not enough, so I worked more, and then more still. I was writing a weekly arts column for the American U student newspaper. I was sidelining as a freelance research hack for a couple of papers. I was going to school full-time, pulling a 4.0 grade average, and galloping full-tilt toward the finish line in some odd little private race.

As a rule, I am and always have been a hyperkinetic person. I am always busy, no matter whether I'm working one job or five. I like being busy. It keeps the brain agile. Also, I can't help it. Diagnostically speaking, I'm manic. Very. To this day, I fidget and run around most of the time. If I'm not busy, I start wondering what's wrong with me. I start feeling lazy, and I search for something to do. I do not have an off switch. But while I was in Washington, this became extreme. The activity was desperate. And I still can't tell, in retrospect, whether it was a desperate attempt to stay busy enough to keep myself alive, or an attempt to work myself to death. I became very afraid of sleep, and of stillness. As if I was afraid I might not wake up.

Fall in Washington was cool and breezy, bright, a sort of promised land of blue skies and teeming streets, the sprawling diplomatic mansions that lined the street where the American campus sat, smug and landscaped. I woke in the mornings, in the bed by the window of the dorm room I shared with another young woman. I went to breakfast with a few people I knew from the floor, ate a bowl of cereal, drank my coffee, went to my classes, ran from the campus to the Tenleytown Metro station, ducked into the subway, ducked out, raced up the long escalator, excuseme excuseme, elbowing and shouldering my way past a bunch of suits. I was just another woman in a suit and running shoes, and I popped up like a gopher in Dupont Circle. We all went zipping down the streets, our separate and anonymous ways, squinting in the sudden light, past the flower vendors, the fruit vendors, the hot dog and pretzel stands, past the cafés and the shops and the small circular park where men slept on benches with newspapers over their faces, past the men asleep on the grates in the sidewalk where steam rose like a belch from the belly of the city, past the women with signs and tin cups, crouched up against buildings, below eye level. Everyone was gauging the distance between here and there, avoiding eye contact, swinging briefcases in sharp arcs, clutching purses to hips, walking that walk.

I perfected that walk in short order. You walk as fast as possible, even if you're only going to the store for a cup of coffee, even if you're going nowhere in particular, even if you're early for work. You walk as if you're going to be late. You are *definitely* going to be late, for a very important date, and because you are all trying to look important, you walk as if it is important that you not be late, because there are things waiting for your important consideration when you get there, because Washington will come to a standstill if you are even a split second late. You keep your face blank. You do not smile and you do not frown. You look straight ahead, you notice neither the bums you step over without breaking your stride, nor women in multiple coats wandering in your midst, muttering about the terrible state of the world. You do not notice the fruit vendor who wears a different hat every day and lives on the same sidewalk where her fruit stand sits and laughs and laughs the most lovely little laugh and waves to you every day as you pass, Hello, dearie! How are you feeling today? Because you are essentially just a small town girl lost in a big city, it always makes you want to cry. You smile a shy smile and say, Hi, and then straighten your face again and keep your thoughts to yourself and keep going and you race up the stairs to your office, say hello to the staff, pick up the phone and start making calls as you dig through the pile of papers on your desk, scribble notes on your legal pad, hang up, and work until the rest of the staff has long since gone home. Alone in the office, you go out to the coffeemaker and brew another pot, lean back against the wall and rub your eyes with your fists. You turn on the radio. You pour yourself more coffee. You go back to your desk.

Night. The streets still crowded with those who have worked late and are now on their way home. I loved the nights, the night subway, the night walk back to the dorm. Things were good, at first. I made a few acquaintances that one might have called friends, if one was in a generous mood. I don't actually remember any names, but we went down to dinner together, and I ate my carrot sticks with mustard and, on nights when I was feeling particularly brave, frozen yogurt in a coffee cup. It seemed more manageable, somehow, to eat it from a coffee cup than from a bowl—a bowl was simply too much. When I had hunted down the cafeteria manager to make sure, absolutely *sure,* that the frozen yogurt was nonfat, and not low-fat, when I was sure there hadn't been a mistake, and no one had put out the wrong sign just to fuck with my head, I sat at the table and we all argued loudly about politics and philosophy, laughing and shouting. They were nice people. A little wacky. Very ambitious. We were all intensely driven, all of us spent more time working off campus than in school, mostly in politics. After we'd gone our separate ways to study and work, we reconvened late at night in the fifth-floor smoking lounge, turned on the television to the news, sat around a small table and played poker, shouting at one another until dawn.

Weekends, we drank. A lot. The campus was technically a "dry" campus, but that meant diddly-squat. We hit the bars and drank ourselves silly and danced. I once wore a little black dress and we took the Metro to Quigley's downtown and I met a very nice idiot named Jeff. I was drunk enough by the time I got there to think that the name "Jeff" was perfectly hilarious, as was the fact that I was seducing an accounting major from Georgetown, of all things, as was the fact that Jeff was wearing a silk tie and a baseball cap *at the same time*, as was the fact that he bought me drink after drink because, of course, I was underage and couldn't buy my own. We fucked, my body numb, in a dark corner of the bar, behind a curtain, standing up. He gave me his phone number on a napkin. In the cab on the way home, the girls I'd come with and I laughed so hard we could barely walk up the stairs of the dorm, and our friends were all in the smoking lounge and someone said Uh-oh and caught me before I fell over, laughing my ass off, and carried me down the hall to my room (Goddamn, girl, what do you weigh?) and put me into bed. I vaguely remember two guys arguing in the room about whether or not they should undress me, and in the end they just took off my shoes, put the garbage can next to my bed, and left me there. I leaned over and puked up a night's worth of booze with a tremendous slosh. There was not an ounce of food in the puke because I hadn't eaten in a day or so.

The next morning, I woke up, hopped out of bed, and sauntered back to the lounge. There were people in there who hadn't gone to sleep at all, and they all stared at me. I was still in my dress and stockings, makeup still on, hair still neatly done. One of them asked, wryly, How do you feel? I said, Fine. Why? He said, You're not hung over? I said, Nope. Are we going to breakfast or what? We went to breakfast. For breakfast, I usually poured a half-cup of bran cereal in a bowl and poured hot water in it, mashing it around with a spoon.

Then people began to ask me if I was anoretic. My roommate told the resident advisor that she was worried about me. He came into my room one night to talk about it, poor fellow, and I told him blithely that I'd once been anoretic but that was all over now. He said he was glad, and if I ever wanted to talk I could come to him. Sure thing, sez I. Talk began to circulate about me and about the bulimic who lived next door who, it was rumored, was the cause of the constantly flooded bathroom. I stopped going to breakfast and dinner. I'm busy, I said, which was true. I began to spend my evenings alone in my room, at my desk, in front of my computer, listening to National Public Radio, ignoring my whirlwind of a roommate who was having a perpetual crisis.

I, by contrast, was certainly not having a crisis. Not I.

I was, however, intensely lonely. My frequent letters home to my parents say over and over that I'm lonely. This now strikes me as very strange. My relationship with my family had been, until I left, antagonistic at worst and stilted at best, and for years I had been doing my best to hold them as far at bay as I could, myself as hidden as possible. But these letters are soft-spoken and intimate, full of questions about the world I was living in, concerns about my place in it, about what I wanted to do with my life, about my fear of the pace at which I was going. That is maybe the strangest part, the fact that these letters, written almost always in the middle of the night, are so revealing, probably more than I had intended. I do not remember being as contemplative as my words would suggest. I do not, in fact, remember feeling anything at all. Except terrified. And the letters do not do justice to how very afraid I was.

One thing the letters do reflect is my attempt at constructing a picture of health for my parents. Every last one contains some mention of food: "I'm off for a snack," "I'm off to dinner," "Warm and cozy after a bowl of soup," "Just back from pizza with friends." Pizza with friends, my ass. Ha ha. I had no ass. No legs or arms or cheeks or breasts. In fact, I had no friends. Early in the first quarter, my roommate moved out. The thin thread that had connected me to the world of humans was cut off completely. I stopped going to meals. Classes, work, walking up five flights of stairs to my room in the dorm, holding the handrail to pull myself up some nights, into my room, door locked. I flipped on the light, the radio, made a pot of coffee, lit a cigarette, kicked off my shoes, and sat down at my desk to work.

I was drinking between three and six pots of coffee a day. My hands shook terribly. It was almost embarrassing; in classes I'd keep them under the table, where they could tremble in private. My hands, when fall began to fade into winter, turned a funny shade of mottled purple, the tendons jutting out through skin, a small web of blue veins crisscrossing the bones. When I held my hands up to the light, only the knuckles touched, the light shone through the gaps between fingers no matter how hard I pressed them together. I became very concerned with gaps, spaces between bones, absent places where I was certain there had once been flesh but I couldn't quite remember when. When the small voice in my head would not stop hissing, I'd throw down my pen, stand up, go to the mirror, drop my pants, and look at the gaps. Pressing my legs together as hard as I could, I'd look at the gaps between my calves and thighs. I began to measure things in absence instead of presence. Where once I'd stared at my rear end, to see if it had grown or shrunk, now I looked at the space around it, to see if the space had grown or shrunk. I looked at the way the side of my ass sank in toward the hipbone. I'd scrutinize the hipbone, cup the bone in my hand, knock on it, listen to the hollow sound. I'd look at the space between my thighs, my lower body like a wishbone, my pubic hair obscene on a prepubescent frame, legs bowed apart from each other, the bones of my knees touching and then pure space, blank space. I could see the heater behind me through my legs, a little oval of space from knee to crotch. I stared at the place where my torso had been, the space between bones. I took my rib cage in my hands, curved my whole hands around the twin curves of bone, fingers inside the cage, palms on the outside, two fists. When I was satisfied that space had not shrunk, that my body had stayed within its spatial confines and had not encroached, I pulled up my pants, sat down at my desk, swallowed my coffee, and worked. All night.

Early in the year, my parents asked me to go to the doctor, just for a checkup, just as a favor to them. I went to a doctor on campus, correctly assuming that he wouldn't know an eating disorder if it bit him on the ass. I ate a bagel before I went in to boost my weight. As my parents had requested, I did tell him that, at one time, I'd had an eating disorder. A very nice doctor, white-haired and personable. He put me on the scale in my underwear and socks: 82 pounds. I was surprised and hid my grin. He told me I might want to put on a little weight and recommended milkshakes. I left, humming all day long, remembering that once upon a time my ideal weight had been 84, and now I'd even beaten that. I decided 80 was a better number, a nice even number to be. I told my parents, when they asked, that the doctor said I was healthy as could be, and that I weighed 104. See? I crowed. I'm maintaining my weight!

I went down to Virginia to cover the presidential debates. A frantic day and night in the press tent, reporters running around madly, bowls of caramels on the tables. I ate an incredible number of caramels and felt very ill. Packs of cigarettes were provided, as was dinner, but the line for dinner was long, and all that seemed safe to eat were the white rolls, so I decided to skip it. I ran around with the rest, interviewing and scribbling notes, sitting in the pressroom during the debates, the noise deafening. An old man with an Underwood typewriter and a loosened tie who sat next to me, chewing on his cigar, reading over my shoulder, turned to me at one point and said, "Kid, you're gonna be a good reporter," and returned to his typing. Then the debates were over and Mary Matalin and James Carville came into the room, the press jostled for position, and I, being five feet tall and as wide as a twig, ducked under everyone's arms and stood with my tape recorder next to their faces and shouted questions over the din and then back to the hotel, tapping out the story while I gnawed on ancient Dots in order of color, and drank a Coke. I caught a train back to Washington at five-thirty in the morning, sat in my seat watching the fall leaves go by. I got out a notebook, intending to write a poem as I always did on trains, but my brain buzzed a flat ambient empty din. I pressed my fist into my stomach to try to squash the incredible hunger that seemed to be chewing on my ribs. I sipped my coffee. And made small talk with the man next to me, a lonely man in Armani who was looking for a date. I remember thinking, in a rare moment of clarity, that I couldn't imagine who would be attracted to me, as ugly as I'd become.

I had become very ugly. Where was the romance of wasting away? Where was the eerie beauty of pallor and delicate bones? Not on my face. Death by starvation is nasty. I was a strange sallow color, my cheeks sunken back into my face. Mornings, I'd wake up and look in the mirror for a while, thinking how different I looked. More and more often, I'd have the same feeling I'd had as a little girl, when I looked in the mirror and suddenly didn't quite know who that person was, couldn't quite make a connection between her and me. And then I'd lie down on the floor, spread out the paper, and do my exercises, shifting often because the floor pressed into my bones and it hurt. I had bruises on each hip-bone, on the bones at the base of my back, on the coccyx bone, the end of the spine that really isn't supposed to stick out because there's supposed to be a butt there. I clearly remember the day I saw that bone sticking out. It looked like I'd grown a tail.

I stopped going to most of my classes in favor of going to work. I'd walk to the Metro, talking back to my stomach, telling it to be quiet, it wasn't really hungry, it was just fucking with my head. I'll eat at lunch, I promised it, placating. When twelve hours had passed since I'd eaten the night before, I'd go down to a little yogurt shop across from the office. They had the best yogurt. It wasn't that nasty icy kind, but the creamy kind, even the fat-free stuff, and they had fat-free peanut butter-flavored yogurt, which was the finest because it fooled the tongue into believing it was in contact with food. I even entertained the notion that it might have protein in it. Being a dairy product, and peanut-flavored to boot. I would order a small yogurt, after shrilly grilling the woman who worked there to be certain the flavor I was ordering was nonfat, and then I'd sit at a table facing the street so no one could watch my erotic encounter with a plastic spoon.

I would spread my paper out in front of me, set the yogurt aside, check my watch. I'd read the same sentence over and over, to prove that I could sit in front of food without snarfing it up, to prove it was no big deal. When five minutes had passed, I would start to skim my yogurt. Try this at home, kids, it's great fun. You take the edge of your spoon and run it over the top of the yogurt, being careful to get only the melted part. Then let the yogurt drip off until there's only a sheen of it on the spoon. Lick it—wait, be careful, you have to only lick a teeny bit at a time, the sheen should last at least four or five licks, and you have to lick the back of the spoon first, then turn the spoon over and lick the front, with the tip of your tongue. Then set the yogurt aside again. Read a full page, but don't look at the yogurt to check the melt progression. Repeat. Repeat. Repeat. Do not take a mouthful, do not eat any of the yogurt unless it's melted. Do not fantasize about toppings, crumbled Oreos, or chocolate sauce. Do not fantasize about a sandwich. A sandwich would be so *complicated*.

Imagine a woman in a suit, reading the *Post* on her lunch hour. Pushing her glasses up on her nose. Then imagine her pulling the yogurt toward her, bending over it as if she is examining its atomic makeup, watch her dip a spoon into the yogurt, then shake the yogurt off and lick a naked spoon. If I saw a woman like this, I'd be very tempted to walk over and shove the whole cup of yogurt in her face. But I was her, and having eliminated breakfast, all I ate for several months was that small yogurt, in the afternoon, and a fat-free muffin late at night. It's astonishing to see just how desperate you are to make those two things last, before they get taken away. Picture a starving dog, gnawing and licking at a dry bone.

The classes I did attend I worked at with an absurd level of dedication, getting into heated arguments and discussions about journalism and philosophy, staying up alternate nights to work on articles for reporting classes and papers in philosophy. It was the philosophy that got me. I became obsessed with philosophy, with Hume in particular, and with materialist ontology. I clung to the doctrine of disembodiment so furiously that it's odd I didn't notice the connection. Instead, I wrote letters to Julian, arguing madly that Hume was right, that life was but a dream and any sort of order in life was purely a product of the imagination and our minds were only a stage upon which perceptions played. My caffeine-and-mania-induced papers were returned to me with As. I reread them and furrowed my brow at arguments I didn't remember making. Then my mother came to visit Washington for a conference.

I didn't even bother to eat. I stayed with her in her hotel room while she was there. She brought me food, yogurt and muffins from her morning meeting. I left it all sitting on the table, sat in a big soft chair with my laptop on my lap, and tapped out a virulent argument against Kierkegaard. When I was finished, I sat in the windowsill with my knees pulled up against my chest, smoking and willing my mother to come back to the room. I wanted my mother. I wanted her to stay in Washington forever. I wanted my mother to hold me very tight and make everything stop spinning. She was visibly worried by the state I was in, tried to talk about it—We thought you were doing so well, she'd say, her voice fading. She tried very hard to simply be there, to find some piece of me underneath my layers of false cheer, exuberant ambition, palpable fear.

When I wrote her to ask how she remembers the trip, she replied that she would not say she thought I was relapsing. She and my father knew I was sick when I left but thought it was better to give me a chance to try and make it without imposing external controls, a decision that I am ultimately grateful for. She talked of how isolated I was, making no effort at all to connect with people at school or work, disinterested in doing things (anoretics, especially when their condition has become severe, tend to completely isolate themselves). She describes me as "depressed, disengaged, wrapped up in whatever mental quest you were on. . . . It was difficult to leave. I felt you very small and angry and determined to be alone." I asked her if she felt she was letting go of me. She wrote, "I was not leaving you psychically but I was leaving you to make some decisions about yourself that I felt only you could make."

Those decisions were, I think, primarily about whether to live or die, and I was making the choice by default. In the past few years, my mother's presence had changed for me. She no longer seemed distant and cold, but calming; and, if not always warm, always connected to me, always tethering me to the ground. That October, the sudden shock of being connected to another human being left a knot in my throat that I could neither express nor undo. We had two days of, for me, a semblance of peace. Then she left. I went back to my dorm room, lay down on my bed, and sobbed.

It is only in retrospect that I understand why her presence was so painful: though she was there, I could feel myself slipping away from her, falling backward into space. It was a presence I reached for but could not grasp. When someone is dying, there is nothing left to say or give. All you can do is hold their ephemeral body, carefully, and then let them go.

I began to lose it.

Shortly after she left, I went to work one day and something was wrong. Not with work. Something was wrong in my head. This was the beginning of what I believed to be a nervous breakdown. I couldn't concentrate on the computer screen. I paced in the office. This happens. Starvation does eventually hit the brain. First it eats all your fat. Then it eats your exoskeletal muscles. Then it eats your internal organs, one of which is the brain. I couldn't think straight, I kept getting distracted, kept telling myself that I was just a lazy brat who didn't have the wherewithal to work like an adult. Then I'd talk back to myself. Hey, I'd say, I'm tired, I'm stressed, I'm working a lot, this is natural when you're working too much. I finally went into my boss's office and said I needed a vacation. My boss was a very cool fellow and had expressed, privately, a genuine concern for my health. He had attempted, on a number of occasions, to take me to lunch, and had drawn me aside to say, Hey, you really don't need to work so hard. Delegate. You're the managing editor. You can give some of this work to the staff. I shook my head no. He'd pat me on the back and say, Well, you let me know if you need a break. So I walked into his office and said, very abruptly, "I'm freaking out and I'm leaving for a few days." He said, Good, good, by all means. I left the office, went back to campus, packed a bag, went to Union Station, and took a train to Boston to visit Lora.

Though she and I had ended the year at Interlochen on a bad note, as soon as she heard I was in the hospital that summer, she called and wrote. Our letters, fat with drawings and clippings and poems and quotes, flew back and forth over the next few years, through all my hospitalizations and the loony bin and the year at home in Minneapolis. In my head, no matter where I was, I saw a thin red line connecting me to the East Coast—Lora—and the West Coast—Julian—therefore keeping me suspended somewhere in this world. They were the only things in the world that made sense to me. I suddenly, fiercely, needed Lora's bouncing, shrieking, busting-with-life self.

We hadn't seen each other since her graduation the summer before. A funny thing had happened in the meantime: She'd transformed from a twiggy wild-haired girl to an absolutely beautiful woman, curvy and graceful. And I had transformed from a thin girl to a skeletal ghost wearing a plum-colored hat that hid my eyes and the purple half-moons below them. She picked me up at the station and we hugged and danced around and she tried, all weekend, in her gentle way, to get me to eat. Hey Max, she'd say as I stared at the muffins in a case at a café, the way one might stare at the crown jewels on display behind glass. Max, she'd say, poking me in the back, Get something to dunk in your coffee. Max, come on. You're way too skinny. I'd shake my head. Not hungry.

It was a painful trip. We crashed about like electrons, racing toward each other and bouncing off, one minute curled in our pajamas in her dorm room, laughing and bawling and hooting and hollering, another storming off scowling and pissy, the way it had always been with us. But there was one difference. I was half-dead, and she knew it and I suspected it, and it had changed me, brought a certain shiftiness to my eyes and motion, an odd heavy breathing when I walked. Hey, I'd say, can we stop and sit a minute? We'd sit in Harvard Square, watching the pigeons and the people strutting about. I'd huddle into my coat, fists shoved in my pockets, fingers rasping against themselves. She'd look away, speak in tight sentences: Max, this isn't cool. (What isn't?) She'd shake her head, furious and silent. Then: Jesus, Max, could you just talk to me? Tell me what the hell is up? (What do you mean?) I looked at the grounds of Harvard, thought about graduate school. Let the thought float off into the white winter sky like a balloon.

I wrote to Lora, asking her to tell me how she remembered that trip, and this is her reply:

> Here we go. You stepped off the train and you looked like a porcelain doll who thought she was bulletproof. And you were very much the fashion plate of a Lois Lane. I mean you would have looked awesome if you had had your health. I was surprised at how little you had gotten or how much I had grown. I guess people who eat grow more. And your head looked really too heavy for you to be carrying it around on your bones like that. And your bags for that matter were about to make you collapse like a Slinky. . . . And then you needed a back rub and I swear I felt like I was giving a back rub to a bird. Absurd to give a back rub to a bird. And maybe your bones were that light and hollow and that was how you managed to carry them around with no muscles and fat like normal regular non-bird humans have. . . . And anyway. Wow. I remember my friend Ryan thinking you were like terminally ill and me saying I hope the hell not. You know?

I remember eating only once the entire time I was there. One night, Lora went out for a few hours to a party that I didn't want to go to. I'd become very afraid of new people. I put on my pajamas. I lay down to read. There was a bag from a bakery on the floor. I couldn't stop thinking about it. I turned my pages, not registering the words. Finally I dove at the bag, peered in. Stale muffins, half-eaten. I agonized. I pulled the muffins out, minimuffins. I said, Just a bite. I'll have a bite, one bite. I took the bite. I took another bite from a different muffin, what if Lora saw I'd been eating? Cranberry muffins, crumbling in my hands. I bit and bit. And then I cried. Having eaten less than the total of one normal-size muffin, I began crying, standing up to look in the mirror, checking my bones, feeling for signs of softness, my brain veering back and forth from pig-pig-pig-fat-pig to stop-it-you're-okay-it's-okay-okay-okay. When Lora came back to the room, I cried and confessed. The look on her face, confusion and horror, I remember clearly, her voice saying, Max, chill, it's fine, it's really fine, stop crying, Max. Max—

One night, Lora and I ran into a childhood friend of mine who stared at me for a minute, then spent the rest of the brief, awkward conversation looking away. In my head, I said good-bye to her. The morning I left, Lora and I sat in a café, she eating, me wrapping the muffin I'd ordered in a paper napkin, putting it into my purse. For later, I said, There's nothing to eat on the train. We sat in the train station, talking only a little. The train was late, and we stared into our coffee cups, waiting to let go. The pain in my chest was sudden and so intense I could barely breathe. I wanted, more than anything to say, Lo, I'm really scared. But I didn't say that, I talked about the classes I was taking and the work I was doing and she didn't say anything at all. When the train came, we hugged and I walked onto the train. I sat in my seat a minute, leaning my head on the window, clenching my jaw, saying to myself: Don't cry. Don't cry. People go away, it happens, it happens, don't cry. The train started moving. I sat up in my seat and wrote a very good paper on Dostoyevsky and got up at one point to throw away the muffin in my purse because it was distracting me with its presence. I sat down feeling much better, much more contained, stronger, the way one might feel if one had just eaten a good solid meal. Back in D.C., I got off the train and walked through the station, and took the subway home. I went to work the next morning feeling empty, and lost, and light, as if I'd untethered myself from something that had been holding me down.

Winter rushed in fiercely and seemed suddenly malevolent, as if winter was after me in particular, the winds scraping against my skin. In reality, Washington is not all that cold, certainly not as cold as Minnesota. I knew that, and it seemed funny that I would be so cold. It snowed one day—Washington is always very surprised when it snows, they're never prepared for it, so everything shuts down. I returned from a day of Christmas shopping and decided not to take the shuttle bus from the station to campus, I could use the exercise. I walked the few blocks, near tears with cold, my bags too heavy, the muscles of my arms burning from what can't really have been so very much weight. Halfway home I began to run, a faltering, stumbling run, eyelashes fluttering with snowflakes, face numb, hair falling into my face with the weight of wet snow. I slipped and fell and could not get up. I sat there in a heap in front of the vice president's mansion, I, up-and-coming young journalist, A student, maniac, starving artist, invisible basket case, me. I cried with an impotent fury at my legs for refusing to stand when I told them to and thought of my cousin Brian as my hands, pure white, indiscernible in the white snow, scrabbled about trying to collect the contents of my bags which had spilled. I thought of my brilliant and wonderful cousin, dear friend and lifelong confidant, who'd been in a wheelchair since he was small. I thought of how he must feel every day, legs refusing to work, through no fault of his own, through some miserable joke of God, and I thought: *This is your own fucking fault. Get up. GET UP.* I hated myself with a pure and fierce energy and wished myself dead.

Back in my room, I put down my bags, undressed, wrapped myself in blankets, put on Christmas music, and watched the snow fall outside my window, a picture-perfect postcard winter scene, wide lawns of white, thin black arms of trees holding up the white sky. I thought of writing. But what would I have said? I'd long since stopped writing, real writing, my own writing. No words ever came anymore. I'd lost the sense of first-person, the sense of being in the world that writing requires. I guess I had nothing to say for myself. I turned my face into the pillow and slept.

Finals week hit. I studied night and day, chatted briefly with the few acquaintances whom I still spoke to in halls or in class. I ate only bagels and yogurt, from the little campus store. One bagel, one yogurt a day. I took them up to my room, set them down on the floor on top of a book, got a pillow from the bed to sit on, and peeled the bagel. I pulled off the bottom part first, dunked it piece by half-inch piece into my coffee, chewing it slowly while studying, stopping my meal often, as proof that I could stop eating, that I didn't need to eat quickly, that I wasn't really hungry. I underlined passages, made rapid notes in my notebook, and then I peeled a bit more of the skin of the bagel and nibbled on it like a rabbit. When the entire skin was gone and I had only the naked bagel before me, I ate it bit by bit, pressing it into a pile of salt before I put it in my mouth: I'd lick the bit of bagel, then coat it with salt, then pop it in my mouth and chew. This process took so long that I usually didn't want to bother with the yogurt. Then the yogurt would get warm, and I wouldn't want it, and I'd throw it away. Some days I ate a can of green beans, drowned in salt. I'd wander into the lounge, microwave the green beans while I made more coffee, and ignore the silence that fell over the room when I came in.

One night, as I was leaving with my bowl of green beans, I heard someone I'd known earlier in the year say: Jesus, I wish she would just fucking *eat*. It infuriated me, and my fury surprised me. It used to make me swell with pride when people noticed that I didn't eat, that I was thin. All along, part of the point of disappearing was to disappear visibly, to wear my thinness like a badge of courage, an emblem of difference from the rest of the world. But then, it pissed me off. Something had changed. I didn't want to be seen anymore. I wanted to be left entirely alone.

But I was not. Well-intentioned people began to approach me. My former roommate stopped by and said she was worried. I said, quite baffled, that I hadn't lost any weight, I was exactly the same as I'd been before, and she shook her head and said, No, Marya, you're not. Another young woman—who I'd always wished I could be friends with—knocked on my door one day, came in and sat down on my bed. I remember she was eating a carton of yogurt. I remember watching the way that she ate it, in normal bites, not licking it from the spoon like some people. I remember thinking how incredibly pretty she was. I remember her talking to me, warmly, about this and that, before she declared, You're an anoretic. And she looked me straight in the face.

I was sitting in my chair at my desk, knees pulled up against my chest. No, I said. No, I'm really not.

She looked at me for a minute and then said, You're severely anorexic and I think you should get some help.

It was snowing outside and I was holding my breath so as not to cry. I wanted to cry. I wanted to talk to her, and sit in the room all day with her, to tell her things, to have someone near me, to go to a movie, to talk about life, to be a human being again. I stared at my knees.

She put her hand out, as if to touch my arm, but left it in midair. She said, I want to help if I can.

I said, flatly: Why.

She said: I don't know.

I said: You can't help.

I said: I'm going to die.

I said: Please go away.

And she looked up at the ceiling. I remember the way her red hair fell over her back and I thought of Lora and my mother and she touched my shoulder as she stood to go and as the door clicked shut I bit my knee and thought:

I'm sorry.

I went home for Christmas break, and it was hell. I was only just beginning to realize that beyond the visible change in me, I had become an entirely different creature in my few months in Washington. Serious and quiet. Eyes that moved only rarely to meet other eyes. Slow in my movements, oddly still.

I took a cab from my dorm to the airport, watching the mansions in their holiday-lit glory glow as the cab hurtled along in the midst of the rest of the nighttime traffic, and wrote a story in my head for the holiday party my parents were having that weekend, a storytelling party. I wrote a story about the sadness of cities and the small solitary happiness of one woman at Christmastime. As usual a story for the benefit of my parents. As usual a lie. At Dulles, I dragged my suitcase behind me because I couldn't lift it and slept all the way to Minneapolis. It was freezing bloody cold when I got there. My parents had brought me a coat, and we went to a café and I began eating. Out of nowhere. I ate what seemed to me a vast amount of food, two raspberry muffins. Nothing had ever tasted so good in my life. We talked. They listened to me and watched me strangely as I spoke about Washington, the work I was doing, the way I felt I was growing as a person. This must have seemed a terrible irony to them. I weighed, at most, seventy-five pounds and was eating like a starved cat, apologizing for eating so much, it was just that I was so hungry, I hadn't eaten, I said, since lunch. Lunch indeed. They let me be for a day or so. Then the fights about food began.

The worst of it was that it did seem to me that I was eating enough. It seemed to me, in fact, that I was eating too much, and I had to at least go through the motions of appearing normal for my parents. My father and I screamed at each other about food. He hollered that I wasn't eating. I hollered, indignantly, that I'd *just eaten*, I just had a muffin, and I turned to my mother for support, didn't I just eat a muffin? Mom? Just this afternoon? She said, yes, but honey, now it's dinnertime, you should eat dinner, you can't just eat a muffin and call that dinner, come on, and my father said Goddammit, and slammed out of the kitchen.

My stepbrother Paul was there for Christmas. One night he invited me for a walk, after a fight about food with my father. As we walked outside, bundled to the eyes, I said to him, Paul, I'm not better. And we walked a while more. He said, I know. I said, I'm worse than ever. And I shook my head and looked at the sky and counted stars, wondering how far this could go. We walked a block. Then I was too tired to keep going, and we turned back.

There was the party and everyone politely ignored the fact that I was disgustingly thin. I had given myself permission to eat, for the party, so as not to embarrass anyone, and I did eat, many carrot sticks and celery sticks and fruit from the fruit tray with fat-free fruit sauce that I'd made. We all told stories and sang carols and it was very warm in the house and there was a fire in the fireplace. My friend Sibyl pulled me aside and said, You're sick. I said, No no. I'm fine. She said, Marya, you look like you're about to die. I said, No no. And went back to the party where there was noise and laughter and singing and everything was warm.

My parents, Paul, and I went for a walk one afternoon in the countryside with the dogs romping through the deep snow, and I think that was the day I finally lost my mind. I mean, above and beyond the previous incremental losing of my mind. We hadn't been walking for more than a half hour when suddenly I wanted to lie down in the snow and go to sleep, just bury myself in the snow. I'd read somewhere that if you made yourself a snow cave you could keep warm, the snow itself would keep out the cold of the snow, and I was so incredibly tired, willing my legs to keep walking. We were having a family outing and I didn't want to ruin it but I was so *fucking* cold. I wish I could find words to explain what this kind of cold is like—the cold that has somehow gotten in underneath your skin and is getting colder and colder *inside you*. It isn't an outside sort of cold; it's a cold that gets into your bones and into your blood and it feels like your heart itself is beating out the cold in hard bursts through your entire body, and you suddenly remember that you have a body because you can't ignore it anymore. You feel like an ice cube. You feel like you're naked and have fallen through thin ice on a lake and are drowning in the ice water underneath. You can't breathe. At some point I turned and stumbled back to the car, yelling at God in my head for letting me get so fucking cold, Why aren't you saving me? Save me, you bastard! I screamed in my head as I went, the snow very deep and heavy against my legs and I felt like I was running through water, that clumsy slow-motion slogging you do when you're playing water games at the shore as a child. This is different because you're thinking, Hypothermia, I'm gonna fucking get hypothermia, and my family, in a furious silence, drove home as I apologized over and over for ruining their day, but it was just that I was so *cold*.

Back home, I sat in a chair at the dining room table, still wearing my coat and my hat and my scarf, hands chapped and red, fingers wrapped around a cup of tea held close to my face so that the steam would warm my skin. I thought, spring will come. It's going to be all right. I switched on my laptop and worked.

Vacation ended and I was at school again. When I opened the door of my dorm room upon my return, I realized there was someone living with me. There were clothes in the other closet, pictures on the dresser, books on the desk. I panicked. How the hell was I supposed to get any work done? How was I going to do my morning and nightly exercises? How was I going to peel my bagel in peace? How was I supposed to go back and forth, from mirror to desk to mirror to desk, all day, all night, as I'd been doing for months? Shit. Shit shit shit.

Unfortunately, she was one of the nicest, most genuine, most wonderful people I've had the privilege of meeting in my entire life, and we actually came to care a great deal about each other, such as I was able to care about anything at that point, and that ruined everything.

Having a normal person around me made it poignantly clear to me that I was out of control. No, that had not in fact occurred to me before this point. She ate. She slept. I watched her do both, as if watching the fascinating habits of an exotic beast. In the long and quiet nights, when she slept in the shadow of the small circle of light cast by the lamp on my desk, I watched her yellow hair cast over her pillow, her mouth slightly open and curved in a very small smile. I watched as she dropped butter in a pot, marveling at the existence of butter and all of its implications, which seemed so separate from me: the idea of buying butter in a store, the idea of touching butter without fearing that the oils would seep through the skin of your fingers and make a little lipidy beeline for your butt, the idea of eating food that you knew, you *knew* had butter in it, of having butter in your possession that did not haunt your waking and sleeping hours, that did not wear a little invisible sign that only you saw: EAT ME. ALL OF ME. NOW.

In her presence, I was reminded again of why I was an anoretic: fear. Of my needs, for food, for sleep, for touch, for simple conversation, for human contact, for love. I was an anoretic because I was afraid of being human. Implicit in human contact is the exposure of the self, the interaction of selves. The self I'd had, once upon a time, was too much. Now there was no self at all. I was a blank.

But the thing that was most amazing to me was that she was perfectly beautiful. Her skin had the most curious softness, and a funny sort of gold-rosy color lit her cheeks. Her hair was thick and shiny. And she had tits and an ass that were startlingly appealing. Not that it would have occurred to me that I might be attracted to her. I had long since stopped having the vaguest sexual feelings. It was simply the contrast that got me. Where my breasts had been, persistently bouncing even at my theretofore thinnest, there were now only small brown-button nipples stretched over a rib cage, skin sunken inward between each bone. Where my derriere had been, there was nothing at all, a straight line from the nape of my neck to my legs, ending in a tiny bone in the center of the bow of pelvic bones, which jutted out fore and aft in an odd flat sweep. My face was the strangest, cheeks sunken so far deep that you could see all of my teeth through the skin, throat taut and concave below my chin, eyes seeming to move farther and farther back into my head with each day.

I looked like a monster, most of my hair gone, my skin the gray color of rotten meat.

I double-folded my skirt across my front and pinned it shut. I put toilet paper in my shoes so the ground wouldn't slam back at the bones of my feet when I walked, jarring me and making me dizzy. I waited.

While I waited, I applied for internships at newspapers across the country, wondering, as I put my applications together in my office when everyone else had gone home, making my piles of recommendations, essays and clips that all seemed so separate from me, a pile of lies, why I even bothered. I stood at the window of the office, looking down on Dupont Circle and the circling figures, mocking myself for being too weak to jump.

I went in search of a scale.

Seventy.

I took off my belt and shoes.

Sixty-seven.

That's when I began bingeing. It was all over then. From there on out, everything is a blur.

Nothing in the world scares me as much as bulimia. It was true then and it is true now. But at some point, the body will essentially eat of its own accord in order to save itself. Mine began to do that. The passivity with which I speak here is intentional. It feels very much as if you are possessed, as if you have no will of your own but are in constant battle with your body, and you are losing. It wants to live. You want to die. You cannot both have your way. And so bulimia creeps into the rift between you and your body and you go out of your mind with fear. Starvation is incredibly frightening when it finally sets in with a vengeance. And when it does, you are surprised. You hadn't meant this. You say: Wait, not this. And then it sucks you under and you drown.

Sixty-five.

The blur, the spinning of the sky above my head as I wandered through Washington, D.C., getting lost and trying to walk off the need for food, sucking up the smells of restaurants as I passed as if the smell itself might be enough, talking to myself, gripping my wallet and trying to fight off the thoughts of food, food, food, trying to clench my teeth hard enough to satisfy the longing for something between my teeth, the longing to chew, to bite down, to swallow. And then the binge, in and out of fast-food restaurants, half-running as I tried to hide my face while I stuffed my mouth with food, and more food, and more food, and then threw up in bathroom after bathroom. I began to carry Kleenex in my pockets so that when the coughing started, the blood-coughing, I could politely cough into my Kleenex and then stuff it up my sleeve, unseen. I began to have trouble walking, the sky always tilting at funny angles and pressing down on one side of my head, the edges of my vision shrinking and then widening without warning, and everything seemed very, very big, and the sky was incredibly wide and bright, and it scared me, the sky did. It seemed unpredictable.

My roommate was very worried, tried to get me to talk to her, and I did talk, a little bit. I told her when I'd made it through a day without bingeing. I told her how proud I was if I had made it. I would refuse her offers of food. Once I start bingeing, I can't deal with the idea of keeping food down, any food. The less I eat, the more I want to binge. It does make some biological sense. It did not make sense to me then, though. Nothing did. I stopped going to my classes, saving up my energy for work, where I sat staring at my computer screen, managing to work a little before I became frantic again and went out in a manic search for food.

You can subsist a long time, eating just a little. You can stay alive. That's how we all stay alive as long as we do, because we eat, just a little. Just enough to feign life. You can't stay alive very long when you're not eating at all, or when everything you eat is thrown up.

Sixty-one.

And then the last shoe dropped. I bought laxatives. I bought laxatives and began eating a box of them every day. Trouble was, there wasn't any food in my system. I was shitting water and blood. This is an eating disorder; and this is how crazy it makes you; and this is how you kill yourself by accident. Accident? Yes, by accident, because we are running through the streets of the city in the middle of the night, trying to find an open store where we can find more food. We are buying ipecac. We are missing the presidential inauguration that we are supposed to be covering because the sky is too big and we have shoved our way through the crowd, camera cracking against our ribs as we will our legs to walk and then run with the unfed energy of madness into Union Station. We are buying food and more food and we eat on the subway all the way home and people are staring and we drag ourselves up the stairs of the dorm and sit down on the floor and stuff the rest of the food into our mouths, choking on each bite as we sob horrible tearing sobs and then we stand up and drink the whole bottle of ipecac, smug in our mastery of ourselves and we think of how we will write an article when we've thrown up and then the floor comes flying at our heads.

I lay there, praying with all my might, curled fetally into myself, stomach tearing, praying that I might be allowed to either throw up or die, dear God just please let me throw up or die, throw up or die, and then I threw up horribly and blacked out again.

Soon I cannot get out of bed in the morning. I try. I valiantly try. I put both hands on the desk by the bed. I pull. I pull harder, trying to lift myself upward to sitting. I lose my grip and fall backward. I pick up the phone and call into work sick.

I hang up and laugh at how funny it is to be calling into work, sick.

And then I call Mark, who might understand. I hide under the covers with the phone and whisper, Mark, I'm scared. And Mark talks to me, but I can't hear what he's saying, I just listen to the music of a voice. And I say again, Mark, I'm scared.

My roommate was beginning to panic, and I didn't want her to be so worried, so I got a therapist. I sat in the therapist's office and tried to talk. I don't remember a word that was said. I remember the office: a beige leather couch into which I sank, feeling small, her desk and chair and windows and plants. And I remember her: platinum blond, heavily made-up face, cheekbones jutting, black leggings, and a long sweater with gold lamé whatsits sewn to the front. I looked at her with suspicion. She looked at me with pity, which annoyed me. Then I left, got lost in the building, got confused about whether going down the stairs would burn calories, guessed that it would, slipped on my way down, cracking my tailbone on a stair. I went bingeing, lost in unknown parts of the city, often looking up from my plate and realizing that I had no idea where I was or how I'd gotten there. I went to work when I could get out of bed. Otherwise I lay there, tossing uncomfortably. The bed was hurting my bones. The bed was giving me bruises.

Fifty-nine.

One day I was sitting in a Burger King eating six orders of Tater Tots and then I was in the bathroom throwing up and then I decided I was definitely having a nervous breakdown. This had to be a nervous breakdown. I called my mother from work. It was a Saturday morning and I was alone in the office and working maniacally and calling my mother and sobbing over the phone that I was having a nervous breakdown and what was I going to do? What was I going to do? I don't remember what she said. I only remember the sound of her voice, low and soothing, asking, Do you want to come home? No, I don't want to come home, I don't know what I want, I'm losing my mind, I just wanted to hear your voice. When we hung up I put my head down on the keyboard and cried for a while more and then I worked.

My therapist convinced me to see a doctor. So I went to the doctor, who examined me. I'd been drinking huge amounts of water all day, so the scale read sixty-nine, and I guess he wasn't too worried because that was a pretty normal weight, apparently, and I was in the prime of health.[2] I left and ate bag after bag of candies and threw up and made my way back to the dorm, squinting under the sky, wishing I was dead, wishing and wishing I was dead and it was much too sunny and I wanted so badly to be dead.

Fifty-five.

One night, in the coffee shop above the Dupont Metro station, I sat drinking my coffee and couldn't read. I was reading *Newsweek,* or attempting to read it at any rate. I realized that I couldn't read the words. I stared at them harder. I stared at them very hard, trying to make them cohere. They wouldn't cohere. At first they marched along in an unreadable row, and then they scattered all over the page. I slapped the magazine shut and thought, I'm out of my mind.

The boy at the top of the escalator steps was waving the *Washington Times* and it was night and nothing made sense, now that I'd lost my mind. I was feeling rather calm about it all, and the boy was waving the paper and everyone was moving very quickly and someone caught my

---

[2] A doctor who would fail to freak at a fully grown woman with the weight of a nine-year-old is extremely unusual. While the frequency with which nonspecialists fail to diagnose eating disorders is alarming, most doctors can spot something this obvious. This doctor did not freak in part because I told him point-blank that I had an eating disorder and was Working on It; I guess he assumed someone else was keeping an eye on me, so he did not even give me the usual battery of tests one would have at a normal physical.

arm at some point and said, Hup, steady now, and kept walking. I wondered why he caught my arm and the boy was swimming in front of my face and saying, Ma'am? Ma'am? Hey, can somebody help? and I was getting shorter, somehow, Alice shrinking without warning, and HEY, can somebody HELP? and I fell down the escalator steps at Dupont Circle and then I hit bottom and thought:

I think I'm dead.

Finally.

Fifty-two.

Then everything goes white.

From here on out things are very blurry. Sitting in my room with my roommate, who started to cry and said, Marya, I'm sorry, I called your parents. I was just so worried. It took me a minute to register. Then I picked up the phone, it was the middle of the night I think, and called my parents and said, I'm really sorry, but I've got to come home. I hope you don't mind.

They minded.

My father explains this minding, years later: "I had said to you for so long, 'You're not eating enough, you're looking deadly ill again.' We said it and said it and said it, you said, 'I'm fine, I'm fine, I'm fine,' you lied, you lied, you lied. When you wanted to come home, something in me said, 'She damn well better be sick.'"

If I put myself in my parents shoes, I can understand. After four years of watching your child play an infantile game of chicken, watching her stand at the edge of a cliff, teetering and laughing, almost falling and almost falling but never quite flinging herself over the edge, I can see how a worried audience might eventually get a little sick of this particular game. I can see how people might need to, for their own sanity and for simple reason's sake, let go.

And I can see, too, how a person's brain might refuse to accept that this time, she's actually gone over the edge.

My father flat-out did not want to believe that this was it. Neither did

I. My own behavior at this point was entirely contradictory: I knew that I needed to get home, but I didn't want to admit that I was really sick. Like, really fucking sick. I lied about my weight and said I was just so stressed that I thought a short break from school would do me some good. My father suggested I work fewer hours. I was continuously hysterical, terrified that my one chance to get saved was out of my reach. The girl who cried wolf. I talked to my mother occasionally, incoherent, trying to get her to convince my father to let me come home, just for a break, I said. There was a lag time—a few days? a few weeks? time unravels in my head here—while my father and I argued in a series of phone calls about whether or not I should come back, my therapist pleaded with them, my roommate did. Then I just up and dropped out of school. I walked into my counselor's office and said I was an anoretic and needed a leave of absence. She was incredibly understanding and very supportive. She, too, called my parents and told them I—haha—visibly needed a bit of a rest. I packed my things and sent them home, quit my job, and hopped on a plane to Minneapolis.

Let us say that my reception was not exactly warm.

I can understand that. I think it would be unpleasant to look at your child and realize she is going to be dead very shortly. My father was furious and my mother was terrified into a chilling silence. The night I got home, my mother sat at the kitchen table with me while I ate several bowls of cereal in a row and then cried because I'd eaten too much, and she just said, Honey, oh, honey, don't say that. Lifting my head from the place mat, I looked at her, searching her eyes for an answer, and I asked: Mom, do you think I'm crazy?

There was an excruciating silence. The clock ticked. I was still wearing my coat.

She said, looking out the window, "I think you're very sick."

It took me a minute to realize that she'd just said: Yes.

I've never been so terrified in my life. I had registered, to some extent, that this was the end, that I was honest-to-God about to push my leaky little rowboat away from shore and really truly *die*. The idea began to sink in, more than it ever had, that I might be crazy, in the traditional sense of the word. That I might be, forever and ever amen, a Crazy

Person. That what we'd suspected all along, what I'd been working so hard to disprove, might be true. I preferred, by far, being dead.

I spent the next few days sitting on the couch in a quilt, looking out the window, thinking about madness while my parents pleaded with me to go to the doctor, just to get a checkup.

I agreed to go. The night before I went, I drove—yes, drove—over to the university district to read in a café. I couldn't read, of course. I kept thinking about the fact that I'd just eaten dinner, a bit of dinner, and it was making noise and jumping around in my stomach and I thought about throwing up but decided that as long as I was going to throw up I might as well throw up something besides the three bites of skinless chicken I'd eaten. I bought a few muffins and walked around eating them, the old familiar adrenaline rush pumping through me, propelling my legs into a Burger King, writing a check from an account that was empty, chewing calmly. Then I was off, running through the town, stopping here and there and eating and throwing up in alleyways and eating and blacking out and standing up and running and eating as I walked, impervious to the cold, hand to mouth and hand to mouth. I bounced checks worth $200 in a few hours eating and running and purging and finally getting into the car and stopping on my way home at a Perkins, my last supper, I thought. I ordered pancakes with whipped cream and bacon and eggs and hash browns. I threw up in the bathroom, bought a slice of pie, ate it in the car and threw up when I got home. I got into bed, too tired to do my exercises.

It was the worst night of my life. It is the only lucid memory of this entire time. I dreamed I was eating and eating in a dark, hellish restaurant, and everyone was staring but I couldn't stop eating and then I'd jerk awake and think it was real and panic and then remember it wasn't real. I hadn't really eaten, everything was okay, and then, horribly dehydrated, I'd take huge swallows from the bottle of diet orange soda I had by my bed, crash back into sleep, return to the restaurant, and keep eating, and wake, and panic, and drink, and sleep and dream, hours and hours of dream eating and the echo of people laughing as I ate and ate. When morning came I was essentially broken. I could hardly talk.

My father drove me to the hospital for my checkup. For some reason it didn't register with me that I was seen in the emergency room. For some reason, when I walked in, the woman at the triage desk took one look at me as I came through the door, picked up the phone, and said something I couldn't hear. Then there was a sound like a pummel of hoofbeats and someone's voice on the loudspeaker. There was a flurry of people. I was taken to a room. I lay down on the little bed and someone put a blanket on me. Someone came in and poked at me, then helped me sit up, handed me a little can of juice. It said BLUE BIRD APPLE JUICE. Apparently I was supposed to drink it. When the somebody left, I poured it down the sink, thinking, Why am I pouring this down the sink? What does this prove?

That thought was my downfall.

A doctor came in. She was brisk. She told me she was going to admit me. I said I had to go, I was meeting friends for breakfast, which was true. I'd been worried all morning about how I was going to get out of eating at breakfast, wondering if the restaurant had yogurt, and whether it was fat-free or low-fat, and I asked if I couldn't come back later? wondering if in the meantime I could gain enough weight to keep myself out of the hospital, something in the range of fifty pounds, and I was very tired and I lay my head on the pillow and closed my eyes for a minute. She waited. I pushed myself up from the bed and smiled and asked, Okay? I can go?

She said: You aren't going to make it down the block.

I thought about that for a minute.

I thought it was possible that she was right.

I asked if I could go have a cigarette while I thought about this. She humored me. I walked outside, holding the wall as I went. It was too cold to smoke, so I ground the cigarette out with my heel, turned, got dizzy, bent over, and waited. While I waited I counted my bones. They were all still there. Then I thought, my God.

I straightened up, held the cold brick wall while the dizziness came in waves and washed away. I walked very slowly inside, placing my feet carefully on the floor. I went to the desk and signed myself in.

Afterword

The Wreck: Now

I came to explore the wreck.
The words are purposes.
The words are maps.
I came to see the damage that was done
and the treasures that prevail.
I stroke the beam of my lamp
slowly along the flank
of something more permanent
than fish or weed

—Adrienne Rich, "Diving into the Wreck," 1973

I have not enjoyed writing this book. Making public what I have kept private from those closest to me, and often enough from myself, all my life, is not exactly my idea of a good time. This project was not, as so many people have suggested, "therapeutic" for me—I pay my therapist a lot of money for that. On the contrary, it was very difficult. I wrote in stops and starts, trying to translate a material object, a body, into some arrangement of words. Trying to explain rather than excuse, to balance rather than blame. The words came bitten-off, in quick gusts and then long ellipses. After a lifetime of silence, it is difficult then to speak.

And even when you have spoken, you find your lexicon vastly insufficient: the words lack shape and taste, temperature and weight. *Hunger* and *cold*, *flesh* and *bone* are commonplace words. I cannot articulate how those four words mean something different to me than perhaps they do to you, how each of these has, in my mouth, strange flavor: the acid of bile, the metallic tang of blood.

You expect an ending. This is a book; it ought to have a beginning, a middle, and an end. I cannot give you an end. I would very much like to. I would like to wrap up all loose ends in a bow and say, See? All better now. But the loose ends stare back at me in the mirror. The loose ends are my body, which neither forgives nor forgets: the random half-hearted kicking of my heart, wrinkled and shrunken as an apple rotting on the ground. The scars on my arms, the gray hair, the wrinkles, the friendly bartender who guesses my age, smiling, saying, "Thirty-six?" The ovaries and uterus, soundly asleep. The immune system, trashed. The weekly trips to the doctor for yet another infection, another virus, another cold, another sprain, another battery of tests, another prescription, another weight, another warning. The little yellow morning pills that keep one foot on the squirming anxiety that lives just under my sternum, clutching at my ribs.

The loose ends are the Bad Days: my husband finding a bowl of mush on the kitchen counter, cereal I poured and "forgot" to eat, my husband arguing with me about dinner (No, honey, let's *not* have rice cakes with jelly). The loose ends are the nightmares of hunger and drowning and deserts of ice, the shivering jolt awake, the scattering of cold sweat. They are the constant trips to the mirror, the anxious fingers reading the body like Braille, as if an arrangement of bones might give words and sense to my life. The desperate reaching up from the quicksand of obsession, the clawing my way a little farther out, then falling back. The maddening ambiguity of "progress," the intangible goal of "health."

It does not hit you until later. The fact that you were essentially dead does not register until you begin to come alive. Frostbite does not hurt until it starts to thaw. First it is numb. Then a shock of pain rips through the body. And then, every winter after, it aches.

And every season since is winter, and I do still ache.

February 18, 1993. I am given a week to live.

Four years (approximately 169 weeks, 1,183 days, 28,392 hours) pass.

March 11, 1997. I am alive.

There will be no stunning revelations now. There will be no near-death tunnel-of-light scenes, no tearful revelatory therapy sessions, no happy family reunions, no cameo appearances by Christ, M.D., no knight on a white horse galloping into my life. I am alive for very menial reasons:

1. Being sick gets singularly boring after a while.
2. I was really annoyed when told I was going to die and rather petulantly went, Well fuck you then I won't.
3. In a rare appearance by my rational self, I realized it was completely stupid and chicken-shittish of me to just check out of life because it ruffled my feathers.
4. It struck me that it was entirely unoriginal to be starving to death. Everyone was doing it. It was, as a friend would later put it, totally passé. Totally 1980s. I decided to do something slightly less *Vogue*.
5. I got curious: If I could get that sick, then (I figured) I could bloody well get unsick.

So I did. Am. However you want to put it. Obstreperousness, which as a character trait is extremely exploitable in the energetic annihilation of one's own body and individual self, is also very useful in other pursuits. For example, life.

My eating disorder was not "cured" the minute I rolled—was rolled, rather, in a wheelchair with an IV in my arm, head nodding and heart lurching in my chest—onto the eating-disorders unit one bitterly cold day, February 18, 1993. It was not cured during the three months I stayed there, or during the years that have passed between then and today. I sit here now, eating dry cereal from a bowl because going to the store for milk seems somehow complex. It was not cured. It will not be cured. But it has changed. So have I.

I am precisely twice the size I was then. Which means I am still underweight. Which also means that in the mess of the last four years, I did a few things right. I am three inches taller than I was then, which means, maybe, that the body surges upward toward light, like a plant seeking sun. I am classified as (Axis I) 1. Atypical Bipolar II, cyclothymic, hypomanic 2. Eating Disorder Not Otherwise Specified (ED-NOS), (Axis II) 1. Borderline?, which means, essentially, nothing. I have scars all over my arms that were not there in 1993, which means some sadness came alive as my body did, and I, mute, etched it into my skin. It also means that we do not keep razors in my house. I am married, which means many things, including but not limited to the fact that I've learned a thing or two about love, and patience, and faith. It means I have a responsibility to stay here, on earth, in the kitchen, in the bed, and not seep slowly back into the mirror.

And I am all right. We will not deal here with words such as *well*, or *recovered*, or *fine*. It took a long time to get all right, and I like all right quite a bit. It's an interesting balancing act, the state of all right. It's a glass-half-empty-or-half-full sort of place, I could tip either way. It's a place where one can either hope or despair: Hope that this will keep getting easier, as it has over the past few years, or despair at the infuriating concentration balance requires, despair at the fact that I will die young, despair that I cannot be "normal," wallow in the bummerish aspects of my life.

Blah blah blah. I'm sick of despair. It's so magazine-model-looking-apathetic-and-underfed-and-stoned-and-exactly-the-same-as-all-the-other-wan-sickly-models. Forgive me for being chipper, but despair is desperately dull.

So I guess what happened is that I got tired of being so dull.

This is what happened: I went to the hospital and stayed there for a very long time. I got out of the hospital and threw myself into life with precious few tools and made a big mess and broke a bunch of things. Learned to be more careful. I worked, made friends, had a messy love affair, moved into a crack house apartment downtown and got a cat. Learned that in order to live, plants need water. That girl cannot live by cereal alone, though I go back and forth on that one still. That friends are a good source of food and soul when one has not yet gotten the hang of cooking or living (as opposed to dying) alone. That nothing—not booze, not love, not sex, not work, not moving from state to state—will make the past disappear. Only time and patience heal things. I learned that cutting up your arms in an attempt to make the pain move from inside to outside, from soul to skin, is futile. That death is a cop-out. I tried all of these things. I shaved my head, attempted suicide in November 1994, got forty-two stitches in my left arm, which hurt like a sonofabitch, and decided that was enough of that. I wrote and published and read and researched and taught and went to school from time to time and drank a lot of coffee and had a lot of really macabre dreams and played Trivial Pursuit and went to therapy and found myself extremely wrapped up in the business of life. I learned, gradually, to just fucking *deal*.

There is, in fact, an incredible freedom in having nothing left to lose.

In my limbo period after leaving the hospital the last time, I was grasping at straws. If you do that long enough, you eventually get a hold of some, enough, anyway, to keep going. I no longer had anything that I understood or could believe in. The situation I was in then is not at all uncommon. The experts say, What did you do *before* your eating disorder? What were you like before? And you simply stare at them because you can remember no before, and the word *you* means nothing at all. Are you referring to Marya, the constellation of suicidal symptoms? Marya, the invalid? Marya, the patient, the subject, the case study, the taker of pills, the nibbler of muffins, the asexual, the encyclopedia, the pencil sketch of the human skeleton, the bearer of nightmares of hunger, the hunger itself?

It is impossible to sufficiently articulate an inarticulate process, a very wordless time. I did not learn to live by words, so I have found myself with few words to describe what happened. I've felt rather like I was dubbing in voices and adding Technicolor to a black-and-white silent film. This history is revisionist in that same way: I have added words, color, and chronology to a time of my life that appears to me a pile of random frames scattered over the floor of my brain. I am sometimes startled, now, when I stand up and turn to the door to catch myself in the mirror. I'm often surprised that I exist, that my body is a corporeal body, that my face is my face, and that my name has a correlation to a person I can identify as myself. But I suppose it's not so strange to create a collage of memory—clippings that substitute for a linear, logical narrative. I did a very similar thing with myself.

There is never a sudden revelation, a complete and tidy explanation for why it happened, or why it ends, or why or who you are. You want one and I want one, but there isn't one. It comes in bits and pieces, and you stitch them together wherever they fit, and when you are done you hold yourself up, and still there are holes and you are a rag doll, invented, imperfect.

And yet you are all that you have, so you must be enough. There is no other way.

I make it sound so simple: I say it got boring, so I stopped. I say I had other things to do, so I stopped. I say I had no other choice but to stop. I know all too well that it is not that simple. But in some ways, the most significant choices one makes in life are done for reasons that are not all that dramatic, not earthshaking at all—often enough, the choices we make are, for better or worse, made by default. It's quite true that there was no revelatory moment. Mostly what happened was that my life took over—that is to say, that the *impulse* for life became stronger in me than the impulse for death. In me, the two impulses coexist in an uneasy balance, but they are balanced enough now that I am alive.

Looking back, I see that what I did then was pretty basic. I took a leap of faith. And I believe that has made all the difference. I hung on to the only thing that seemed real to me, and that was a basic ethical principle: if I was alive, then I had a responsibility to stay alive and do something with the life I had been given. And though I was not at all convinced, when I made that leap of faith, that I had any sensible reason for doing so—though I did not fully believe that there was anything that could possibly make as much sense as an eating disorder—I made it because I began to wonder. I simply began to wonder, in the same way I had wondered what would happen if I began to lose weight, what would happen if I stopped. It was worth it.

It *is* worth it. It's a fight. It's exhausting, but it is a fight I believe in. I cannot believe, anymore, in the fight between body and soul. If I do, it will kill me. But more importantly, if I do, I have taken the easy way out. I know for a fact that sickness is easier.

But health is more interesting.

The leap of faith is this: You have to believe, or at least pretend you believe until you *really* believe it, that you are strong enough to take life face on. Eating disorders, on any level, are a crutch. They are also an addiction and an illness, but there is no question at all that they are quite simply a way of avoiding the banal, daily, itchy pain of life. Eating disorders provide a little private drama, they feed into the desire for constant excitement, everything becomes life-or-death, everything is terribly grand and crashing, very Sturm und Drang. And they are distracting. You don't have to think about any of the nasty minutiae of the real world, you don't get caught up in that awful boring thing called regular life, with its bills and its breakups and its dishes and laundry and groceries and arguments over whose turn it is to change the litter box and bedtimes and bad sex and all that, because you are having a *real* drama, not a sitcom but a GRAND EPIC, all by yourself, and why would you bother with those foolish mortals when you could spend hours and hours with the mirror, when you are having the *most interesting* sadomasochistic affair with your own image?

What all this grandiosity covers—and not very well, I might add—is a very basic fear that the real world will gobble you up the minute you step into it. Obviously, the fear is incredibly large or you wouldn't go to all the trouble of trying to *leave* it, and certainly not in such a long, drawn-out manner. The fear, too, is a fear of yourself: a completely dualistic and contradictory fear. On the one hand it is a fear that you do not have what it takes to make it, and on the other hand, a possibly greater fear that you *do* have what it takes, and that by definition you therefore also have a responsibility to do something *really big*. It's a little daunting, going out into the world with this state of mind. Most people go out with a general idea that they'll do something or other and that it will be okay. You go out with the certainty that you will be a failure from the outset, or that you will have to do something utterly stellar, which implies the potential for failure anyway. When I was growing up, I always felt there was an expectation that I would do one of two things: be Great at something, or go crazy and become a total failure. There is no middle ground where I come from. And I am only now beginning to get a sense that there is a middle ground at all.

I had to decide that whatever happened, I would be all right. That was the hardest decision I've ever made, the decision to protect myself no matter what happened. My entire life, I've turned on myself the minute something went wrong, even a tiny little thing. It is not an uncommon habit among women. Among those of us who see in all-or-nothing terms, it seems as if you have only two choices: either lash out at the world and label yourself as interminably hysterical, shrill, unstable, and otherwise flawed, or lash out at yourself. With eating disorders, that lashing out at yourself is unfortunately rewarded—temporarily—by the world and thus is all the more tempting. But then the whole thing goes sour.

My leap of faith was more a negative reaction against the idea of wasting my life than it was a positive, gleeful run into the arms of the world. I'm wary of the world, even now. But I would not say I am wasting my life.

There is a difficult factor in deciding to end the game, and that is that most women are playing it at some level of intensity or another—and all of those levels have sublevels of dangers, not just the over-the-top-mortality-stat type of disorder. Eating-disordered people, for the most part, don't talk to one another. It is usually not a little sorority where it's all done in a very companionable way. It's usually intensely private. And when you decide you are tired of being alone with your sickness, you go out seeking women friends, people who you believe can show you by example how to eat, how to live—and you find that by and large most women are obsessed with their weight.

It's a little discouraging.

I can think, in retrospect, of all sorts of ways in which I might have avoided an eating disorder, and thus avoided the incredibly weird journey through the darker parts of the human mind that my life, essentially, has been. If I had been born at a different point in time, when starving oneself to death did not seem such an obvious and *rewarding*—Oh, you've lost so much weight! You look fabulous!—way of dealing with the world, of avoiding the inevitable pain of life. If I had been a different sort of person, maybe less impressionable, less intense, less fearful, less utterly dependent upon the perceptions of others—maybe then I would not have bought the cultural party line that thinness is the be-all and end-all of goals. Maybe if my family had not been in utter chaos most of the time; maybe if my parents were a little better at dealing with their own lives. Maybe if I'd gotten help sooner, or if I'd gotten different help, maybe if I did not so fiercely cherish my secret, or if I were not such a good liar, or were not quite so empty inside, maybe maybe maybe.

But all this is moot. Sometimes things just go awry. And when, after fifteen years of bingeing, barfing, starving, needles and tubes and terror and rage, and medical crises and personal failure and loss after loss—when, after all this, you are in your early twenties and staring down a vastly abbreviated life expectancy, and the eating disorder still takes up half your body, half your brain, with its invisible eroding force, when you have spent the majority of your life sick, when you do not yet know what it means to be "well," or "normal," when you doubt that those words even *have* meaning anymore, there are still no answers. You will die young, and you have no way to make sense of that fact.

You have this: You are thin.

Whoop-de-fucking-dee.

But when you decide to throw down your cards, push back from your chair, and leave the game, it's a very lonely moment. Women use their obsession with weight and food as a point of connection with one another, a commonality even between strangers. Instead of talking about *why* we use food and weight control as a means of handling emotional stress, we talk ad nauseam about the fact that we don't like our bodies. When you decide not to do that, you begin to notice how constant that talk is. I go to the gym, and women are standing around in their underwear bitching about their bellies, I go to a restaurant and listen to women cheerfully conversing about their latest diet, I go to a women's clothing store and the woman helping me, almost universally, will launch into a monologue about how these pants are very slimming, how lucky I am to have the problem of never being able to find clothes that fit, "Because you're *tiny*!" she'll squeal. I have to remind myself that it's not a conversation I want to get into. I refuse to say, "Gee, thanks." I don't necessarily *want* pants that are slimming, I don't want to look like the photos of skeletal models on the walls. Wanting to be healthy is seen as really *weird*.

So I'm weird. So what?

I want to write a prescription for culture, some sort of tranquilizer that will make it less maniacally compelled to climb the StairMaster right into nowhere, and I can't do that. It's a person-by-person project. I do it, you do it, and I maintain the perhaps ridiculous notion that if enough people do it we will all get a grip. I want to write about how to Get Well, but I can't do that either. I want to do a sidebar here with little pie charts breaking health down into statistical slices, showing the necessary percentages of therapy, food, books, baths, work, sleep, tears, fits, trials, and errors, and I can't. I find this maddening. If I were to describe the path between point A and point B, I would have to detail a convoluted, crisscrossed, almost blind stumble through a briar patch: the doublings-back, the stumbles into different, smaller rabbit holes, the sudden plunking down and howling with rage. In the end, I will have to point out that my stumble is specific to me. Your stumble will be different. You will avoid potholes I fell headlong into and find yourself tripping into quicksand I missed.

It is not a sudden leap from sick to well. It is a slow, strange meander from sick to mostly well. The misconception that eating disorders are a medical disease in the traditional sense is not helpful here. There is no "cure." A pill will not fix it, though it may help. Ditto therapy, ditto food, ditto endless support from family and friends. You fix it yourself. It is the hardest thing that I have ever done, and I found myself stronger for doing it. Much stronger.

Never, never underestimate the power of desire. If you want to live badly enough, you can live. The greater question, at least for me, was: How do I decide I want to live?

That is a question I'm still working on. I gave life a trial period, six months, and said that when the six months were up, I could get sick again if I really wanted to. In that six months, so much happened that death seemed, primarily, inconvenient. The trial period was extended. I seem to keep extending it. There are many things to do. There are books to write and naps to take. There are movies to see and scrambled eggs to eat. Life is essentially trivial. You either decide you will take the trite business of life and give yourself the option of doing something really cool, or you decide you will opt for the Grand Epic of eating disorders and dedicate your life to being *seriously* trivial. I kind of go back and forth, a little Grand Epic here and a little cool trivial stuff there. As time goes by, I take greater and greater pleasure in the trivial stuff and find the Grand Epic more and more dreary. It's a good sign. And still, every goddamn day I have to think up a reason to live.

Obviously I've come up with something.

I do not have a happy ending for this book. I suppose I could end it with my wedding—Former Anoretic Catches Man! Ex-Bulimic Saved from Gastric Rupture by Pretty White Dress!—but that would be ridiculous. I could end it with the solid relationship I have with my parents, but that seems less than relevant. I cannot end it with assurances of my own Triumph Over Adversity, because (1) we're a ways off from Triumph yet, and (2) the Adversity was, um, me. I cannot end it with my blooming health or stable weight because neither exist. I cannot sum up and say, But now it's over. Happily Ever After.

It's never over. Not really. Not when you stay down there as long as I did, not when you've lived in the netherworld longer than you've lived in this material one, where things are very bright and large and make such strange noises. You never come back, not all the way. Always, there is an odd distance between you and the people you love and the people you meet, a barrier, thin as the glass of a mirror. You never come all the way out of the mirror; you stand, for the rest of your life, with one foot in this world and one in another, where everything is upside down and backward and sad.

It is the distance of marred memory, of a twisted and shape-shifting past. When people talk about their childhood, their adolescence, their college days, I laugh along and try not to think: that was when I was throwing up in my elementary school bathroom, that was when I was sleeping with strangers to show off the sharp tips of my bones, that was when I lost sight of my soul and died.

And it is the distance of the present, as well—the distance that lies between people in general because of the different lives we have lived. I don't know who I would be, now, if I had not lived the life I have, and so I cannot alter my need for distance—nor can I lessen the low and omnipresent pain that that distance creates. The entirety of my life is overshadowed by one singular and near-fatal obsession. I go to great lengths now to compensate for a life of sadness and madness and a slow dance with death. When I leave my house, I put on a face and a dress and a smile and wave my hands about and talk brightly and am terribly open and seem to have conquered my monsters with great aplomb.

Perhaps, in some ways, that's true. But I often feel as though they have conquered me. As I write this, I am only twenty-three. I do not feel twenty-three. I feel old.

I have not lost my fascination with death. I have not become a noticeably less intense person. I have not, nor will I ever, completely lose the longing for that *something,* that thing that I believe will fill an emptiness inside me. I do believe that the emptiness was made greater by the things that I did to myself.

But to a certain extent—the extent that keeps me alive, and eating, and going about my days—I have learned to understand the emptiness rather than fear it and fight it and continue the futile attempt to fill it up. It's there when I wake in the morning and there when I go to bed at night. Sometimes it's bigger than at other times, sometimes I forget it's even there. I have days, now, when I don't think much about my weight. I have days, at least, when I see properly, when I look in the mirror and see myself as I am—a woman—instead of as a piece of unwanted flesh, forever verging on excess.

This is the weird aftermath, when it is not exactly over, and yet you have given it up. You go back and forth in your head, often, about giving it up. It's hard to understand, when you are sitting there in your chair, having breakfast or whatever, that giving it up is stronger than holding on, that "letting yourself go" could mean you have succeeded rather than failed. You eat your goddamn Cheerios and bicker with the bitch in your head who keeps telling you you're fat and weak: Shut *up,* you say, I'm *busy,* leave me alone. When she leaves you alone, there's a silence and a solitude that will take some getting used to. You will miss her sometimes.

Bear in mind she's trying to kill you. Bear in mind you have a life to live.

There is an incredible loss. There is a profound grief. And there is, in the end, after a long time and more work than you ever thought possible, a time when it gets easier.

This is the Hour of Lead—
Remembered, if outlived,
As Freezing persons, recollect the Snow—
First—Chill—then Stupor—then the letting go—

—EMILY DICKINSON

There is, in the end, the letting go.

Present Day

Mornings, I sleep through the alarm. My pulse in sleep is something like thirty-nine; it's hard to get back into your body when it slides into half-life in the night, a pale corpse rolling into dark waters without a splash. I wake up when Julian shakes me. Mar. MAR. MARYA WAKE UP GET UP COFFEE HELLO. I open one eye at him. Fuck off, I say. NO UP GET UP ARE YOU UP? Yes. Go away. YOU'RE NOT UP.

I slide my hands under the covers and take my pulse: good day or bad day? In the fifties, a fine and bright morn, up without falling. Bad day, forties or lower: feet on the floor. Sit up slowly. Head spin. Better than acid, this. Head swim and nausea. Hand on the wall, stand up. Catch yourself. Look in the mirror, check the butt. Still there. Dismay. Into the bathroom, lean head on wall. Pee. Stand up slowly.

Go to the gym. Stand on the scale. Do I? Yes. I confess. Everyone says not to. I do it anyway. Just to be sure that I've not overstepped my limits. Limits? Who set them? A question we have yet to answer. Lately have lost weight. Am scared by how this pleases me—I'm well! I'm better! I'm all right! I'm alive! And I have lost weight and I get on the treadmill and run for an hour and a half, until my bad knee feels like it's exploding with every step, but I have lost weight! More weight, lose more—I get off the treadmill and sway. Hallo. Steady, girl. I have gotten used to speaking to myself as if I were a horse. Steady. Into the showers.

Pass out in the showers.

Do not tell Julian this.

Because Julian is afraid, more than anything, I think, that I will die.

I have tried to tell him. I have said: I will die first. You will have to get married again, after me, and have a lovely golden years romance and how picturesque and honey don't think of it now, just have now with me. See? I'm here.

See? See? See? Look at me. *Look at me.*

How long? My love, I don't know. I can only guess but I guess alone.

We know that I am here. See? We do not know how long. We know that last night, many nights, I wake up: heart tripping the light fantastic, manic heart, stumbling about in a jester's cap and bell-toed shoes, swaying this way and that, tachycardiac frantic heart, trying to get out, my chest is thumping outward cartoonlike, a big red Valentine's Day heart pushing out from my ribs, ragtime tiptapping, calm down CALM DOWN MARYA maybe you're just hearing Julian's heart, maybe you're having a heart attack STOP IT, maybe you're hot, maybe you're dying DON'T SAY THAT, maybe you're holding your breath in your sleep, maybe maybe maybe—you sit up, too fast, head spins. You stagger from bed, hit your head on the sink, lay your cheek on the cold porcelain like a drunk, turn on the water, put your mouth under the tap, try to breathe nice and slow. Slow. Slow.

Some nights, many nights, I crawl back into bed and curve tight up against Julian, who sleeps like a smooth beating heart, hot, skin steaming, mouth just open as if in awe of his dreams, hands making the small abstract gestures of sleep. I fit myself into his chest and listen to his heart. And try to memorize his heart. And speak severely to my heart: Listen, I say. Like that. Steady. Strong. Julian mutters. My heart sinks back. Sits up and patters, wide-eyed, once more: the last shudder of coming, the last shaking sob of a child who's cried a long time. I count it tapping thirty-eight by the green light of the clock. I count it tapping thirty-five. And then it tumbles into sleep, grabbing me by the hair and pulling me down into these watery sleeps that are so terribly deep and cold.

Bibliography

Because the articles in scholarly, medical, and psychiatric journals consulted for this book would be too numerous to cite, and because they are of such varying degrees of relevance and specialization, I have elected to include only book-length texts in this bibliography. I would direct the reader to the *International Journal of Eating Disorders* for extensive and in-depth research perspectives on both the medical and psychological aspects of eating disorders.

Anderson, A. E. *Males with Eating Disorders.* New York: Brunner/Mazel, 1990.

Banner, Lois. *American Beauty.* Chicago: University of Chicago Press, 1983.

Bartky, Sandra. *Femininity and Domination*. New York: Routledge, 1990.

Bell, Rudolph. *Holy Anorexia*. Chicago: University of Chicago Press, 1985.

Bemporad, J. R., and D. B. Herzog, eds. *Psychoanalysis and Eating Disorders.* New York: Guilford, 1989.

Blinder, B. J., B. F. Chaiting, and R. Goldstein, eds. *The Eating Disorders: Medical and Psychological Basis of Diagnosis and Treatment*. New York: PMA Publishing Group, 1988.

Bordo, Susan. *The Flight to Objectivity: Essays on Cartesianism and Culture.* Albany: State University of New York Press, 1987.

———. *Unbearable Weight: Feminism, Western Culture, and the Body.* Berkeley and Los Angeles: University of California Press, 1993.

Bourdieu, Pierre. *Outline of a Theory of Practice.* Cambridge: Cambridge University Press, 1977.

Brown, C., and K. Jasper, eds. *Consuming Passions: Feminist Approaches to Weight Preoccupation and Eating Disorders.* Ontario, Canada: Second Story Press, 1993.

Brownell, Kelly, and John Foreyt, eds. *Handbook of Eating Disorders.* New York: Basic Books, 1986.

Brownmiller, Susan. *Femininity.* New York: Linden Press, 1984.

Bruch, Hilde. *Eating Disorders: Obesity, Anorexia Nervosa, and the Person Within.* New York: Basic Books, 1973.

———. *Eating Disorders.* London: Routledge & Kegan Paul, 1974.

———. *The Golden Cage: The Enigma of Anorexia Nervosa.* Cambridge, Mass.: Harvard University Press, 1978.

———. *Conversations with Anorexics.* (Posthumus). Edited by D. Czyzewski and M. Suhr. New York: Basic Books, 1988.

Brumberg, Joan Jacobs. *Fasting Girls: The History of Anorexia Nervosa.* New York: 1989.

Butler, Judith. *Gender Trouble.* New York: Routledge, 1990.

Bynum, Caroline Walker. *Holy Feast and Holy Fast: The Religious Significance of Food to Medieval Women.* Berkeley and Los Angeles: University of California Press, 1987.

Cash, Thomas, and Thomas Pruzinsky, eds. *Body Images: Development, Deviance, and Change.* New York: Guilford Press, 1990.

Chernin, Kim. *The Obsession: Reflections on the Tyranny of Slenderness.* New York: Harper & Row, 1981.

———. *The Hungry Self: Women, Eating, and Identity.* New York: Harper & Row, 1985.

———. *Reinventing Eve: Modern Woman in Search of Herself.* New York: Harper & Row, 1987.

Chesler, Phyllis. *Women and Madness.* San Diego: Harvest, 1972.

Crowther, J. H., D. L. Tennenbaum, S. E. Hobfoll, and M. A. P. Stephens. *The Etiology of Bulimia Nervosa: The Individual and Familial Context.* London: Hemisphere Publishing Corporation, 1992.

Currie, Dawn, and Valerie Raoul. *The Anatomy of Gender: Women's Struggle for the Body.* Ottawa, Canada: Carleton Universtiy Press, 1992.

deRiencourt, Amaury. *Sex and Power in History.* New York: David McKay, 1974.

Dijkstra, Bram. *Idols of Perversity.* New York: Oxford University Press, 1986.

Dinnerstein, Dorothy. *The Mermaid and the Minotaur: Sexual Arrangements and the Human Malaise.* New York: Harper & Row, 1976.

Eichenbaum, Luise, and Susie Orbach. *Understanding Women: A Feminist Psychoanalytic Perspective.* New York: Basic Books, 1983.

Ewen, Stuart, and Elizabeth Ewen. *Channels of Desire: Mass Images and the Shaping of American Consciousness.* New York: McGraw-Hill, 1982.

Fallon, Patricia, Melanie A. Katzman, and Susan C. Wooley, eds. *Feminist Perspectives on Eating Disorders.* New York: Guilford Press, 1994.

Faludi, Susan. *Backlash: The Undeclared War against American Women.* New York: Crown, 1991.

Featherstone, Mike, Mike Hepworth, and Brian S. Turner, eds. *The Body: Social Process and Cultural Theory.* Newbury Park, Calif.: Sage Publications, 1991.

Findlen, Barbara, ed. *Listen Up: Voices from the Next Feminist Generation.* Seattle: Seal Press, 1995.

Fiske, John. *Television Culture.* New York: Methuen, 1987.

Foster, Patricia, ed. *Minding the Body: Women Writers on Body and Soul.* New York: Anchor Books, 1994.

Foucault, Michel. *Madness and Civilization: A History of Insanity in the Age of Reason.* New York: Vintage, 1965.

———. *Discipline and Punish.* New York: Vintage, 1979.

———. *The History of Sexuality.* Vol. 1, *An Introduction.* New York: Vintage, 1980.

———. *The History of Sexuality.* Vol. 2, *The Use of Pleasure.* New York: Vintage, 1985.

Furst, Lilian R., and Peter W. Graham, eds. *Disorderly Eaters: Texts in Self-Empowerment.* University Park, Pa.: The Pennsylvania State University Press, 1992.

Garfinkel, Paul, and David Garner. *Anorexia Nervosa: A Multidimensional Perspective.* New York: Brunner/Mazel, 1982.

Garner, Shirley, Claire Kahane, and Madelon Sprengnether, eds. *The M(O)ther Tongue.* Ithaca, N.Y.: Cornell University Press, 1985.

Gilligan, Carol. *In a Different Voice: Psychological Theory and Women's Development.* Cambridge, Mass.: Harvard University Press, 1982.

Goffman, Erving. *Gender Advertisements.* New York: Harper & Row, 1976.

Gordon, Richard. *Anorexia and Bulimia: Anatomy of a Social Epidemic.* Cambridge, Mass.: Basil Blackwell, 1990.

Grimshaw, Jean. *Philosophy and Feminist Thinking.* Minneapolis: University of Minnesota Press, 1986.

Hansen, J., and E. Reed. *Cosmetics, Fashions, and the Exploitation of Women.* New York: Pathfinder Press, 1986.

Harvey, Elizabeth, and Kathleen Okruhlik, eds. *Women and Reason.* Ann Arbor: University of Michigan Press, 1992.

Hatfield, E., and S. Spreche. *Mirror, Mirror: The Importance of Looks in Everyday Life.* Albany: State University of New York Press, 1986.

Henry, Jules. *Culture Against Man.* New York: Alfred A. Knopf, 1963.

Hesse-Biber, Sharlene. *Am I Thin Enough Yet?: The Cult of Thinness and the Commercialization of Identity.* New York: Oxford University Press, 1996.

hooks, bell. *Yearning: Race, Gender, and Cultural Politics.* Boston: South End Press, 1990.

Hornyak, L. M., and E. K. Baker, eds. *Experiential Therapies for Eating Disorders.* New York: Guilford, 1989.

Iggers, Jeremy. *Garden of Eating: Food, Sex, and the Hunger for Meaning.* New York: Basic Books, 1996.

Irigaray, Luce. *Speculum of the Other Woman.* Ithaca, N.Y.: Cornell University Press, 1985.

Jackson, Linda. *Physical Appearance and Gender: Sociobiological and Sociocultural Perspectives.* Albany: State Universtiy of New York Press, 1992.

Jacobus, Mary, Evelyn Fox Keller, and Sally Shuttleworth, eds. *Body/Politics: Women and the Discourses of Science.* New York: Routledge, 1990.

Jaggar, Alison, and Susan Bordo, eds. *Gender/Body/Knowledge: Feminist Reconstructions of Being and Knowing.* New Brunswick, N.J.: Rutgers University Press, 1989.

Johnson, C. L. *Psychodynamic Treatment of Anorexia Nervosa and Bulimia.* New York: Guilford, 1989.

Johnson, Craig, and Mary Conners. *The Etiology and Treatment of Bulimia Nervosa: A Biopsychosocial Perspective.* New York: Basic Books, 1987.

Kaplan, Louise J. *Female Perversions.* New York: Anchor Books, 1991.

Kristeva, Julia. *Black Sun: Depression and Melancholia.* New York: Columbia University Press, 1987.

Laqueur, Thomas. *Making Sex: Body and Gender from the Greeks to Freud.* Cambridge, Mass.: Harvard University Press, 1990.

Lasch, Christopher. *The Culture of Narcissism: American Life in an Age of Diminishing Expectations.* New York: Warner Books, 1979.

Lawrence, M. L. *Fed Up and Hungry: Women, Oppression and Food.* New York: Peter Bedrick Books, 1987.

Lloyd, G. *The Man of Reason: The Male and Female in Western Philosophy.* London: Methuen, 1984.

Mead, George Herbert. *Mind, Self, and Society.* Chicago: Chicago University Press, 1934.

Miles, Margaret. *Carnal Knowing: Female Nakedness and Religious Meaning in the Christian West*. Boston: Beacon Press, 1989.

Millman, Marcia. *Such a Pretty Face: Being Fat in America*. New York: W. W. Norton, 1980.

Minuchin, Salvador, Bernice L. Rosman, and Lester Baker. *Psychosomatic Families: Anorexia Nervosa in Context*. Cambridge, Mass.: Harvard University Press, 1978.

Mitchie, Helena. *The Flesh Made Word*. New York: Oxford University Press, 1987.

Nietzsche, Friedrich. *The Will to Power*, edited and translated by Walter Kaufmann. New York: Vintage, 1968.

Nicholson, Linda, ed. *Feminism/Postmodernism*. New York: Routledge, 1989.

Orbach, Susie. *Hunger Strike: The Anorectic's Struggle as a Metaphor for Our Age*. New York: W. W. Norton, 1986.

Robertson, M. *Starving in the Silences: An Exploration of Anorexia Nervosa*. New York: New York University Press, 1992.

Rodin, Judith, and Ruth Streigel-Moore. *Body Traps: Breaking the Binds That Keep You from Feeling Good About Your Body*. New York: William Morrow and Co., 1992.

Rogers, A. G., ed. *Women, Girls, and Psychotherapy: Reframing Resistance*. New York: Haworth, 1991.

Rosaldo, Michelle Zimbalist, and Louise Lamphere, eds. *Woman, Culture and Society*. Stanford, Calif.: Stanford University Press, 1974.

Rosen, Marjorie. *Popcorn Venus*. New York: Avon, 1973.

Sault, Nicole, ed. *Many Mirrors: Body Image and Social Relations*. New Brunswick, N.J.: Rutgers University Press, 1994.

Schaef, Ann Wilson. *When Society Becomes an Addict*. San Francisco: Harper & Row, 1987.

Schwartz, Hillel. *Never Satisfied: A Cultural History of Diets, Fantasies and Fat*. New York: Free Press, 1986.

Seid, Roberta Pollack. *Never Too Thin: Why Women Are at War with Their Bodies*. New York: Prentice Hall Press, 1989.

Showalter, Elaine. *The Female Malady: Women, Madness and English Culture, 1830–1980*. New York: Pantheon, 1985.

Steele, Valerie. *Fashion and Eroticism: Ideals of Feminine Beauty from the Victorian Era to the Jazz Age*. New York: Oxford University Press, 1985.

Steiner-Adair, Catherine. "The Body Politic: Normal Female Adolescent Development and Eating Disorders," Ph.D. dissertation, Harvard University Graduate School of Education, 1987.

Suleiman, Susan, ed. *The Female Body in Western Culture.* Cambridge, Mass.: Harvard University Press, 1986.

Synnot, Anthony, ed. *The Body Social: Symbolism, Self and Society.* New York: Routledge, 1993.

Thompson, Becky W. *A Hunger So Wide and So Deep: American Women Speak Out on Eating Problems.* Minneapolis: University of Minnesota Press, 1994.

Turner, Bryan. *The Body and Society: Explorations in Social Theory.* New York: Oxford University Press, 1984.

Weibel, Kathryn. *Mirror, Mirror: Images of Women Reflected in Popular Culture.* New York: Anchor Books, 1977.

White, Michael, and David Epston. *Narrative Means to Theraputic Ends.* New York: W. W. Norton, 1990.

Woodman, Marion. *The Owl Was a Baker's Daughter: Obesity, Anorexia Nervosa and the Repressed Feminine.* Toronto, Canada: Inner City Books, 1980.

Yager J., Gwirtsman H. E., C. K. Edelstein. *Special Problems in Eating Disorders.* Washington, D.C.: American Psychiatric Press, 1992.

Zerbe, Kathryn J. *The Body Betrayed: A Deeper Understanding of Women, Eating Disorders, and Treatment.* Carlsbad, Calif.: Gurze Books, 1993.

Acknowledgments

Thanks to my agent, Sydelle (Saint of Perpetual Patience) Kramer, and to Frances Goldin and Lillian Lent for the incredible work they put into this and the unwavering support they gave. Also for not laughing at and answering weird questions and providing becalming influence throughout. But most of all for taking the chance. There aren't enough ways to thank you for that.

Thanks to my editor, Terry Karten, for unfailingly hitting the nail on the head, for patiently weaseling out the rest of the story, and for very, very patiently explaining each step of the way. Thanks also for support all along, and again, my undying thanks for going way, way, way out on a limb. Many, many thanks to Kera Bolonik, who gave this book the uber-edit, for which I am extremely grateful.

Thanks to the readers whose insights were invaluable for cutting the dross and smoothing the rough edges and asking the questions and giving the much appreciated help all along; you are all very fine and I thank you more later.

To Paul Trachtman, who said it could be done, whatever it was, and without whom this book would not even exist, since it was his idea. Also for his friendship, editorial insight, and general How to Live example for these many years, all thanks. To Michele Hodgson, for giving me a start and supporting me all along, I am forever grateful. To Britt Robson for suggesting the title for the original article. To Terry Cazatt and Jack Driscoll who taught me to write in the first place.

To all of the women who generously allowed me to interview them and use their immeasurable insight in this book. Special thanks to Megan for not only stories but also general brilliance and friendship.

To my parents for raising me right, for not throwing a fit about the airing of family laundry in public, for keeping me alive on several occasions, for support throughout all kinds of weirdness, not the least of which was the writing of this book, for staying sane and believing in me despite all evidence, with that obstinacy specific to parents and midwesterners.

To all the people to whom I owe quite literally my life, especially Kathi Jacobsen, Dave Auge, Jan Johnson, Ruth Davini, and the staff at Lowe House, especially Kim, Janet, Paul, Tara, John. Thanks somehow fall short of what I mean to say but nonetheless, thanks.

To all the people who put up with me and then again the ones who didn't: To Ruth Gila Berger, Daniel Casper, Jeremiah Chamberlain, Lora Kolodny, Jeremy Norton, Josie Raney, Kari Smalkoski, Mark Trockman, Kristen van Loon, Craig Welsh, and Arwen Wilder, for many, many things, including but in no way limited to dogged friendship, constant inspiration and example, highly caffeinated conversation, prolific advice on and support during the writing of this book, et al.

To Brian Nelson especially for teaching me to live right, for asinine jokes, for calling in the middle of the day and night to see if I'm still ticking, for a lifetime of friendship, for everything.

Finally, most of all, to my husband, Julian, for being you, etc., for making me laugh, for sticking around all these years, for ineffable patience throughout the writing of this book, for being who you astonishingly are, and here as usual words fail me, thank you, love.

Paula

Isabel Allende

'Listen Paula, I am going to tell you a story,
so that when you wake up, you will not feel lost.'

In December 1991, Isabel Allende's daughter Paula, aged 28, fell gravely ill and sank into a coma. This book was written during the interminable hours the novelist spent in the corridors of a Madrid hospital, in the hotel room where she lived for several months, and beside Paula's bed at home in California, during the summer and autumn of 1992.

Faced with the loss of her child, Isabel Allende turned to the thing she does best, to her art, to storytelling to sustain her own spirit, but also to convey to her daughter the will to wake up, to survive. The story she tells is that of her own life, her family history and the tragedy of her nation, Chile, in the years leading up to Pinochet's brutal military coup.

Paula is a testament to the ties which bind mothers and children, a brave, enlightening, inspiring book filled with the insight, passion, humour and magic which characterises the work of one of the world's greatest stroytellers.

HarperCollins*Publishers*

Doris Lessing

Under My Skin

Volume One of
My Autobiography, to 1949

'By reclaiming her life from fiction and polemic, Doris Lessing has written the most impressive book of her career.'

PENELOPE MORTIMER

Under My Skin is the first volume of Doris Lessing's long-awaited autobiography, beginning with her childhood in Africa, taking us through her marriages, the birth of her children, involvement in communist politics, and ending on her arrival in London in 1949 with the typescript of *The Grass is Singing* in her suitcase.

More distinctive and challenging, more revealing of the mind of its creator than any other autobiography of recent times, *Under My Skin* tells the story of a young woman uncompromising in every respect, who battles at every turn against her upbringing and environment in Southern Rhodesia, who fights for her individuality and self-determination at any cost.

'A wonderful book. One of the most vivid autobiographies I have ever read: frighteningly candid and with a stinging intelligence.' *Daily Telegraph*

'Doris Lessing forges backwards and forwards through the ideas and events of our times, and in everything she says or does she remains about twice the size of most other writers.'

Independent

0 00 654825 8

flamingo

Suzannah Dunn

Venus Flaring

'Suzannah Dunn is a gifted writer' *The Times*

Ornella and Veronica are the very best of friends, inseparable throughout the trials and minute details of their lives, sharing everything, hiding nothing. They grow up and find their way into the world together – Ornella, flamboyant and domineering, becomes a doctor, Veronica, observant and self-possessed, a journalist. But then something goes horribly wrong between them, and what was once the truest of friendships disintegrates into an obsessive nightmare of smouldering resentment that can barely be controlled. As Ornella's loyalty fades, Veronica's desperate need for reconciliation becomes a matter of life and death – and if you can't trust your best friend with your life, then who can you trust?

In prose that soars and fizzes with startling truths, Suzannah Dunn has created a deliciously disturbing and stylishly compelling tale of loyalty, love, memory, obsession and ultimate betrayal.

'Dunn writes with a warm attentive style which makes her characters compellingly real.' *Time Out*

'Suzannah Dunn writes in loaded and knowing prose, like a hip Edna O'Brien or Muriel Spark in a gymslip.'
Glasgow Herald

flamingo

Melanie McGrath

Motel Nirvana

Dreaming of the New Age in the American Desert

'McGrath is a cool-eyed chronicler of a dispossessed generation – philosophical, astute and ultimately unforgiving. This is no pseudo rock'n'roll trip, but an accessible and insightful study of the modern condition. The final autobiographical chapter is breathtaking.' DEBORAH BOSLEY, *Literary Review*

'McGrath meets the nation's lost souls of the New Age. A 267-year-old princess from the tribe of Atlantis, a technoshaman, an alien who talks to Barbie dolls, an overweight angel and a prince who will never die all impress her with their certainties as much as they depress her with their chronic self-awareness. It's an ambitious debut: McGrath has a keen sense for deadpan descriptions of off-kilter encounters and an acute knack for deflating the Myth.' EMER BRIZZOLARA, *Ikon*

'McGrath has a fine, questing mind, a splendid eye for detail and a healthy cynical attitude. Confronted at every turn – in her deliciously sardonic picaresque travelogue through America's south-western desert states – by the strange, the sinister and the just plain barmy . . . she maintains a fine, dense and colourful narrative that brings the desert landscape and the loony-tune New Agers to life.'

NICK CURTIS, *Financial Times*

ISBN 0 00 654715 X

flamingo

Hunter S. Thomas

Fear and Loathing in Las Vegas

A Savage Journey to the Heart of the American Dream

'We were somewhere around Barstow on the edge of the desert when the drugs began to take hold . . . And suddenly there was a terrible roar all around us and the sky was full of what looked like huge bats, all swooping and screeching and diving around the car, which was going about a hundred miles an hour with the top down to Las Vegas . . .'

So begins *Fear and Loathing in Las Vegas*, the now legendary quest by ace Gonzo journalist Hunter S. Thompson into the heart of the American Dream. As knights of old on hazardous quest for the Holy Grail buckled on armour of supernatural power, so Hunter Thompson entered Las Vegas armed with a veritable arsenal of 'heinous chemicals'. His perilous, drug-enhanced confrontations with casino operators, bartenders, police officers and other representatives of the Silent Majority have a hallucinatory humour and nightmare terror rarely seen on the printed page. This is the true story of a man who passed through hell – and lived to tell the tale.

'*Fear and Loathing in Las Vegas* is a scorching epochal sensation. There are only two adjectives writers care about any more . . . 'brilliant' and 'outrageous' . . . and Hunter Thompson has a freehold on both of them' Tom Wolfe

'What goes on in these pages makes Lenny Bruce seem angelic . . . the whole book boils down to a mad, corrosive prose poetry that picks up where Norman Mailer's *An American Dream* left off and explores what Tom Wolfe left out' *New York Times*

ISBN 0 586 08132 1

flamingo

Martin Amis

The Information

'Any other writer would kill to reach this high style. Amis can stroll the heights at his leisure – the writing is on fire.'

ALLISON PEARSON, *Independent on Sunday*

How can one writer hurt another where it really counts – his reputation? This is the problem facing novelist Richard Tull, contemplating the success of his friend and rival Gwyn Barry. Revenger's tragedy, comedy of errors, contemporary satire, *The Information* skewers high life and low in Martin Amis's brilliant return to the territory of *Money* and *London Fields*.

'This is a book of brilliant energies, a comedy of the enraged passions, and a comedy of humiliation. *The Information* sparkles with Amis's distinctive rage, disgust, stylistic observation, language . . . Amis admires the big American writers. His writing shares their grandeur.'

MALCOLM BRADBURY, *The Times*

'Quite dazzling – you're never out of reach of a sparkly phrase, a stiletto metaphor or drop-dead insight into the human condition. And there is the humour: Amis goes where other humorists fear to tread – he is the crown prince of literary hipness.'

CHRISTOPHER BUCKLEY, *New York Times Book Review*

flamingo

Paul Martin

The Sickening Mind

Brain, Behaviour, Immunity & Disease

'A fascinating account, based on the ways in which mental states affect the individual's liability to disease . . . Martin has admirably succeeded in demonstrating "that our mental state and physical health are inexorably intertwined" He is a highly civilised scientist who seasons his text with witty parentheses. He also provides many examples from literature, ranging widely from Shakespeare, Goethe and Hardy to Tolstoy, Dostoevsky and Kafka . . . Interesting, informative and a pleasure to read.' ANTHONY STORR, *Sunday Times*

'A masterpiece of popularization . . . Martin's lucid account of possible mechanisms of the connections between mental states and personality traits and illnesses is a notable triumph of his book . . . Excellent'

RAYMOND TALLIS, *Times Literary Supplement*

'Excellent . . . Martin's book is a powerful reminder of the need for disciplined thinking in the face of the irreducible complexity of our bodies and minds, in sickness and in health.' JON TURNEY, *Financial Times*

ISBN 0 00 655022 3

flamingo

Douglas Rushkoff

Children of Chaos

Surviving the End of the World as We Know it

'The case is argued headlong. Hold the book in one hand, your hat with the other' *New Scientist*

The Information Age is over. Welcome to the Age of Chaos. Our world is getting more complex every day. Faced by a media run amok, a rapidly expanding global economy, the collapse of national and social boundaries and the profound impact of technology on our lives, we all feel like immigrants to a very new territory. Gone are the organized, hierarchical civilization, overwhelmed by a seemingly random and disjointed wave of change.

Douglas Rushkoff, acclaimed as 'the brilliant heir to Marshall McLuhan', believes that this is the moment we have all been waiting for – not an apocalypse at all, but a renaissance in which children's popular culture will lead us through despair and powerlessness towards a new sort of hope.

In *Children of Chaos* he deconstructs the culture of the generation he calls the 'Screenagers' in his search for strategies on coping with, and thriving amidst, the discontinuity of the post-modern experience.

'Whatever changes may be ahead for the human race, Rushkoff offers us a recipe for survival'

MARK EDWARDS, *Sunday Times*

ISBN 0 00 654879 2

flamingo